LORD LIVERPOOL AND
LIBERAL TORYISM
1820 *to* 1827

D1477235

Robert, 2nd Earl of Liverpool

BY SIR THOMAS LAWRENCE

LORD LIVERPOOL AND LIBERAL TORYISM
1820 *to* 1827

by

W. R. BROCK, B.A.
FELLOW OF TRINITY COLLEGE, CAMBRIDGE

CAMBRIDGE
AT THE UNIVERSITY PRESS
1941

CAMBRIDGE
UNIVERSITY PRESS

University Printing House, Cambridge CB2 8BS, United Kingdom

Published in the United States of America by Cambridge University Press, New York

Cambridge University Press is part of the University of Cambridge.

It furthers the University's mission by disseminating knowledge in the pursuit of education, learning and research at the highest international levels of excellence.

www.cambridge.org
Information on this title: www.cambridge.org/9781107425767

© Cambridge University Press 1941
Thirlwall Prize Essay 1939

First published 1941
First paperback edition 2014

A catalogue record for this publication is available from the British Library

ISBN 978-1-107-42576-7 Paperback

CONTENTS

PLATES

TO MY MOTHER

PREFACE

THIS ESSAY formed the Thirlwall Prize for 1939; but, in
the months which followed the award of the prize, it has
been rewritten and some new material has been added.
I must hope that the reader will not bear too hardly upon
any minor errata which he may notice, for the final stages
of rewriting were carried out during the anxieties of
autumn 1939, the revision has been unduly hurried
owing to the imminence of military service, and the
proofs have been read in a barrack room. I would not,
however, claim any indulgence for the views expressed,
and I hope sincerely that they may at least occasion some
thought upon a period of English history which has not
always been considered with sympathy and understanding,
and that, in particular, they may rouse some interest in a
Prime Minister who, though his talents were not brilliant,
has suffered an undeserved eclipse, and who had a considerable though not an ostentatious influence upon the
course of nineteenth-century English history.

I should like to express my thanks to Professor G. M.
Trevelyan, Mr J. R. M. Butler, and Mr G. Kitson Clark for
their advice and encouragement, and my profound regret
that the illness and death of Professor H. W. V. Temperley
prevented me from gaining the full benefit of his advice.
Mr K. Scott of St John's College has given me valuable
assistance in reading the proofs and in verifying some
references.

W. R. BROCK

CHAPTER I

INTRODUCTION. THE EARLY CAREER OF LORD LIVERPOOL

IF there is a dark age in nineteenth-century England it is the period of five years following the battle of Waterloo. It was a period dominated by the fears of the upper classes and the discontents of the working classes; it was a time in which national glory had grown stale, in which the propertied classes were conscious of fighting a rearguard action, and in which a bitter populace lacking education and understanding of political affairs was ready to follow any inspiring leader. In retrospect it may be seen that the working class had not the sustained vigour to make a revolution, and that the upper classes were not brutal tyrants. Yet it remains the one period during the nineteenth century in which a revolution could have taken place, and the significant and sinister figure is that of "Orator" Hunt, a born demagogue and a born autocrat. With a little more luck, with a little more cleverness, and with a phalanx of devoted and desperate followers, Hunt might have been the leader of the English revolution.

Very different is the change which did take place. With the return of prosperity there was also a change in the whole tone of Government; within a few years the very suspicion of revolution had vanished, and the broad outlines of Victorian England had been sketched by a Government which has some claim to be called the first of the great improving ministries of the nineteenth century and one of the mainsprings of later political thought and action. Approbation took the place of execration, ministers who had gone in fear of their lives found themselves objects of national respect, and the Prime Minister of a Government which had been accused of truckling to continental despots was threatening to "play the whole game of liberal institutions". Parliament was still unreformed, the Catholics still went under galling and outworn restrictions, but, in its foreign and economic policy, the Government was winning the approval of thinking men and has retained the admiration of posterity. This is the period which may be called that of Liberal Toryism. The name is artificial—that is to say it is not found in the mouths of contemporaries—but because the High Tories accused the Government of "liberalism", then a suspect and dangerous thing, because the "liberals" who dominated the Cabinet felt acutely their estrangement from the "ultras", and because the meaning of the phrase is readily intelligible to a later age, it is not inappropriate to speak of "Liberal Toryism".

Liberal Toryism is usually associated with the name of Canning, and Canning certainly struck the public eye more than any other minister. Yet Canning was primarily a Foreign Secretary, he stuck fairly closely to his own department, and Liberal Toryism must mean a good deal more than Canning's foreign policy. Canning's peculiar contribution was his use of public opinion as a political weapon; but in that age politicians could not live by public opinion alone, and Canning himself could not have remained in power a day had he not had the unswerving support of the Prime Minister, Lord Liverpool. The view taken in the following pages is that Liverpool as much as Canning was responsible for the experiment of Liberal Toryism. Within the Cabinet Liverpool was the mainstay of "liberal" opinion, he was perhaps the only man who could persuade the Tory party as a whole to sanction such opinions, and he was certainly the only man who could hold together the Cabinet between 1822 and 1827.

A modern estimate of Liverpool's services as a statesman is long overdue, and this work deals only with his work as Prime Minister during the last few years of his Government. Nevertheless, there is some excuse for this limited treatment in that Liverpool's main claim upon the gratitude of posterity must derive from these last few years. Before 1820 Liverpool had fulfilled useful and important duties, but they were duties which would not earn him more praise than many another administrative statesman; he had held the premiership under conditions which any moderately capable politician could have fulfilled; after 1820 he performed services which no one else, at that time, could perform. Before 1820 the Tory Government had been the only possible Government, after 1820 Liverpool alone made possible the Government he desired.

Lord Liverpool was born, as Robert Banks Jenkinson, on 6 June 1770. His life thus covered the whole period of the Tory ascendancy; his earliest memories were those of Lord North and the American war; he had grown to maturity and entered public life under the mighty shadow of Pitt; his own administration carried England to the eve of Catholic Emancipation, Parliamentary Reform, and the breaking of the old Tory party. His father was Charles Jenkinson, sometime the private secretary of Bute, who rose to sinister eminence as the leader of the "King's Friends", acquired respectable fame as Pitt's President of the Board of Trade, became a peer and lived to write an authoritative work upon the currency. The spiritual descendant of Charles Jenkinson is the modern civil servant, and his son, though fifteen years Prime Minister, has often more in common with the permanent head of a department than with a modern democratic statesman.

From the first Charles Jenkinson destined his son for high political office, and to his father the son's character owed much. Years afterwards it was said of him that "he always quotes his father"[1], and it seemed indeed that the lives of father and son had blended together to form an unrivalled experience of fifty years in high politics. The early years of his life were completely dominated by his father. If Liverpool lacked imagination, he lost it following his father's precepts; if he compensated for this deficiency by perseverance and industry, it was his father who instilled in him these virtues. Young Jenkinson was sent to Charterhouse, and a letter written to him in 1784 survives.[2] It deserves quotation, for, in the paragon which Charles Jenkinson wished his son to be, may be seen the lineaments of the future Prime Minister: "You should not be satisfied in doing your exercises just so as to pass without censure, but always aim at perfection; and be assured that in doing so you will by degrees approach to it. I hope also you will

1 Add. MSS. 38743, f. 266, Arbuthnot to Huskisson.
2 Yonge, *Life of Lord Liverpool*, I, 7.

avail yourself of every leisure moment to apply yourself to algebra and the mathematics: you will thereby attain not only a knowledge of those sciences, but by an early acquaintance with them you will acquire a habit of reasoning closely and correctly on every subject, which will on all occasions be of infinite use to you. The hours which are not employed in the manner before mentioned you will give to the reading of history and books of criticism, and here the knowledge you have of the French language will furnish you with many excellent books." And, lest the fourteen-year-old schoolboy should become frivolous even in his reading, his father adds: "I would wish you for the present not to read any novels, as they will only waste your time, which you will find not more than sufficient for the pursuit of more useful and important studies." By the time he reached Oxford in 1786, Jenkinson was an exceptionally well-educated young man; it is in fact surprising to find that he retained any youthful spirits at all. The impression he made at Christ Church is told by one with whom he was intimate:[1] "When at the University he was not only a first-rate scholar, but he had confessedly acquired a greater share of general knowledge than perhaps any undergraduate of that day. He was an excellent historian and his attention had been directed so early by his father to the contending interests of the European nations, that intricate political questions were already familiar to his mind."

It is interesting to contrast the impressions which he made at this age with those made in the last fifteen years of

1 J. F. Newton, *Early Days of the Right Honble George Canning*, London, 1828.

his life. As a Prime Minister he is praised for kindness, for amiability, for fairness, and for consideration; as an under-graduate the impression is that of a pushful and self-important young man. Lady Stafford, who saw him in his father's house during 1787, found him "well educated, well informed, and sensible", but she found him too ready, in the presence of Pitt and Thurlow, to put forward his own ideas rather than attending to theirs.[1] His tutor also seems to have found him too opinionative,[2] and at all times he was ready to put his ideas into a flood of language. He himself realised this fault: "Though I had contracted a habit of disputing in company during the first two or three terms I was here, I have been long since convinced of the bad effects arising from that habit, and I have prevented these bad effects in the most particular manner by avoiding as much as possible all mixed companies and living as much as possible with a few particular people."[3] Even so Leveson Gower found his "excessive importance" had become "very disgusting", spoke slightingly of his abilities, but thought that "a wonderful fluency of words and no share of mauvaise honte may cause his making some figure in the House of Commons".[4]

But there was also something in Liverpool's character which prevented him from becoming a mere prig. A Christ Church contemporary speaks of the "benignity of his personal intercourse", and remarks that his "temper was extremely conciliatory".[5] There was also a habitual dis-

1 *Private Correspondence of Lord Granville*, Leveson Gower, i, 8.
2 Yonge, i, 9: "My tutor has frequently thought that I have been too
much run away with by general ideas."   3 *Ibid.*
4 Leveson Gower, i, 35.   5 Newton, *op. cit.*

regard of his own dignity which contrasted strangely with his self-conscious importance. His father had told him while at school that he should pay proper attention to his person, for "every failing in this respect creates disgust or exposes a man to ridicule in such a manner as to defeat the advantages which he could otherwise derive from his parts or learning".[1] The fault, if it can be called a fault, remained with him through life, and years afterwards Mme Lieven found him "the oddest figure imaginable, full of the most amusing blunders". And when he was a rising star in the political horizon, one who had known him well said: "It is very odd that in all the time I have known him I never observed what a very plain and awkward man he is."[2] This did perhaps lose him some of the respect he might have enjoyed, and Leveson Gower, from whose bitter remarks jealousy was not absent, said that those who had known him well at Oxford "cannot certainly look up to him with any great admiration".[3] But it was this combination of amiability and gaucherie which won him the friendship of George Canning, whom he met for the first time at Oxford.

Canning could well appreciate the solid qualities of Jenkinson, and he looked upon him as a future rival. Both belonged to a select "speaking society", where "looking forward to some distant period when we might be ranged against one another on a larger field, we were perhaps neither of us without the vanity of wishing to obtain an early ascendancy over the other".[4] But the pleasant temper of both converted the possible rivalry into a close, though

1 Yonge, I, 7.   2 Leveson Gower, I, 345.   3 *Ibid.* I, 217.
4 Newton, *op. cit.*, quoting a letter received later from Canning.

not always an easy, friendship. Canning was always ready
to exploit his brilliant and slightly malicious wit, Jenkinson was always apt to turn suddenly from a genial companion to an offended and pompous young man, and, in the
words of the Dean of Christ Church, they were "quarrelling
and making it up all day long".[1] Still they made it up and
the intimacy endured even though its most frequent inci-
dents were the injuries of one at the apparent unkindness of
the other. The irritation which both felt at times was born
of affection, and Jenkinson retained a sincere admiration
for Canning. In the future there was to be a serious
estrangement which was not completely healed for nine
years, but the permanent result of this friendship was seen
in 1821 and after, when Liverpool looked to Canning,
though his fellow-Tories would gladly have seen Canning
consigned to the outer darkness.

Oxford was followed by foreign travel. Here perhaps the
rigour of his education was relaxed, though even the
beauties of Italy did not prevent him from studying
Blackstone. But naturally it was the Roman poets, and
Virgil above all, who commanded attention in such a place.
"I have travelled with Aeneas through the grotto of the
Sybill and the lake of Avernus; I have passed with him from
Tartarus to Cocytus and from Cocytus to Elysium. I have
drunk Falernian wine in the villa of Hortensius, contemplating from the same spot the Temple of Venus, the
houses of Cicero and Caesar, and the reputed (though
falsely so) tomb of Agrippina. I have visited the baths of
Marius and the famous ruin of the temple of Jupiter.

1 Dorothy Marshall, *The Rise of George Canning*.

Virgil has been my constant companion; I have found him not inferior in geography to poetry, and I shall in a few days pay my homage at the tomb of the divine poet, remembering with a grateful heart the luxurious moments his verses have so lately afforded me."[1] Did Liverpool turn in later years from affairs of state to the "divine poet"? Perhaps he did, but the classics were not for him the constant solace that they were for Canning or for Gladstone. He who has had to turn the long folios of Liverpool's official correspondence may also wish that he had retained the vigorous style of this early letter, but the parenthetic "though falsely so" is symptomatic of the cautious phrasing which was to rob his writing of all force and character.

In the summer of 1789 his travels led him to Paris, and there he stood as a spectator at the first scene of the Revolutionary Epic, the taking of the Bastille. It was not an experience which inspired him with any respect for the wisdom of the mob. In the years which followed the war it was not without importance that the Prime Minister had seen the infuriated men and women marching upon the Bastille.

In 1790, while still under age, he was returned for the borough of Appleby by Sir John Lowther. But it was another year before his voice was heard at Westminster. When the time came for him to speak it was not necessary for him to force his way forward, for he was chosen by Pitt to defend the Government against a vote of censure on what was known as the Russian armament question. Russia had embarked upon war with Turkey, and Pitt had announced

1 Yonge, I, 12.

an increase in the navy with the avowed object of opposing Russia if necessary. Jenkinson drew attention to the designs of Russia, which threatened not only the neighbouring states but the whole balance of power in Europe; he made a long and careful examination of the situation, and his conclusion was voiced in the fine phrase, "Great Britain is constitutionally the foe of all wars of ambition and wanton aggression, and a stable peace is equally her interest and her inclination". The speech was more successful than its author could possibly have hoped. "I cannot resist", wrote Dundas to Charles Jenkinson, "the impulse I find to inform you that your son has just made one of the finest speeches I have ever heard. Mr Pitt thinks exactly as I do with regard to it." And Pitt praised it publicly as "not only a more able first speech than had ever been heard from a young member, but one so full of philosophy and science, strong and perspicuous language, and sound and convincing arguments, that it would have done credit to the most practised debater and most experienced statesman that ever existed". It cannot be said that Liverpool fulfilled entirely the promise of this maiden speech, but it is usually forgotten that he remained a Parliamentary speaker of a very high order. In later years, in the House of Lords, he was equal to the task of bearing almost the full burden of debate upon the Government side. As a speaker Wellington placed him alone with Pitt, and, even if it be granted that Wellington probably shut his ears when Canning spoke, it is still high praise from one whose Parliamentary experience extended over so many years.

In the years which followed, Jenkinson did not take a

frequent part in debate, but when he did speak it was upon important questions. His reputation grew steadily and was confirmed in 1793 by a seat at the India Board. In 1796 he obtained election for Rye, so freeing himself of a patron and establishing a connection with the Cinque Ports which was to last until his death. His frequent absences from Parliament can be accounted for by two things: he was a conscientious colonel of the Kentish Militia, and he had become a lover. The Kentish Militia was employed upon garrison duty, and was stationed for a considerable time in Scotland, where, he told his father, "the style of living is rather gross, though very hospitable. The servants are few, and very dirty; but there is a great quantity of meat put upon the table, and after dinner the bottle passes rather quicker than I like." The story of his courtship is told in Dorothy Marshall's *Rise of George Canning*, and in Canning's own words.[1] The object of his choice was Lady Louisa Hervey, daughter of the Earl of Bristol, and the affair went smoothly to the declaration and acceptance, but in obtaining the consent of the two fathers unexpected hazards arose. The Earl of Bristol acquiesced and promised a dowry of £10,000, but Hawkesbury[2] raised difficulties. He thought the match "imprudent and ineligible in many respects", and would have his son unmarried until he was thirty unless "he should marry a fortune indeed"; the Herveys were Whigs and a young Tory would not profit by marrying one. Canning busied himself on Jenkinson's behalf, but it was Jenkinson himself who discovered the right form of

1 Pp. 135 ff.
2 Charles Jenkinson had become Lord Hawkesbury in 1786.

pressure. Hawkesbury valued his son's career before all things, and Jenkinson now gave out that he was so broken in spirit that he must absent himself from Parliament. Before this threat Hawkesbury gave way, consent was given, and the marriage took place on 17 March 1794 ("Jenkinson in such spirits and such fidgetts that it was quite uncomfortable to sit near him"). In spite of the help which he had given, Canning found the marriage not entirely to his liking; Lady Louisa was something of a prude, she imposed upon the buoyant spirits of Canning an uncomfortable restraint, and Jenkinson's house ceased to be a centre of Canningite society. It is from the time of his marriage that the warmth of Jenkinson's intimacy with Canning began to cool. Jenkinson, however, was extremely happy with his wife, she suited exactly that solemn side of his character which Canning was so fond of ridiculing, and she was an admirable if not a very interesting young woman.

In 1796 two events occurred to advance the fortunes of the Jenkinson family. Hawkesbury became Earl of Liverpool, Jenkinson assuming the courtesy title of Hawkesbury; and the latter was made Master of the Mint. He was now definitely on the road to Cabinet office, occupying one of the chief subordinate offices; but his further promotion might have been delayed for some years. He was young and could afford to wait; his seniors were but in middle age and were not likely to move. But all prospects were put out of joint, and Hawkesbury's were immensely improved, when Pitt resigned over the Catholic question. The Jenkinsons had both been opponents of the Catholic claims, and both were prepared to serve under Addington, who, faced with a dearth of experienced ministers, made Hawkesbury, just thirty years of age, his Foreign Secretary.

It is not here intended to refer more than briefly to the twelve years which now elapsed before Liverpool became Prime Minister. As Foreign Secretary under Addington it was his duty to negotiate the Peace of Amiens, and his career at this time belongs to the controversies which surround that peace. By his period as Foreign Secretary it cannot be said that he added greatly to his reputation, but he did not, on the other hand, lose, and, by occupying such an important position, he established a claim which would entitle him to consideration in any future Government. Thus, when Pitt succeeded Addington, he became Home Secretary; there was perhaps a slight lessening of the esteem in which he was held, but there was nothing tangible, nothing which would retard seriously his future career. In addition, he had, under Addington, taken up that position which he was to hold until his retirement, Tory leader in the House of Lords.[1] Addington, weak in both Houses, had found himself especially weak in the Lords where no speaker of merit could oppose the Whigs, Grenvilles, and Pittites; he had, then, raised Hawkesbury to the House of Lords, and Pitt had continued him as Government leader in that House.

It was during Pitt's second ministry that there occurred a serious quarrel between Hawkesbury and Canning; and Canning, with the bitter frankness of an injured friend,

[1] Portland was Prime Minister over Liverpool, but he is said never to have spoken in the House of Lords.

told Pitt that Hawkesbury "is not either a Ninny or a great and able man. He has useful powers of mind, great industry, and much information." Pitt was more kind: "With his information...and the habits of reflection which he has acquired, he is by no means a contemptible adviser"; he confessed that he could not do without him in the Lords; but he added that he was not a man "to whose decisions, singly, I would commit a great question of policy".[1] These were not perhaps the warmest of recommendations for a man who was to take up the burden of Pitt, and under whom Canning was to serve for eleven years. But to compensate for this he had grown into great favour with the King who, on the death of Pitt, offered him the premiership. To a man of thirty-five it was a tempting bait; to refuse might mean long years of waiting, until he was too old to enjoy the great heritage, or until some other young man had risen in the political firmament. It says much for the calm judgment of Hawkesbury that he read the omens aright—and the omens said that no man save Pitt could succeed where Pitt had almost failed—that he did refuse, and that he advised the King to waive his objection to Fox. This advice the King followed, and the ministry of All Talents was formed, but not before he had forced Hawkesbury to accept another legacy of Pitt, the splendid and profitable Lord Wardenship of the Cinque Ports. This ensured him a sufficient income until his death and gave him a pleasant house at Walmer Castle.

Hawkesbury led the Opposition to the Talents, and, upon their fall, the King hoped once more that he would

1 Marshall, *op. cit.*, p. 290.

take the Treasury. But it had been decided previously that the best way of reconciling the factions and jealousies within the Tory party was to entrust the lead to the Duke of Portland, who had not the ability to raise a faction, and whose part in politics had, of late years, been too obscure to arouse any jealousies. Under Portland the Government was virtually that of a committee, with Liverpool, Canning, Castlereagh, and Spencer Perceval as its members. It was a system which could not endure for long, particularly when one of the members was possessed of Canning's restless ambition. The quarrel between Canning and Castlereagh brought about the fall of Portland and placed the premiership once more within Liverpool's reach. Portland had become deeply involved in the quarrel; he had promised Canning that Castlereagh should be replaced by Wellesley, but he had concealed this promise from most of his colleagues. At the beginning of September Canning called upon Portland to fulfil his promise, and it was not Portland's honour alone which was involved, for Portland had backed his promise with a promise which he had— "most unfairly", says Liverpool—extracted from the King. With Canning's demand the whole transaction came to light and the rest of the Cabinet objected to a step upon which they had not been consulted and of which they did not approve. A complete dissolution of the Government seemed imminent, and Liverpool decided that the best course would be to hasten the dissolution in such a way as to relieve them of some of their difficulties. "The promise, however, was absolute," he wrote, "and, having been made in the King's name, must necessarily be fulfilled. The state of the Duke of Portland's health had become more critical every day; and it occurred to me that the best means of obviating the various difficulties with which we were surrounded, was by persuading the Duke of Portland to retire, and by making, in consequence, an entire new arrangement of the administration."[1]   In a new administration there would be an initial difficulty to be overcome in the House of Commons: the lead would be disputed between Canning and Perceval.   Canning had held the key position of Foreign Secretary and he had a longer administrative experience than Perceval, but the latter had been "entrusted with the general direction of business in the House of Commons" and was not prepared to serve under Canning.   Perceval proposed a sensible solution: that both should serve under a peer.   Liverpool was implied though not mentioned by name, but Canning replied that he would resign if Portland resigned, that the Prime Minister must be in the Commons, that he was willing to serve as Premier, but in no other situation. When this deadlock became apparent Liverpool and Perceval obtained the King's permission to negotiate with Grey and Grenville.

What this offer to the Whigs might have been is not known, for the mere proposal to negotiate was met by Grey with an instantaneous refusal. The Whigs were, in the severe words of their most recent historian,[2] "well content to leave Perceval to flounder on in office—to allow him to carry on the Government of the country at a very critical moment of the war, with the assistance of such incompetents as Ryder, Westmorland, and Mulgrave—and to

1 Yonge, I, 287.   2 Michael Roberts, *The Whig Party*, 1807-12.

supplement purely destructive criticism by a stiff intracta-
bility in negotiation". The duel between Canning and
Castlereagh put both out of the question so far as office was
concerned, and Perceval was left to face the future with only
a sad rump of the great Pitt party to support him.

Nevertheless, this ministry endured for three troubled
years; it was able to carry on the war, to resist a strong
Parliamentary Opposition, and to stop the rot which seemed
to be eating its way into the Tory party. It cannot be said
that it was a good Government, but it was a useful one and
might have led on to greater things. It refused the Bullion
Report, it imposed the Orders in Council which caused
great domestic distress and brought the United States into
the war, and the irritation with which the Foreign Secretary, Wellesley, regarded the pedestrian methods of his
colleagues was not entirely unwarranted. But, at this time,
vigorous government was almost a fair substitute for good
government; and vigorous government Perceval supplied.
He was a lawyer and a High Tory, which was not perhaps a
combination likely to recommend him for popularity, but
he was also a man of spirit and determination, and, in a
House of Commons which saw little spirit or determination
on either front bench, he commanded respect and support.
"Perceval's character", Liverpool told Wellington, "is
completely established in the House of Commons; he has
acquired an authority there beyond any minister within my
recollection except Mr Pitt."[1] Had the Tories found, in
fact, another Pitt, and would Perceval rise phoenix-like
from the ruins of 1809 as the great man had risen from the

1 Yonge, I, 372.

ruins of Empire and Coalition? Prophecies and prognosti-
cations were cut short with the life of their subject, for, on
12 May 1812, Perceval was shot dead in the lobby of the
House of Commons by the lunatic Bellingham.

The confused period of negotiation which followed has
been recently examined with accuracy and detail;[1] this fact
and the scope of the present work make unnecessary more
than a brief résumé. The circumstances of the time seemed
to point directly to the formation of a "mixed administration", and the Regent would probably have welcomed such
a result provided that the formula "Tory bloc plus independent supporters" could be maintained, and that he
would not have to accept a predominantly Whig administration. The Prince had thrown over the friends of his
youth too recently to allow one to approach the other
without bitterness; he was convinced that Whig rule
would mean ruin to the country, the Whigs were convinced that they could not accept office save on their own
terms and as a single united party. He first hoped that
the remaining Tory ministers would be able to carry
on, and he employed Eldon to discover their sentiments.
The consensus of opinion was that the prospects of the
Government as it stood were doubtful but not desperate
"if the administration is known to possess the entire confidence of the Prince Regent". Consequently the ministers
chose Liverpool as their head, and he was entrusted with
the Government by the Prince Regent.

Liverpool had now entered upon the situation which he
was to hold for nearly fifteen years; he had been placed in

1 Michael Roberts, *op. cit.*, pp. 382–405.

that position by the unanimous vote of his colleagues—in itself something of a novelty—and with the approval of the Prince. But it seemed at first that his premiership would be short and inglorious. Liverpool sought the support of Canning and Wellesley; he offered them good offices and upon the Catholic question a compromise—rendered necessary even without their participation by the number of Catholic sympathisers among the ministerial Tories—that this question should remain "open", all Government supporters being free to speak and to vote upon it as they wished. There was certainly considerable difference between leaving the question to its fate in a House of Commons where anti-Catholics could command a small majority, and making it a Government measure and placing all the resources of ministerial management at the service of the "Catholics"; and this compromise did not satisfy Canning and Wellesley. Canning hinted that a larger arrangement was necessary, entertained "a most anxious wish that His Royal Highness would send for Lord Moira",[1] and thought that Wellesley "ought to receive authority to make some specific proposal to the Opposition which might bring over to us some of the best of that body".[2] The fact was that Canning would not come in as an ally to an established Government, and he required a Government in which he and his friends would have the central and controlling interest. On these vague grounds the negotiation was broken off, and Liverpool determined to stand alone; but optimism was not enough and on 21 May Stuart Wortley carried a motion in the House of Commons

1 Roberts, *op. cit.*   2 *Ibid.*

praying the Regent to form an efficient administration. Wortley was a Tory, an admirer of Perceval, and member for Yorkshire; a number of his supporters upon this motion were country gentlemen of the same type. The significance of the vote of 21 May was that it was not a party victory, and so far as the country could speak it had spoken against the continuance of the weak Tory ministry. The resignation of the ministers followed as a matter of course, but they continued with their departmental business until successors could be found.

The Prince had now to fulfil his constitutional function of finding a Government capable of governing. It is possible to blame him for not applying directly to the Whigs, but it is also fair to remember that the Whigs could not command a majority in the Commons, that only the most unscrupulous use of patronage could have procured them a majority from the electorate, and that the chief objection to them was not their ideas of reform but their defeatist attitude to the war. There were, on the other hand, influential members of both Houses attached to neither party, and it was to Wellesley that the Prince now entrusted the formation of a "mixed administration". Here an unexpected obstacle arose: Wellesley had just sanctioned the publication of an explanation of his resignation in February, which reflected bitterly upon Perceval; the colleagues of the late minister now refused, in duty bound, to serve under Wellesley. Wellesley then hoped to coalesce with the Whigs, but the Prince urged the ministers to reconsider their decision. They replied adhering to their refusal, and from the explanations which the Prince demanded there emerges an interesting fact. The majority of the ministers were in favour of negotiation with Wellesley and Canning, but they concurred with the minority, headed by Liverpool, in order not to split the party. There are hints that Liverpool himself felt that his withdrawal from politics for a few months—until the Catholic question had passed—would be the best solution of everybody's problem; but his colleagues stood by him, and thus early the position of Liverpool was made the cardinal point in the composition of a Tory ministry.

Wellesley now pressed to be allowed to make an approach to the Whigs, and at last, on 1 June, the Regent gave him full powers and he immediately made the Whigs an offer. They were to have four or five places in a cabinet of twelve or thirteen; Canning, Moira, Erskine, and Wellesley himself would fill four more places; and the remaining four might be filled from among the old ministers. The Whigs would secure the passage of Catholic Emancipation, their favourite measure, and, with two sympathisers in Erskine and Moira, they would be able to dominate the Cabinet. But the Whigs refused Wellesley's offer outright: they would come in as a party and in sole control, or they would not come in at all; it was to the principle of disunion and jealousy that they objected; to the supposed balance of contending interests in a Cabinet so measured out by preliminary stipulation. The Whigs had been asked to come forward as individuals and to unlearn the lessons of party government; their refusal may be justified in principle but it was impolitic in practice.

Wellesley had failed, and the Prince now turned to his

friend Moira who might make a ministry from the moderate men of all parties. Moira was convinced that nothing could be expected from the Whigs, but in order "to take from them the last shadow of excuse which they might attempt in saying that I had made no overture to them", he made them an offer. He sought an interview with Grey and Grenville, at which both sought a convenient excuse for the termination of the negotiations. The excuse was found in Moira's attitude to the household officers, for he refused to allow the Whigs to exercise their right of dismissing these officers, insisting, not that it was beyond their powers, but that such an action would constitute an insulting and unnecessary triumph at the Prince's expense. On the refusal of the Whigs, Moira began to plan a ministry with the Canningites. By 7 June he had a Cabinet outlined and had obtained a promise of support from Liverpool; at this seemingly favourable juncture he suddenly resigned his commission, and Liverpool succeeded quietly to that situation which he had seemed to lose irretrievably on 21 May.

Moira's sudden relinquishment of his chances remains something of a mystery. To his cousin, Sir Charles Hastings, he explained that it was necessary to have a ministry ready immediately as the Treasury was almost empty, that Erskine and the Duke of Norfolk had suddenly drawn back, that this would have meant bringing in two more of the old ministers, and that this in turn would have "appeared to compromise my principles for the sake of being at the head of a ministry". It is also probable that the Prince played upon Moira's doubts and fears, and persuaded him to withdraw in favour of Liverpool. Moira was certainly devoted to the Prince; he believed that he "had just done the good of proving that the Prince has bent himself fairly and frankly to the wishes of the Commons"; and a little later he was complaining that "my attachment to the Prince has barred the field of fame against me". It seems, moreover, that Moira had some arrangement with the ministers before he withdrew. In 1815 Liverpool reminded Vansittart of the time when "Lord Moira assisted us so *materially* in 1812", and the fact that he also mentions Colonel Doyle as "one of the only two for whom he seriously pressed" seems to point to some hurried arrangement. The facts seem to be that Moira would have wished to launch a ministry, but that, at the last moment, he encountered new difficulties; that the Prince encouraged his timidity, emphasising the absolute necessity of having a ministry in power immediately; and that Moira agreed to see Liverpool, and to connive at the resurrection of the old ministry as a stopgap. He continued to hope for a further change, and was soon advising Wellesley not to associate with the Whigs as he might soon be called upon by the Prince. But he misread the motives of the Prince, whose chief wish was for a "safe" ministry commanding a Parliamentary majority. The House of Commons having asked for a stronger ministry was now convinced that no better ministry could be found, and a steady majority supported Liverpool.

So, as an admitted second best, the ministry, which was to rule for almost fifteen years, entered upon its heritage. Liverpool was shortly to make a bid for the support of Canning, but the negotiation broke down upon Canning's inveterate jealousy of Castlereagh. In 1814, however, Canning made peace with the Government and was definitely reconciled to Liverpool; in that year his followers accepted subordinate office and he himself went on a mission to Lisbon; in 1816 he consented to enter the Cabinet by the back door and succeeded Buckinghamshire at the Board of Control on the latter's death. In 1818 the Duke of Wellington was persuaded to enter the Cabinet, and these were the sole changes during the next eight years, and, in all its essentials, the Government which had been considered hardly strong enough to rule for a day remained without alteration for that period.

A general election in the autumn of 1812 strengthened the Government slightly, but more important to its situation were the victories of Wellington which silenced criticism of war policy and turned the attention of the public from domestic complaints to military success. When the Government reached the period of the peace treaties it was as strong as any Government of the century. After the war, however, a reaction set in and the country began to demand a return to pre-war conditions which could not be accomplished; the expenses of Government had risen during the war, and it was never possible to bring them back to anywhere near the figures of the 1790's. Caught between the upper and nether millstones of public demand and expenditure which could not be reduced, the Government nearly perished; it just survived, and the radical agitation rallied independent Tories around the Government once more. At the very time, however, that it was possible to look forward to a new and happier era in domestic politics, the melancholy business of the Queen cut across political affairs and reduced the Government to impotency. Once more the Government just managed to survive, but it was clear that if it was to survive for any length of time it must be transformed in personnel and, far more important, in spirit. It is with that transformation, with its effects upon the course of government, and with the pre-eminent part played by Liverpool both in that transformation and in the new policy which resulted, that this work is principally concerned. First, however, it is necessary to examine the character of Liverpool, his methods as Prime Minister, and the state of politics which produced the phenomenon known as Liberal Toryism.

CHAPTER II

THE CHARACTER AND OPINIONS OF
LORD LIVERPOOL

"HIMSELF immovable in his hostility to the demands of the Catholics, it was still he who had introduced into office Mr Canning....The alterations in the Silk Trade, the Navigation Laws, the Corn Laws, in the whole system, in short, of the duties and prohibitions had taken place under Lord Liverpool's authority and with his approval. His character at the same time was to the public a sufficient pledge that love of novelty and theory would not be allowed to run into extravagance—for seldom has a minister, not distinguished by any striking brilliancy of genius, and greatly inferior to more than one of his colleagues in popular oratory, gained so much weight and conciliated so much universal favour by the mere force of his personal character. He possessed a sound, cautious mind; a long political life had stored it with all the political knowledge that a minister requires....Above all the country trusted his pure and unquestioned integrity." In these words, and without undue bias, the writer of Liverpool's obituary in the *Annual Register* summed up his character. A combination of pure Tory and Liberal opinions, long experience in Government, and a high moral character which had helped to convince people that the politician was not dishonest by definition, were the principal features which impressed his contemporaries; they were also the qualities which fitted him for the premiership.

His many years as Prime Minister had merged the man into the trained administrator. He had become an institution, and with his seizure it seemed as though some pillar of the constitution had fallen, but he had acquired also much of the impersonality which belongs to an institution. His private life contained no scandal and few anecdotes which might endear him to the public mind, his virtues were not those upon which men would lavish extravagant praise, his failings were not those which would be attacked with violence. It is these things which account for the slight hold which Liverpool has had upon the memory of posterity. Other ministers, with far less service to recommend them, are remembered if only for some particular action or some particular mistake; Liverpool, with fifteen years as Premier to his credit, gives his name to a ministry and nothing more.

Something has already been said of Liverpool's early career; he had gained a wider experience of Government than any other statesman, and he had proved himself an effective speaker. But able men have not always shown the qualities required of a Premier; in Liverpool's case the asset of his own character, which fitted him for the business of managing a Cabinet, far outweighed his abilities as an executive statesman. To begin with a negative quality: the frankness and amiability of his character made him a man whom others forbore from hurting if they could. He was extremely sensitive to the opinions of others, and, when accused of harshness or injustice, he suffered the greatest anguish of mind, and this might in turn precipitate periods of gloom and depression. His friends, who were accustomed to his behaviour when at ease with life, refrained from harassing him unduly, and those who met him only in an official way were still struck with his straightforward and honest manner. Those who worked with him display a respect which amounted˙to affection. In 1822 Huskisson, contemplating resignation, wrote: "I could not conclude this letter without entreating you to believe that however much that connection by creating opportunities of frequent intercourse has strengthened the personal sentiments which I entertain towards you, they could not be impaired by its interruption, and I shall at all times set the same high value on your friendly regard and retain the same feelings of esteem and respect for your character both public and private."[1] And the sincerity of this is shown by a letter to Canning: "In respect to the personal feelings which I shall retain towards Lord Liverpool it is more easy to state them to you than to himself. My sense of his kindness during the last seven years as well as of his individual good will and friendship at all times will remain unabated."[2] Arbuthnot, who worked for many years under Liverpool at the Treasury, became almost extravagant in his expressions of devotion: Lord Liverpool could have commanded his very life.[3] Others who knew him less intimately also paid their tributes of respect: W. H. Fremantle, for instance, entertained for him the "highest personal respect and warmest feeling", and would have been pleased to work under him at the Treasury.[4] This respect and his "kindness" could play an important part

1 Huskisson, *Papers*, p. 137.   2 *Ibid*. p. 120.
3 *Ibid*. p. 159.   4 Buckingham, I, 257.

in the running of a Government. Thus in 1822 Arbuthnot, after talking with Canning of the ways in which Wallace, Vice-President of the Board of Trade and a man with a grudge, could be soothed, wrote to Liverpool: "We both thought that a communication to him from yourself would gratify the most, and would give us the best chance.... We, either of us, should be ready to lend you all our aid for the purpose; but, as I have said, we strongly feel that kindness expressed by yourself would carry far more weight."[1]

Publicly Liverpool enjoyed a respect which few disputed; some might disparage his abilities, none doubted the integrity and honesty of his character. At no time is this more noticeable than in the months immediately after the Queen's "trial", when ministers were not likely to be lightly praised even by their friends. Lord Dacre, who had presented the Queen's petition in the Lords, said that Liverpool was "very able and the honestest man that could be dealt with. You may always trust him...and though he may be going to answer you after a speech, you may go out and leave your words in his hands and he will never misrepresent you."[2] From the west country a Tory clergyman wrote that even political enemies "very generally agreed to praise the great good conduct and talent of Lord Liverpool in a situation of peculiar difficulty".[3] Greville thought him "a model of fairness, impartiality, and candour";[4] while a Tory who complained of the ministry as a whole wrote that Liverpool's conduct was "quite unexceptionable, and be-

1 Add. MSS. 38191, f. 233.   2 Phipps, *Memoir of R. P. Ward*.
3 Add. MSS. 31232, f. 255, Dean of Bristol to Vansittart.
4 Greville, I, 108.

coming a judge as well as a statesman".[1] This respect was
an important qualification for his office, and it gave to the
ministry a prestige which usually escapes comment in accounts of the period. When Liverpool told Stuart Wortley
that he would resign if the Queen's name was not excluded
from the Liturgy, Wortley replied: "Upon this ground
I applaud your determination of giving up your office
rather than give way. Retirement upon such grounds will
only add to the weight of your character, which now stands
so high that I will venture to say this, even if you do retire,
you will not remain out of office."[2] In Liverpool's personal
reputation Canning saw the chief hopes of the ministry at
this time: "Nothing but plain management, or rather absence of all management, will suit the crisis; and happily
Liverpool stands in a situation in which *his own* word will
carry him through."[3] During the long premiership of
Liverpool an imperceptible change took place in one aspect
of English manners: at the end of the eighteenth century,
and in spite of Pitt's great name, the average Englishman
endorsed Adam Smith's verdict upon that "insidious and
crafty animal, vulgarly called a statesman or politician"; by
the time of the great Reform Bill there is already found the
alliance between politicians and the respectable middle
class. Victorian Governments would have been utterly different in character had not politics become the profession
for honest men as well as the recreation of landed aristocrats. In the eighteenth century an honest politician had
been, in the public eye, an extraordinary and praiseworthy

1 Colchester, III, 181, F. Burton to Colchester.
2 Yonge, III, 117.   3 *Ibid.* p. 181.

exception to a general rule; in the nineteenth century the corrupt time server was singled out for reprobation because he was an isolated case and not the symbol of a class. In accounting for this change something must be allowed to the hold which Liverpool established in the esteem of the respectable middle class, and to the honesty with which his Government was administered.

Liverpool was never a social success. He "had no habits of any but official employment", and it was impossible to imagine him being happy in retirement.[1] To Madame Lieven he appeared gauche, and at Brighton Pavilion he was "the oddest figure imaginable", making "the most amusing blunders".[2] He had been a great favourite at the simple court of George III, he was out of place amid the splendours and frivolities of his son. In spite of this Madame Lieven seems to have liked him, and he, in his turn, provided a rare breath of scandal by his liking for her—"It is a common joke in this circle of society that he takes a very great interest in me; I quite like Prime Ministers"—and one evening, after a "long and solemn dinner, he amused us by the odd fancy of jumping over the back of a big sofa, on which I was seated, and establishing himself on a little footstool in front of me. The great Liverpool hovered and then settled on the ground, looking very comic."[3]

If Liverpool lacked social graces, he was a very different man in the company of those who understood him. There he could shake off his reserve and delight them with "the benignity of his personal intercourse". No trace of humour

1 Buckingham, II, 85. Wynn found Coombe Wood "unquestionably the dullest house in which I ever passed a day". *Ibid.* p. 33.
2 Lieven, p. 160.   3 *Ibid.* p. 195.

appears in his correspondence, and, indeed, private and intimate correspondence did not come easily to him ("Jenkinson never writes when he can possibly help it"[1]), but in conversation he does not seem to have been without the art of amusing. Thus at a visit to Dropmore "he was chatty, full of anecdote, and evidently anxious to please".[2] He was one of those whose chance actions have the knack of becoming grotesque—whether it was vaulting over a sofa to alight at the feet of Madame Lieven, or meeting Canning at Bath in "a huge pair of jack-boots, of the size and colour of fire buckets"—and, without certain real abilities, he would certainly have become buffoon or butt in ordinary to Canning and his friends.

The figure which emerges from the scanty references to his private life is that of a likeable man, modest, shy, and sometimes awkward, not easy to know, but repaying the effort of making his acquaintance with the pleasantness of his personality. He was honest and he was conscientious, but this last virtue was apt to run to excess and bring on a terrible and wearing anxiety. His pain at the thought of offending others and his troubled thoughts for the morrow produced depression or irritation which seriously affected his health and temper. At fifty he was already an old man with many of the failings of old age; and Huskisson in his letters to his wife made frequent mention of Liverpool's fidgets—"Liverpool is in one of his grand fidgetts"— "Liverpool beats Binning at figitatis. He ought to be the Grand Cross of the Order"—"I am so worried with the

1 Dorothy Marshall, *The Rise of George Canning*, p. 135.
2 Buckingham, II, 19.

grand figitatis at Fife House"[1]—and the King thought him "in the highest degree irritable without having any feeling".[2] In 1824 Eldon found him "damned ill and damned cross",[3] and in 1826 he had become more than usually peevish and was careless of the opinions of others when things were left to his decision.[4] This irritability became more common as the years went on, as his mind was more and more distracted with the dissensions of his colleagues, but, fortunately, it was an acquired, not an inherent characteristic, and his periods of irritability contrasted strongly with his normal equanimity.

Men will not suffer for long the leadership of a man who is no more than an amiable party manager, and the backing for authority must be sound principles and solid ideas. Again his correspondence gives little clue to the man, for his deviations from the strict path of administrative business are rare. But, particularly in his early life, there are references to his "habits of reflection", and the man who, at Oxford, impressed his contemporaries with the wealth of his general knowledge must have had thought and reason behind his actions. Sound judgment was one of his principal qualifications for high office, it was this which could take him out of the politician and make him a statesman. He was slow, but not afraid, to decide, and he adhered to a decision once made; "I have been long enough in life", he told Arbuthnot, "to know the advantages of a straight course on the one hand, and all the inconveniences

1 Add MSS. 39949, fs. 38, 42, 50.
2 Croker, I, 199. 3 Buckingham, II, 31.
4 Buckingham, II, 126. Not a first-hand opinion, being that of Lord Lonsdale.

which arise out of contrivencies on the other."[1]   He considered each question fully, but his mind was not clogged,
as were those of so many Tories, by outworn sentiment; he
attempted to consider each question on its merits, and the
result was that he was neither "liberal" nor "ultra", but
remained in an intermediary position. He was representative of his age in a way that few statesmen have been, for he
reflected both its prejudices and its enlightenment in exact
proportions, and, like the early nineteenth-century world
around him, his mind was a curious mixture of High
Toryism and the new ideas of "economists" and "philosophers". He seems, at one moment, to be looking back to
the eighteenth century, at another to have set his face towards the prosperous commercial world of the high nineteenth century. In his mind these ideas were reconciled,
and he succeeded in reconciling those ideas within his
ministry; there is no sign that he saw the deep antagonism
between the spirit of Canning and the spirit of Eldon, to
him both were true within their limits; at this blend of
ideas within Liverpool's mind it is possible to rejoice, for it
made possible the brilliant last period of his ministry.

The Tories acknowledged two masters, Burke and Pitt.
Yet there was, in this ancestry, an inherent conflict, and two
renegade Whigs could hardly provide a consistent body of
doctrine for the flamboyant creed of "Church and King".
The old Pitt went ill with the young Pitt, the Burke of the
Reflections was hard to reconcile with the Burke of the
Rockinghams. To these cross strains in their ancestry most
Tories were impervious, but they were nevertheless prolific

1 Yonge, III, 147.

of conflicts and misunderstandings within the party. All Tories were united in their opposition to Parliamentary Reform; the majority of Tories were opposed to the Catholic claims, but some of the most eminent were not; the majority despised the notions of political economists without a foot of land to their names, but a few were converts to the new doctrines. All were united once more in the basic sentiment of Toryism, which was a sense of the harmony of society. Neither King, Lords, Commons, nor people should govern, but each had an allotted sphere, and each could disturb the balance by venturing beyond that sphere; but these spheres were, of course, quite without definition, and attempts to define might once more set Tory against Tory. Generally speaking the Tories fell into two divisions, between which the line of demarcation became clearer after 1822: there were first the old or High Tories, who resisted reform wherever it appeared, who supported the old penal code, the old commercial system, and the old representative system; against them were the "liberals" who wished generally for administrative and legal reform, for Catholic Emancipation and for Free Trade, but who would still join in a defence of the Unreformed Parliament. Liverpool was able to keep both High and Liberal Tories within his Cabinet because he belonged completely to neither party, he shared important opinions with both, and between the two he was prepared to mediate.

The Radical disturbances of 1816 to 1819 retarded rather than advanced the cause of Parliamentary Reform. The Tories were more convinced than ever of the wickedness of reformers, and the Whigs became lukewarm in a cause which they saw so supported. After 1820 the question of Reform was quiescent, and the Tories were allowed to retain, without responsible criticism, their time-honoured objections to Reform just as the Whigs retained their traditional adherence to it. It is, however, interesting to turn back to one of Liverpool's earliest speeches, and to see in it a defence of the representative system couched in moderate, reasonable, and philosophic language. "The effects of government on the people do not so much depend on general principles and general theories as on little accidental circumstances which are frequently not even perceptible; and consequently, if plausible theories ought never to be an objection to Reform when practical grievances are felt, so defective theories ought not to be a ground for Reform, when not only no practical grievance, but every political advantage, is felt. ...In the first place...every person would agree that the landed interest ought to have the predominant weight. The landed interest is in fact the stamina of the country. In the second place, in a commercial country like this, the manufacturing and commercial interest ought to have a considerable weight, secondary to the landed interest but secondary to the landed interest alone. But is this all that is necessary? There are other descriptions of people, which, to distinguish them from those already mentioned I would style professional people, and whom I consider as absolutely necessary to the composition of the House of Commons." Among these professional people he included those eminent in the army, navy, and law, and those "who wished to raise themselves to the great offices of the state", for the representatives of the landed and commercial interests were not usually by experience fitted or by temperament inclined towards the business of government. These persons could find their way into Parliament by way of the rotten boroughs, and to say that the rotten boroughs had brought into Parliament many hard-working administrators is a far better justification than the traditional excuse that they had brought in a few brilliant young men. "The House of Commons, as the democratic part of the constitution, as the virtual representatives of the people, certainly to a degree, ought to be affected by public opinions in their operations. It must, however, never be forgotten that the first quality of the House of Commons is that of being a deliberative assembly. If public opinion is necessarily to affect their decisions on every occasion, it will cease to be a deliberative assembly, and the members of it would have nothing to do but to go to their constituents, and desire to be directed by them in the votes they are to give on every important subject. Public opinion ought then to have certain weight in the conduct of that House; but public opinion ought never to have so great a weight as to prevent their exercising their deliberative functions." And finally the reformers attributed to the representative system effects which must be part of every system: "Form a House of Commons as you please—assemble the people on Salisbury Plain—you cannot prevent their having improper attachments and improper aversions. The defect is not in the representation; it is in human nature, and our eyes had better be turned to the improvement of that."[1]

During the whole of Liverpool's Government—in spite

[1] *Parliamentary History*, xxx, 810ff.

of the expressed willingness of Tories to reform in specific instances where corruption was proved—there was but one change in the detail of the representative system; and that was the disenfranchisement of Grampound in 1819 when the patron, Sir Manasseh Lopez, was imprisoned for gross corruption. To the Tories the smallest change—the extension of the franchise to the neighbouring hundreds—would have been most acceptable; but this was rendered impossible by local conditions. The Whigs then suggested that the franchise should be transferred to Leeds, and in this form the disenfranchisement bill passed the Commons. In the Lords Liverpool succeeded in amending the measure to transfer the two members to the county of Yorkshire instead of to the town of Leeds. His reasons for doing so are interesting: "I should say that the giving of the right of election to the populous manufacturing towns was the worst remedy which could be applied. In the first place, it would be the greatest evil conferred upon these towns, it would subject the population to a perpetual factious canvass, which would divert more or less the people from their industrious habits, and keep alive a permanent spirit of turbulence and disaffection amongst them. Against such a measure the most respectable inhabitants of those towns would, I am convinced, protest....I do not wish to see more of such boroughs as Westminster, Southwark, and Nottingham. I believe them to be more corrupt than any other places when seriously contested...and the persons who find their way into Parliament from such places are generally those...who are least likely to be steadily attached to the good order of society." He added that he would prefer a project of borough reform to any other provided that it should substitute a "pure and well-conditioned borough for a corrupt one".[1]

Parliament was supposed to provide a virtual representation of the people, in other words it represented interests if it did not represent numbers. The support for which the Tories hoped was that of the educated classes, of the Church, of the Universities, of the gentry, and of respectable tradesmen or men of commerce. Most Tories affected to despise public opinion, but they were not consistent, for, at times, they were frankly opportunist: in 1827 Croker wrote, "You know how I despise popularity, and I set no store upon so hollow and fugacious a support, but it will in this instance probably last long enough to enable Mr Canning to form a Government strong enough to forfeit it with impunity", and in 1825 Wellington wanted Liverpool to dissolve Parliament while advantage might be taken of a wave of anti-Catholic feeling. The Tories thought popularity an odious thing—when the Whigs were popular—but they were ready to use it when the occasion arose.

This was the first article of Liverpool's Tory orthodoxy; during the years of his ministry the second was to be of far more immediate importance. The fact that Liverpool opposed the Catholic claims not only postponed Catholic Emancipation until after his death, but also enabled him to keep the precarious allegiance of the "ultras". A "Catholic" alliance to carry the question had been a possibility in 1812, and that it was still a possibility was shown in 1822

1 Yonge, III, 137-44.

when a meeting of the sponsors of the relief bill was
attended by Tierney, Newport, Parnell, Canning, Grant,
Phillimore, Plunket, and Wynn.[1] Because the Catholic
question remained open the Tory "Catholics" could join
without injuring their consciences, but it was only because
Liverpool held also some liberal views that they were ready
to do so. On the other hand, after 1822, the High Tories,
growing loud in their complaints against Canning and Huskisson, remained in office only because Liverpool was the
surest safeguard against Catholic Emancipation. No
Government which did not contain both elements could
man its front bench effectively or gain sufficient support in
the House of Commons. The movement for Catholic
Emancipation was carried on in England by a part of the
upper class—it was unpopular in the country, and "No
popery" could still win elections—in Ireland by the whole
nation save the Protestant minority. The question was
really an Irish one and, when it is so considered, the reason
behind the apparent unreason of the Tories can be seen;
behind the stereotyped arguments of dual allegiance was
the very real fear of Irish demagogues at Westminster, of
Ireland ruled at the dictation of the priests, and of the
English power in Ireland broken for ever. The Tories
claimed that the English rule in Ireland was based upon
Protestantism, and that no securities could safeguard that
power once the Irish peasants could elect their natural
leaders; in that simple argument history has proved them
right, and the present age is still too obsessed with the

[1] Buckingham, I, 314. Similar meetings were held at other times as
the occasion demanded it.

problems of nationality to say whether or not they were right in reason and in justice. Characteristically Liverpool based his opposition on expediency rather than principle, he "expressly stated that circumstances might arise in which in his judgment some alteration in those laws might be advisable", but at the present time he said "I will fairly own that in the present state of the opinions and feelings of the Roman Catholics, I do not believe such a project to be practicable, consistently with the attainment of the avowed objects of really satisfying the Roman Catholics and of affording an adequate security to the Established Church and Constitution".[1]

If Liverpool followed the old and not the young Pitt on the question of Parliamentary Reform, if he deserted his master entirely upon the Catholic question, he went farther than Pitt had ever gone in his allegiance to the economic ideas of Adam Smith. Questions of commercial policy he found most congenial to his mind, and upon them he spoke always with the authority born of long study. He recognised the ability of Huskisson and he invited his close co-operation; how close this co-operation became may be judged from a note which Liverpool sent with the draft of a speech in 1822: "...as there may be a chance of your being able to look it over early tomorrow and I beg you will *cut* and *slash* it as much as you please."[2]

Liverpool was a convinced free trader. In 1812 it is interesting to find him saying: "It has been well said in a foreign country, when it was asked what should be done to make commerce prosper, the answer was *laissez-faire*; and

1 Parker, I, 68.   2 Add. MSS. 39948, f. 53.

it was undoubtedly true that the less commerce and manufacturers were meddled with the more they were likely to
prosper."[1] In the concluding years of the war, and during
the post-war troubles, there was little opportunity for
putting these ideas into practice—save a little done by
Wallace at the Board of Trade towards freeing commerce
from its restrictions—but in 1820 Liverpool was able to
tell a free-trade deputation that he had long been convinced
of the truth of their principles. There were, of course,
difficulties; there were many interests dependent upon
the protective system, and he could promise no immediate legislative improvement; but in spite of this he
delivered, a few days later, one of the first thoroughgoing
free-trade speeches delivered in an English Parliament. He
attacked the principle of agricultural protection; "Some
suppose that we have risen because of that system. Others,
of whom I am one, believe that we have risen in spite of
that system." He brought out remarks, which, coming
from an English Prime Minister, seemed novel to his
hearers, but which were to be the platitudes of the nineteenth century: "If the people of the world are poor, no
legislative interposition can make them do that which they
would do if they were rich", and "our manufacturers must
wait with patience until the supply and demand adjust
themselves"; "he was for leaving capitalists to find out the
way in which their capital could be best employed, being
perfectly convinced that, under such circumstances, the
interests of the public were not distinct from the interests of
the individual"; "on all commercial subjects the fewer

1 Hansard, XXIII, 1249.

laws the better. He was sorry to see so many on our statute book."[1]

Beside the immediate difficulties of putting any free trade ideas into practice, his views were modified by two other considerations. He held strongly that view of the solid and comprehensive nature of the national economy which has been one of the most persistent and most reasonable tenets of conservative economic thought: free development was good, but the balance of economic interests within the community must be preserved, and the whole economic organisation of the nation was a unity within which there should be no conflict. In May 1820 he accused Earl Stanhope of having made "a most dangerous distinction between the manufacturing and the agricultural interests; and by stating the policy of the British Government, which in reality afforded equal protection to both, had hitherto led it to support the former at the expense of the latter interest".[2] On another occasion he returned to this point: "The great interests of the country, the agricultural, the manufacturing, and the commercial interests...must stand or fall together....As on the one hand the agriculture of the country is the basis of its power and wealth, so, on the other hand, agriculture would not be what it now is had agriculture been fostered by manufacture and commerce." This led him, as it led all but the most doctrinaire of economists, to support some measure of agricultural protection, even though, as a general principle, "the thing must be left

1 Hansard, 1 (1820), 576 ff.
2 Hansard, 1, 1119. Note that the Government is accused of favouring the commercial interest.

to right itself". The other consideration which he allowed
to modify his *laissez-faire* views was an honourable one;
it is unfortunate only that he did not allow it to influence
him more generally than it did. In 1818 a bill was introduced to regulate the hours of children in cotton factories;
when this bill was opposed in the House of Lords Liverpool said, "Free labour ought not to be interfered with,
however unwholesome or deleterious might be the nature of
the business or manufacture; but to have free labour there
must be free agents; and he contended that children were
not free agents", no medical evidence would convince him
that the children were unharmed by the excessive labour,
and "it was therefore necessary to resort to some legislative
enactments to prevent them from being exposed to the
excessive labour to which they were at present exposed in
cotton factories".[1]

The "liberal" trait in Liverpool's mind was almost as
pronounced upon questions of foreign policy as it was upon
economic questions. He trusted Castlereagh implicitly,
but he never wholly reconciled himself to Castlereagh's
close association with Metternich; in 1812 he would have
preferred Canning, and after 1822 he fell immediately into
line with Canning's policy. Upon foreign questions he had
a great store of information, but it cannot be denied that he
had no breadth of vision and no guiding principles for the
future—it was perhaps the example of his foreign secretaryship which led Pitt to say, in 1804, that he was a wise
councillor but not the man to decide a great question of
policy—he never comprehended Castlereagh's European

[1] Hansard, xxxviii, 548.

ideals, and he had Canning's insularity without Canning's sense of what was new and powerful and inevitable in the world. His arguments were sound and painstaking, he often arrived at the same conclusions as his two great foreign secretaries without having any of their larger inspiration. But it was perhaps this pedestrian method which made him invaluable to Canning, for the "ultras" might be roused to unreasoning antagonism by Canning's intuitive methods, but they could not help being shaken in their resistance by Liverpool's careful arguments. If all else failed it was finally the simple and self-evident strategic superiority of Liverpool and Canning which won the day; others would have been glad enough to see Canning go, but Liverpool would go with him, and they were "architects enough to know how much the removing a main wall shakes a house, and how little anyone could tell where such alterations might lead".

Liverpool was indeed the keystone of his ministry, and only he could hold together the different elements of his ministry as they gradually diverged in the years which followed. One-half of the ministry remained ultra to the core, the other half were the masters of Melbourne, Palmerston, Gladstone, and Disraeli. Within the Cabinet one member was himself undergoing a slow course of political education, and when Peel came to office in 1841 it was at the head of a government which he had impregnated with the traditions of Liverpool's ministry. The last period of Liverpool's ministry was, in fact, one of the main-springs of nineteenth-century legislation and policy; and this ministry owed not only its existence but also its character to the Prime Minister. No man could be less of a charlatan, no man could veil solid abilities more successfully in a habitual reserve; Canning was a far more striking and brilliant figure, Wellington was a greater man; neither could have done Liverpool's work. The amiable figure of Lord Liverpool does not fill the early nineteenth-century scenc, but that scene would have been very different without him.

CHAPTER III

LORD LIVERPOOL AS PRIME MINISTER

UPON the office of Prime Minister there can be but one final judgment: that it is what its holder makes it. To this the most recent writer upon the Cabinet adds a rider, that the function of the Prime Minister is primarily one of giving advice when it is asked.[1] Liverpool has suffered by comparison with Pitt, the most autocratic of Prime Ministers, and with Peel, the model of all Prime Ministers. With those who followed after Peel he compares more favourably; his control over the general policy of the Government and his influence upon the departments was probably as great as that of Lord Salisbury, of Mr Asquith, or of Mr Baldwin, to name three who have since held office for periods comparable with his own. To the outside world, and to many subsequent historians, he appeared as a dim and elusive figure, as a phantom Prime Minister; for this belief the real foundation is the fact that he did not speak in the House of Commons, and that his influence can only be gauged from ministerial correspondence and from a surmise of private conversations.

"The misfortune of this government is that it is a government of departments," wrote George IV in 1823, and, writing to Liverpool himself, drew the inevitable comparison with Pitt.[2] Liverpool never attempted to exercise a commanding influence over all the departments, and he was

[1] Jennings, *Cabinet Government.*   [2] *George IV*, No. 1110.

often content with a general approval of the policy pursued by the departmental chief; in the great offices of state he was fortunate to have strong and tolerably efficient colleagues. Neither Castlereagh nor Canning required much guidance; Melville[1] at the Admiralty and Bathurst[2] at the Department for Colonies and War were both experienced administrators; Eldon and Wellington were both strong men; Sidmouth as Home Secretary has found few defenders but, as an ex-Prime Minister, he occupied a unique place in the Cabinet, and his deficiencies have been more apparent in retrospect than they were to his contemporaries. These departmental chiefs would not come to the Prime Minister for advice save when some peculiarly difficult question arose, or when the policy of their particular departments seemed to become a matter of national interest.

1 Melville's chief part in Government was the administration of Scotland, where he ruled as virtual dictator, but with fairness and ability. Cf. Cockburn, *Memorials of his Time*, p. 386 (ed. of 1872): "The retirement of Lord Melville from the government of Scotland was not an event for which, *in itself*, any candid Scotch Whig could rejoice; because no man, individually, could have conducted the affairs of the country with greater good sense and fairness, or with less of party prejudice or bitterness."

2 For an estimate of Bathurst see *Exposition and Defence of Earl Bathurst's administration of the affairs of Canada*, by R. Wilmot-Horton, who worked under him for eight years: "The character of Lord Bathurst as an efficient public servant...is very imperfectly appreciated by the English public. Undoubtedly his general politics did not respond to the movement of the latter days in which he lived; yet in all cases where first rate practical good sense, and a rapid yet discreet view of intricate subjects was essentially required, Lord Bathurst possessed a mind far more able to grapple with difficulties than many of those persons who underrated his political efficiency. Lord Bathurst had no affection for political economy *by name*, but to the results of a wise combination of Colonial measures, which in their character might more or less belong to the science of political economy, no man was more alive."

A great mass of detailed administration lies, and must lie, outside the immediate ken of the Prime Minister; for advice on such matters the Under-Secretaries in the various departments will be responsible, and, as Castlereagh once remarked to Croker, "No government was ever better manned in the subordinate departments than ours".[1] Croker himself had an unrivalled knowledge of naval matters, Palmerston was a tower of strength at the War Department, Huskisson had few parliamentary duties as First Commissioner of Woods and Forests, but he acted as an auxiliary upon all economic matters. At the Board of Control the permanent head was T. P. Courtenay, a member of Parliament, of whom Canning said that "no office ever had an individual more completely conversant with every detail belonging to it".[2] In every department the Prime Minister had a reserve of power to be exercised at his discretion or invoked at the discretion of the departmental head; but when there was general agreement upon the principles and methods of government, there was little need to use that discretionary power.

If Liverpool was one of the least dictatorial of Prime Ministers, he was, nevertheless, one of the most experienced. He had held each of the three secretaryships and had also been connected with the India Board. No man would scorn his advice, and, during his premiership, he was always cognisant of even the details of the various departmental business; indeed he had frequently to pilot the various departmental measures through the House of Lords. There his speeches never displayed ignorance of his

1 Croker, I, 251.   2 Add. MSS. 38288, f. 386.

subject, and frequently showed a great wealth of accurate information. It would be necessary for him to go through the various measures with the greatest care and to discuss many points with the ministers concerned; in such discussions it can hardly be doubted that his suggestions would have great weight, but intimate conversations, often the most important part of the business of government, leave few traces upon the records of the time. To estimate the exact influence of Liverpool upon the departments would be impossible; it would be a rash man who declared it to be negligible, and few would care to say with his biographer, C. D. Yonge, that he was "the presiding genius of the Ministry both in its foreign and domestic policy". Such a verdict should be carefully tested even when dealing with the greatest of Prime Ministers, of Gladstone even and of Disraeli it would require qualification.

The three great departments in the state were those of Finance, of Foreign Affairs, and of Home Affairs. The Prime Minister was expected to have most influence in the two former, for current practice demanded that the Home Secretary should be allowed an almost free hand in a department which was, in normal times, concerned entirely with routine business. When the secretaryship had been divided into the Northern and Southern Departments, the Prime Minister had acted as a co-ordinating link between two jealous ministers; but their duties at home were of small importance compared to their duties abroad, where it was necessary to present to the outside world a uniform foreign policy, and it followed that the Prime Minister's work of co-ordination was exercised primarily in foreign affairs.

When the secretaryship became divided into Foreign and Home Departments, the Prime Minister continued to be in the closest contact with foreign affairs, but the Home Secretary succeeded to a heritage of detailed routine business in which the Prime Minister was not accustomed to interfere. Sidmouth conducted the Home Office after his own fashion, and the Prime Minister was called in only when the business of that department faced a crisis, when counter-revolution became a national policy. Peel, when carrying out his reform of the penal code, sent to Liverpool a general outline of the policy he would follow, but for the details of the measure he sought the advice of Henry Hobhouse, the permanent head of the department. But the Prime Minister did exercise a closer control over one sphere of the Home Secretary's duties; that sphere was the government of Ireland. Divided responsibility was not the least of the evils which afflicted the English rule in Ireland: within the Cabinet the Prime Minister, the Home Secretary, and the Lord Chancellor might all have something to say upon the affairs of Ireland; at Dublin it was difficult to fix the division of responsibility between Lord Lieutenant, Chief Secretary, and Assistant Secretary, who, as an Irishman with long experience of Irish government, was often the real director of Irish affairs.

The relationship between Prime Minister and Foreign Secretary was of the closest possible nature. In nearly all modern English Governments the core of the ministry has been the alliance of these two ministers. As effective head of the state, the Prime Minister must accept a full share of responsibility for its foreign policy, and the Foreign Secretary must be one whom he can trust implicitly. The arduous duties of diplomacy must necessarily occupy the whole attention of one man and they must also be considered the exclusive prerogative of one man; if the history of modern nations taught nothing else, it would teach the folly of dual foreign policies. A Prime Minister with a Foreign Secretary whom he cannot trust is in the most lamentable situation, he must either venture out of his proper sphere and attempt the disastrous experiment of going behind the back of his Foreign Secretary to conduct his own foreign policy, or he must precipitate a Cabinet crisis by dismissing the offending minister. Liverpool was fortunate in his generation, for, not only was he given two Foreign Secretaries of first-rate ability, but he was also given two whom he trusted implicitly. With both Castlereagh and with Canning he was on the most intimate and cordial terms, with both he entered into frank and detailed discussions of future policy, and to both he gave an almost free hand in the execution of that policy. He acted as a brake upon what may be called the "oecumenical" aspect of Castlereagh's policy, and upon the rasher moves of Canning. To both he was, as might be expected, the counsel of caution; but, and this too was characteristic, he did not shrink from great risks when he was convinced of a policy's rightness. With Castlereagh the whole Cabinet was in substantial agreement, and Liverpool's task—that of acting as a link between Castlereagh and the Cabinet, particularly during the Congresses—was not an arduous one. But Canning did not find favour with the majority of the Cabinet, and Liverpool had, of necessity, to become a partisan. With Castlereagh the influence of the

Prime Minister lay principally in his criticism of details, with Canning it lay in the support of principles. It has been shown that, towards the end of his life, Castlereagh was moving slowly along the path which Canning subsequently followed, and that the difference between the two men was one of method rather than of measures; it is strange that those who argue for this continuity should not have stressed the fact that both worked in close and cordial co-operation with Liverpool.

Different again was the relationship of the Prime Minister with the Finance Department, which comprised the Exchequer and the Treasury. The Prime Minister was First Lord of the Treasury, and in Liverpool's day the duties of this office were not nominal but real. Of the Treasury Board he was, according to his own definition, "primus inter pares".[1] In 1826 Peel referred to Liverpool as "the Minister who presides over the finances of the country".[2] In 1822 Wellington gave as a reason for not making Canning Chancellor of the Exchequer, that "it would be impossible to place two leading men in the Treasury".[3] And in 1821 W. H. Fremantle, referring to a possible choice between the Treasury and the Board of Control, wrote, "I should certainly prefer acting under Lord Liverpool, for whom I entertain the highest personal respect and warmest feeling".[4] It is clear that the First Lord filled some important place in the financial administration of the country; what that place was is not so clear. In 1813 Liverpool wrote: "If any person were to ask me to

1 Add. MSS. 38576, f. 37.   2 Parker, I, 397.
3 Wellington, I, 277.   4 Buckingham, I, 257.

define the duties and powers of the First Lord of the Treasury and Chancellor of the Exchequer in this country, I could not do it. This very circumstance may have led to the union of these two offices, much oftener than to their separation. They have however, at times, been separated, and the Government has gone on with perfect harmony and concord."[1] In 1823 C. W. W. Wynn said: "Robinson will be a decided improvement on poor Van... but as to measures Liverpool must of course give the orders and he obey."[2] This is probably an overstatement, but it is at least certain that the Chancellor of the Exchequer was looked upon more as the First Lord's assistant than as an independent minister; the position of the Chancellor was still much inferior to that of a Secretary of State.[3] In theory the Chancellor of the Exchequer was concerned with supply, the First Lord with the regulation of expenditure; in practice the Chancellor was probably concerned with the details of raising money, while the First Lord exercised a general supervision over financial policy. Contemporaries were right in attributing to Vansittart the "expedients and ingenious devices" of post-war finance, but to Liverpool is probably due the general outlines of the policy, maintenance of a Sinking Fund and a return to gold when circumstances should allow it.

Beyond the actual direction of financial policy the Prime Minister performed another important function in connec-

1 Parker, I, 109.
2 Buckingham, I, 411.
3 Cf. Croker, I, 364: "The Foreign Office would be a severe test, and perhaps too high a step for Robinson." Robinson had been four years Chancellor of the Exchequer when this was written.

tion with economic matters, he acted as a link between the Exchequer and the general economic policy of the nation. After 1822 it is possible to trace the existence of a small "economic cabinet" consisting of Liverpool, Robinson, Huskisson, and Bexley (Vansittart);[1] at such a meeting would be discussed all matters of fiscal and commercial policy. From 1814 onwards Liverpool always had Huskisson at his side, and this intimacy does not seem to have been interrupted by a momentary coolness over Huskisson's position in the Government during 1821 and 1822. At Liverpool's invitation Huskisson criticised drafts of his speeches, and submitted long plain-spoken memoranda on economic questions.[2] It has usually been assumed that Huskisson was the inspiration of those parts of Robinson's budgets which introduced free trade measures;[3] but no one has explained how it was that Huskisson came to exert this influence. Robinson and Huskisson were not particularly intimate—indeed Robinson had been the follower and protégé of Castlereagh, Huskisson the devoted friend of Canning—and there is no obvious reason why Robinson should have invited the assistance of a man in another office whom he might well suspect of personal jealousy. The problem is solved when it is remembered that both ministers stood in very similar relationships to Liverpool, and that finance was not the exclusive concern of the Chancellor of the Exchequer.

1 Cf. pp. 192–3 below.
2 Add. MSS. 39948, f. 53. Cf. p. 41 above, and p. 180 below.
3 Greville, I, 83: "Everybody knows that Huskisson is the real author of the finance measures of the Government."

It is then in matters of finance and economic policy that the direct and personal influence of Liverpool is most likely to be found. Robinson was an able man, but he was also a lazy one, and frequent solicitation for his wife's health concealed inadequately his own decided preference for the fields of Lincolnshire over the labours of Whitehall. In consequence Liverpool and Huskisson are frequently found acting alone when Robinson might at least have been expected to be present. During the crisis of 1825 the famous banker, Alexander Baring, was called into consultation by Liverpool and Huskisson, but Robinson does not seem to have been at this emergency meeting.[1] His absence on this occasion may have been accidental, but it is certain that, in the following year Liverpool and Huskisson prepared a new Corn Law, and that the plan was communicated to Robinson only when it was complete. Strictly speaking a new Corn Law was not within the province of the Chancellor of the Exchequer, but one would expect him to take part in the preliminary discussions of such an important item of economic policy. It is a safe generalisation to say that, as on foreign affairs the deciding factor was the alliance between Liverpool and Canning, so on economic affairs it was the alliance between Liverpool and Huskisson. But in economic affairs Liverpool played a commanding part which he never assumed in foreign affairs.

However great were the powers of the Prime Minister in practice, however small they might be in theory, he still exercised them at the King's command and with the King's

---

1 *The Financial and Commercial Crisis Considered,* by Lord Ashburton (A. Baring), London, 1847.

permission. All the ministers were the King's servants, the Prime Minister was the servant who possessed the confidence of the King; it was this which distinguished the Prime Minister from the other ministers, it was this which allowed him to make a ministry, and the loss of this precious confidence would be the death-blow to the power of any Prime Minister. In the years before 1812 the Whigs had based their hopes upon the confidence of the Prince; in 1812 the weak remnant of the Tory ministry thought their position precarious but not hopeless "if the administration is known to possess the entire confidence of the Prince Regent"; in 1821 the real point at issue was whether the Government was the real government, whether it possessed the confidence of the King. The King's confidence was a symbol of stability, and, once it was certain that the Government possessed it, then timid men, independent men, careful men, and Grenvilles would rally to the support of the ministers. George III had made the bestowal of his confidence a real expression of the royal wishes; under a fully-fledged constitutional monarchy it was to be merely a confirmation of the strongest party's title to power; during the Regency and reign of George IV it was neither one thing nor the other. In launching a ministry the King's choice was still the deciding factor, but it was also becoming evident that no ministry would willingly be dependent upon the whim of the King, and that the King's confidence, once given, must be given until death or adverse divisions did them part. In 1821 Liverpool suspected "a secret scheme, not to destroy the Government at present, but to have the means of destroying it whenever the oppor-

tunity may be more convenient".[1] Upon such terms no
ministry would continue in office, and, at the end of 1821,
the King was forced to choose whether he would dismiss
his ministers or whether he would let it be known publicly
that they possessed his full confidence.

Into this dilemma the circumstances of party conflict
were forcing the King. Like his father he had hankered
after a "mixed administration": on the one hand it might
be said that a government freed from party would be in the
best interests of the country, on the other it was certain
that such a government would be a royal government, for
the King would be called upon to mediate between the
various parties represented in the Cabinet. The Patriot
King still lingered in the background, but in practice the
Patriot King found his action hampered by the existence of
two parties, each of which were bound together by strong
ties of loyalty, from neither of which was it possible to
detach individual members, and one of which was quite
out of the question. Forced to make the unwelcome choice
between Whig and Tory, the King would always choose the
Tories. He might dally with the Whigs in the days of his
youth, he might flirt with their leaders when Tory ministers
tried his patience, but in the day of trial he must choose
that party which maintained a traditional respect for the
crown, which did not promise to weaken the power of the
crown in favour of oligarchs or radicals, which would not
emancipate the Catholics, and which would not betray the
interests of the country in a vain search after the Holy Grail
of Liberalism. The political nightmare which haunted the

1 Yonge, III, 146.

King was the "day when I may be shut out on all sides from any set of men, as servants, that could make my life tolerable".[1] The Tories might not always give full satisfaction, but, so far as the essential interests of the King and the country were concerned, they were safe. Faced with this situation the King had, at times, to make great concessions to his Tory ministers; and, in a way which was not altogether pleasing to them, the Whigs helped to formulate the modern relationship of a constitutional King and his government.

Liverpool showed that, when the occasion demanded it, he was ready to stand up for the rights and powers of a Prime Minister; he was prepared to press the King far, but his Toryism would not allow him to make the fullest use of his advantage. Toward the King the Tories maintained, through whatever difficulties they might encounter, a kind of impersonal loyalty: a loyalty expressed in the maxim, "The King's government must go on". They might be embarrassed by the King, they might demand concessions from him, but in the last resort they had a higher duty which could not be gainsaid. In this resolution they were fortified by the belief that Whig government would be a disaster for the country. The exact expression of Tory feeling was found, as it was so often found, by the Duke of Wellington: "The question for us is not, whether we shall bear with the many inconveniencies and evils resulting from the King's habits and character, and which none of our predecessors ever bore, or make way for others equally capable with ourselves of carrying on the public service? But, whether

1 *George IV*, No. 880.

we shall bear all that we have to endure, or give up the government to the Whigs and Radicals, or, in other words, the country in all its relations to irretrievable ruin? I believe if it were not for this consideration there are few of us who would stay where we are."[1]

Under Pitt had been consummated the ideal of George III: government by a close working partnership of King and Prime Minister. But if bestowal of his confidence and the ultimate control of patronage gave the King the last word, Pitt had been able to demand and to win the right to control the personnel of his Cabinet. The Prime Minister claimed, and most men felt that he was right in claiming, that the Cabinet must be his and his alone; he must choose whom he liked, he must exclude whom he disliked, and no other minister should claim to interpret the royal policy. The final settlement of these points in the Prime Minister's favour was still in the distant future; under George IV the relationship of King and Prime Minister remained anomalous and ill-defined. Briefly, the King could not choose but he could refuse, the Prime Minister could choose but it was difficult for him to insist. In 1821 George IV warned Castlereagh that he must not deceive himself by supposing "that any expediency shall ever induce me to give up the sacred privilege of naming the personal servants of the crown".[2] In 1821 he was able to sustain his objection to Canning, in 1822 he was forced to yield. From 1821 to 1825 he was able to keep Sidmouth in the Cabinet, but to this arrangement Liverpool had raised no objection. In 1812 there had been no call for royal choice, for the ministry

1 Wellington, I, 195.   2 *George IV*, No. 958.

had been ready-made. In 1823 he objected to the large size of the Cabinet—possibly with the conscious aim of excluding Huskisson—but the question was compromised. On the other hand, Liverpool never found reason to object to the presence in the Cabinet of any minister; always unwilling to treat old friends and faithful colleagues with anything which savoured of ingratitude, he never, save in one instance, dismissed a minister from the Cabinet. The one exception was the dismissal of Lord Maryborough (Wellesley Pole) in 1823, and this was avowedly for the necessities of Cabinet making and not for any political offence. It was necessary to treat any wish of the King with respect, and even his prejudices had to be tactfully circumvented rather than overborne or ignored; on the other hand, the strength of the Prime Minister lay largely in the strategic position of the moment and in the loyalty of his colleagues. For this reason the relative shares of King and Prime Minister in choosing the servants of the crown defy definition, the Prime Minister had by far the larger share, but the King maintained the right of crying "I object", and, given favourable circumstances, he could sustain that objection.

Upon the same plane was the influence of the King upon policy: he had lost the power to initiate, but retained the power to obstruct. The secret of George III's great personal influence upon policy had been his own unremitting industry; George III had been prepared to spend long hours in the consideration, not only of the general principles of national policy, but also of the minute details of patronage and administration. This energy and this industry George IV was not prepared to expend. In 1821 Croker, usually a shrewd observer of men and manners, confessed that "whether it be the King's own popular manners, or the habits into which the Regency has led his Minister, or the levelling temper of the times, the Royal authority and the King's person are treated with a striking degree of levity, and no reformers, if they knew the whole secret, would wish to reduce the monarch lower in real and effective state and power than his ministers place him".[1] Croker overstated his case, but his remarks are some indication of the impression formed by those who had heard tell of George III in his prime. George IV was generally content with the expression of a general satisfaction or a general disapproval of ministerial policy; his excursions into the field of detailed and positive politics were sporadic and were never long sustained; his interference in the workings of the patronage system were infrequent and always to gratify some personal wish.

The ministers consciously disavowed the wish to make the King the prisoner of any party, but, at the same time they viewed with the greatest suspicion any attempt by the King to provide himself with an inner circle of intimate advisers. It was fortunate for the smooth working of politics and for the ease of all concerned that the Carlton House party was dissipated after 1812, and that its members became assimilated to one or other of the two great parties. The party went, but its organiser, the Regent's private secretary, remained, and in the situation of this individual the ministers saw a constitutional menace. The private

1 Croker, I, 211.

secretary had unique opportunities for misusing his position: it was the nature of George IV that he sought always
for a confidant; when doubtful he wished for reassurance,
when he knew he was right he wished for someone to tell
him that he was not wrong; the private secretaries came, in
this way, not only to be cognisant of the most important
state secrets, but also to exercise a great influence over the
decisions of the King. As the channel of communication
between the King and the outside world, as the man whose
commands would be obeyed by a small number of influential men and whose favour would be sought by a great
many more, the possibilities before the private secretary
were almost limitless. Fortunately McMahon was hard-
working, honest, and not particularly ambitious; Bloomfield was tactless and never enjoyed the King's favour to
the full; and Knighton, who enjoyed greater power than
either of the others though without the title of the office,
was watched jealously by the ministers—who refused to
him the rank of Privy Councillor even when it was asked
by the King—and, though he was not above intrigue, he
does not seem to have aimed at higher things for himself.
The private secretary already enjoyed power and privilege
far above the usual expectation of men of his rank; and in
an age which preserved many of the social ideas of the
eighteenth century this was enough for most men.

The private secretary was a threat to the Prime Minister's
situation as the sole possessor of the royal confidence, but
it was a threat which did not develop; another threat, and
one which had been defeated by Pitt when in 1792 he dismissed Thurlow, still raised its head during Liverpool's

premiership. Could the King restrain the Prime Minister's freedom by making one of the other ministers his friend and confidant? The answer, according to the relatively new convention, was that he could not; but the further question is whether this convention would prove strong enough to defeat the attempts of the King. Three ministers were, at various times, singled out for especial favour by George IV; they were Eldon, Sidmouth, and Wellington. There was a persistent rumour that Eldon was a second Thurlow, a rumour voiced in Brougham's jeer, "As to Lord Liverpool being Prime Minister, he is no more Prime Minister than I am....Lord Liverpool may have collateral influence, but Lord Eldon has all the direct influence of Prime Minister." This was ironic nonsense, but still the suspicion lingered. In 1821 Croker thought that the King had been intriguing with the Lord Chancellor in order to exclude Canning,[1] but, at the end of August, Eldon told Bathurst that he had heard nothing of the trouble between King and Prime Minister until a few days previously.[2] In September of the same year the King saw Eldon and refused to see Liverpool, but as he also saw Castlereagh and Bathurst it was not evidence of sinister influence in the Closet, but an example of the King's constitutional right to consult with whom he pleased in a time of crisis combined with a deliberate insult to the Prime Minister. After Castlereagh's death the King again saw Eldon privately, but again it was a time of crisis and the King was entitled to all the advice which he could gather. Eldon was the revered sage of the Tory party, he was also not above intrigue; but, and especially after 1822,

1 Croker, I, 191: 11 June 1821.   2 Bathurst, p. 512.

he counted for very little in the determination of policy. Indeed, in the changing world of the 1820's he was a pathetic rather than a powerful figure: he had grown to maturity in an age of leisurely and remunerative politics, in that world he had made his own career, but now there crowded in upon him new ideas which he scorned to understand and new men who appreciated not his worth. "I cannot conceive why it should signify whether the person who has threatened to resign executes that threat or not,"[1] wrote C. W. Wynn in 1824; and even the Prime Minister, who might have been expected to understand how a gentleman should conduct politics, thought his administration of Church patronage a scandal,[2] and told him that his delay in preparing the report of a Commission upon the Court of Chancery was of the greatest inconvenience to the Government.[3]

Sidmouth, though he had been the close friend of Pitt and a Prime Minister, was a lesser man than Eldon. Almost the last shreds of his energy had been expended in defeating the designs of the villain Hunt and the assassin Thistlewood, in 1824 he protested against the recognition of the South American republics and his protest was ignored; he resigned, and his resignation passed almost without notice. On one or two occasions he was consulted independently by the King, but he never occupied the position of King's confidant. His chief influence derived from the fact that he led a small family "connection" to which Vansittart, Bragge Bathurst, and Hiley Addington

1 Buckingham, II, 66.   2 Add. MSS. 38298, f. 279.
3 Add. MSS. 38301, f. 1.

belonged, and which was the repository of political wisdom for an exclusive band of correspondents—clergymen and respectable magistrates[1]—throughout the country. All the Sidmouths were notable for the purity of their lives rather than for the brilliance of their talents, and all were ageing men: Hiley Addington died in 1814, Brother Bragge was tactfully ousted from the Cabinet in 1822, Vansittart withdrew from the front rank of the battle to the labours of the Chancellorship of the Duchy of Lancaster, Sidmouth himself went out in 1824. This was hardly promising material with which the King might build a secret camarilla, and it must be said for the Sidmouths that not one of them could have been drawn into anything which had the suspicion of dishonesty or disloyalty.

Wellington was in a different position. Bound by a rigid sense of duty he was the last to fail in this respect; but he was guided by the idea that, in view of his national and European position, he was bound to act above mere partisan considerations and sometimes to act as a mediator between King and ministers. Always he was unwilling to sink the saviour of Europe in the minister of state, and, impressed with a sincere desire for European peace, he was betrayed into a position which was hardly in accord with men's ideas of constitutional rectitude. The story of his temptation and fall may be traced in the pages of Madame Lieven's letters to Metternich. In the spring of 1823 the King spoke to her of Canning: "I do not like him any better than I did," he said, "I recognise his talent, and

[1] Beeke, Dean of Bristol and a financial expert of some standing, was one of the most eminent.

I believe we need him in the House of Commons; but he is no more capable of conducting foreign affairs than your baby."[1] And on 19 March he ordered the Duke "not to let a day pass without seeing Canning, and finding out what he is up to in his office".[2] This Wellington was bound to refuse; but during 1824 he did drift into confidential relationship with the King and with the ambassadors of Austria and Russia, and the object of this—the famous "Cottage Coterie"—was to circumvent the foreign policy of Canning, which was also the policy of the Prime Minister, and, whatever the ultras might suspect, of the Cabinet majority.

This attempt to influence policy from outside the Cabinet failed, and it failed in spite of the fact that the King, the two most powerful ambassadors, a woman diplomat with a flair for intrigue, and the greatest living Englishman were all drawn into the meshes of the plot. It failed because the Prime Minister stood behind the Foreign Secretary, and because both were prepared to resign if that policy was not carried out. The convention of collective responsibility and Cabinet loyalty stood the test; and Wellington found that, instead of his close association with the King strengthening his hand, his opinions in the Cabinet were set at a discount. He seems to have been dropped from the most intimate councils of state—"I see the Duke of Wellington every day," Madame Lieven told Metternich in June 1823, "and every day I am more and more convinced that he counts for nothing in affairs"[3]—and his fellow ministers regarded his actions with a suspicion which would never have occurred

1 Lieven, p. 241.   2 *Ibid.* p. 243.   3 *Ibid.* p. 268.

to them but for his unfortunate association with the Cottage Coterie. In 1824 Arbuthnot, who was by this time fully in the Duke's confidence, wrote to Bathurst: "I wish to observe that the only way to keep the Duke right will be to support him in the Cabinet when he delivers an opinion in accordance with your own. I know he thinks he is deserted; and that some of his colleagues, who agree with him, are afraid of saying so lest they should be supposed to be giving support to the *King's favourite*."[1] In 1825 the King and the Duke had to choose between accepting the recognition of the South American republics or breaking the Government; neither was likely to choose the latter alternative. The firm stand of the Prime Minister and the newly founded doctrine of collective responsibility had broken the attempt of the King to control foreign policy; it was an experiment which no one cared to repeat, but Wellington did not forgive Canning and barely forgave Liverpool.

Liverpool ended his long career as Prime Minister in a position as strong as any holder of that office: he had fought for the dignity of his position and, though his victories had not always been swift, they had been sure. For eight years the constitutional difficulties which surrounded the relationships of Prime Minister, King, and fellow ministers came little to the fore; after that time the most important questions for the future of the constitution were agitated and were finally decided in the Prime Minister's favour. The right of the Prime Minister to select his colleagues was not fully settled, and far into the nineteenth

1 Bathurst, p. 565.

century Queen Victoria was to object to ministers and to carry her point; but at least it might be said that, after the happenings of 1821 and 1822 no sovereign would dare to make personal dislike the ground for objection. The King's right to object to measures was still maintained—indeed many would regard that right as a fundamental of the constitution—but his attempt to initiate a personal policy had been decisively defeated. The King's attempt to make Wellington his agent in the Cabinet had failed. Under Liverpool the Cabinet was a more solid body than it had been at any time previously, but this solidarity depended almost entirely upon the Prime Minister; by all he was acknowledged to be indispensable, and all, ultras and liberals alike, feared the day when his shattered health should force him out of public life. Even in the times of greatest disagreement between the various ministers the working of the Cabinet had been relatively smooth and according to accepted constitutional machinery; there had been no open disagreement, and, save for Sidmouth, there had been no resignations. To have kept the Government in being, and to have done so without ostentation and without dictatorial methods, was perhaps Liverpool's greatest achievement; for this reason, and because the smooth working of the machine must be one of the first concerns of every Prime Minister, it is now necessary to examine briefly the methods by which Liverpool obtained and maintained his quiet control.

The Prime Minister was adviser to the departmental chiefs, he was confidential minister to the King, he was also chairman of the Board of Directors known as the Cabinet.

Here the Prime Minister had to preside over the meeting of fourteen gentlemen, most of whom had some departmental axe to grind, and whose collective assent was necessary before any policy could be put into execution; here the Prime Minister had to exercise whatever qualities of tact and management he possessed; and here, in the approval or disapproval of his colleagues, the power of a Prime Minister would be made or broken. It was the business of the Prime Minister to see that the policy he favoured was approved, and to do so without offending any minister beyond hope of reconciliation.

In 1821 Wellington said that "ours is not, nor ever has been, a controversial cabinet upon any subject".[1] Indeed, during the first eight years of Liverpool's ministry there is no record of any serious disagreement within the Cabinet, and certain admirers of Canning have striven in vain to show that he disapproved of any measure of government during these years. The ministers were all men well acquainted with one another, they had all been bred in the same school of official business, and none of them displayed disturbing inspiration or alarming inefficiency. But for the even tenor of the Government's way Liverpool must be given some credit. It was he who first welded the followers of Perceval, the Sidmouths, and the Canningites into one ministry; and it was he who finally accomplished his favourite project—the reunion of the old Pitt party—by drawing in Wellesley and the Grenvilles. With characteristic modesty he outlined his feelings upon succeeding to the premiership: "I have had no resource but to bring

1 Buckingham, *George IV*, 1, 237.

forward the most promising young men, on whose exertions the fate of the Government in the House of Commons will very much depend. I should be most happy to see another Pitt amongst them, I would willingly resign the Government into his hands, for I am fully aware of the importance of the minister being, if possible, in the House of Commons. I can assure you I never sought the situation in which I find myself now placed; but having accepted it from a sense of public duty, I am determined to do my utmost for the service of the Prince Regent as long as I have reason to believe that I possess his confidence."[1] These sentiments were generally known to his friends and colleagues, and it is no small tribute to Liverpool that, in spite of his constant readiness to efface himself, there never was any serious attempt to remove him. They knew he would go, and bade him go not; they knew he stayed from his sense of duty, and they were ever ready to emphasise that duty.

After 1822 the harmony of the Cabinet was dissipated. Upon foreign policy, and, to a lesser extent upon economic matters, meetings of the Cabinet degenerated into furious debates and into angry personal altercations. Years afterwards Wellington gave to Greville a description of Canning in the Cabinet: "he prided himself extremely upon his compositions" but he would "patiently endure any criticisms upon such papers as he submitted to the Cabinet, and would allow them to be altered in any way that was suggested". The Duke himself had "often cut and hacked his papers, and Canning never made the least objection,

1 Parker, i, 32.

but was always ready to adopt the suggestions of his colleagues. It was not so, however, in conversation and discussion. Any difference of opinion or dissent from his
views threw him into an ungovernable rage, and on such
occasions he flew out with a violence which, the Duke said,
had often compelled him to be silent that he might not be
involved in a bitter personal altercation.... Canning was
usually silent in the Cabinet, seldom spoke at all, but when
he did he maintained his opinions with extraordinary
tenacity."[1] When Cabinet meetings became a duel between
Wellington and Canning, or when, which annoyed Canning
even more, Westmorland, "le Sot Prive", obstructed business for hours with persistent opposition to unimportant
details, then the work of the Prime Minister became
vastly complicated. Liverpool was heart and soul behind
Canning, but he had also to think of the Government;
resignation of the ultras would have meant the end of the
ministry, and Liverpool knew that the end of his ministry
would mean the coming of the Whigs. Only Liverpool
prevented the split of 1827 from happening in 1824; he was
successful, but the attempt ruined his health and ruined his
temper.

To some extent Liverpool was helped by his strategic
position: the intense distrust of the Whigs and the fear of
Catholic Emancipation kept the High Tories from pressing
their opposition to its logical limits. But their forbearance
would not last for ever; the future was to see the great
secession of 1827, and behind the seceders were the legions
of Dr Humbug "who had proved Mr Canning to be The

1 Greville (ed. Reeve), I, 107.

Beast in St John's Revelation". When all is taken into consideration it is still extraordinary that the crucial decision upon foreign policy—"that it is the opinion of the Cabinet that the question of any further step to be taken towards the South American States should be decided without reference to the opinions and wishes of the Continental Allied powers"—should have been made with but one dissentient voice.

The success of Liverpool in overcoming the opposition within the Cabinet is largely explained by the fact that the Cabinet frequently did little more than ratify decisions which had already been taken, and that these decisions were really taken in private and less formal meetings. "We all know", wrote Charles Wynn when he was himself a Cabinet minister, "that business can never really be settled in the meeting of so numerous a Cabinet, but that it must be in fact arranged at more private meetings and dinners."[1] Cabinet dinners were an important institution; to them it was not necessary to ask every minister, and in intimate conversation over the dinner table the policy of the country could be freely discussed. But the Cabinet dinner was not the heart of the Cabinet. Wynn gave it as his belief "that the only real and efficient cabinet upon all matters consists of Lords Liverpool and Bathurst, the Duke of Wellington and Canning, and that the others are only more or less consulted upon different business by these four".[2] These were the four ministers who received all

[1] Buckingham, I, 398. In the letter from which the above extract is taken Wynn was complaining that he was not invited to the Cabinet dinners.
[2] *Ibid.* p. 494.

state documents as a matter of course, but to their intimate discussions the Prime Minister could invite, or not invite, whom he pleased. There are signs that, when the Duke of Wellington was moving heaven and earth to defeat Canning's policy he was not invited to the "inner cabinet".[1] Behind the Cabinet, behind informal discussions, behind even the "inner cabinet", there was a still more select council when two or three were gathered together. To his country houses—Coombe Wood, Kingston, or Walmer Castle—Liverpool would invite the minister with whom he wished to talk; there, in the relative seclusion and during the parliamentary recess, the first plan of the policy to be pursued was mapped out. Canning was a frequent visitor, Huskisson another, the remaining ministers came on occasions. The importance of these meetings was that, before the matter even reached the stage of discussion by the inner Cabinet, Liverpool's mind was made up, and he was ready to support the minister concerned against any opposition. It was the unity of aim between Liverpool and Canning which finally defeated all opposition within the Cabinet, and Huskisson's free trade measures were forced through in the same way. Another use of the invitations to Coombe Wood or Walmer was the conciliation of the discontented; in 1823 Wynn's complaints of neglect had risen in volume and in bitterness, the sequel was an invitation to Coombe Wood where he passed two days and was "much pleased".[2] Every measure required these extensive and private preliminaries before it came finally before the Cabinet; if the preliminaries were completely successful

1 Pp. 67–68 above.   2 Buckingham, II, 34.

the formal Cabinet could do no more than agree, but upon some questions—notably the great questions of foreign policy—it was not possible to satisfy all objections before the Cabinet meetings, and it was then that Cabinet meetings became long, tiresome, and angry. But even upon these great questions, which divided the Cabinet into two mutually suspicious parties, much was done, and successfully done, before the measure reached the Cabinet stage. Wellington led the opposition in the Cabinet, but, save for some guerilla attacks by Westmorland, he usually found himself without support; those on whom he counted sat in uneasy silence, for they had already been persuaded and had already committed themselves to Liverpool and Canning. They wished Wellington well, but "the leaders of the two Houses thought otherwise", and they must perforce acquiesce.

These were Liverpool's methods of government, and, of their type, they were successful. They were methods which could have been rendered successful only by a man of great tact and great persuasion, and these were qualities which Liverpool possessed to the utmost. He will never be numbered among the most brilliant of Prime Ministers, but, for his party and for his time, he was a good Prime Minister. His party was bound by loose ties and his time was one of disintegration and new ideas; nothing is more certain than that the rule of an inspired and autocratic Prime Minister would have shattered the party, which suffered already from the malaise of the times. For this reason Canning, though he was the most striking personality in the ministry during the latter years of Liverpool's premiership, was quite out of the question as Prime Minister. The final split was, perhaps, inevitable; it might have been postponed had Liverpool been able to arrange, as he meant to arrange, for the quiet succession of Canning; but this was, perhaps, a task which would have overtaxed even his powers of conciliation. The dissolution of the Tory party could not be long averted, but in averting it for the few years after 1822, Liverpool made possible five years of useful legislation, of legislation which left a great heritage to the succeeding years. The ministry of 1822 to 1827 was the first of those nineteenth-century governments which, without being called "reforming", may certainly be called "improving". It was Liverpool's leadership which made this ministry possible, and, for this reason, it is not altogether fantastic to call this most cautious and least inspired of Prime Ministers one of the architects of the nineteenth century.

CHAPTER IV

GOVERNMENT, PARTY AND PUBLIC
OPINION IN 1820

WHIG publicists of the early nineteenth century were fond of alluding to contemporary politics in the same terms as the historical conflicts of the past. English history was seen as a long struggle between the people and the despotic power, whether a King or a Government wielded despotic powers: the picture which they delighted to draw was that of a ministerial party loaded with places and privileges ruling by means of corruption with a total disregard of public opinion. Modern historians would, of course, modify this over-simplified picture, but this view still colours most accounts of the period. It is, however, a view which will hardly bear investigation, and a most cursory reading of political correspondence will show that the patronage system was on the decline and ceasing to be an effective means of party organisation; that the Government was frequently at the mercy of public opinion expressed through a large independent section of Parliament; and that the ministers themselves were professional administrators who inclined in their opinions to the commercial rather than to the landed interest. The great social and economic changes of the time do not go without reflection in the higher walks of politics, and, with Parliament still unreformed, there is the spectacle of a Tory Government implementing a liberal foreign policy, reforming the criminal code, and acting upon the principles of *laissez-faire*. This last phase of the Tory Government was largely dictated by the state of public opinion in the country, and it is usually supposed to begin in the year 1822. It is here intended to examine the state of the Tory party, of public opinion, and the relation of both to the Government on the eve of this change.

First it may be asked: Who actually governed? The answer is that England was governed by professional politicians. It is the measure of George III's work that, after 1761, the great landed aristocrats never regained control of the state; during his reign there grew up a very large Tory aristocracy, but it was never a governing aristocracy. In the early nineteenth century the road to political power did not lie through great landed possessions or great borough influence, it lay through sheer hard work and an apprenticeship in the lower ranks of Government. Of the ministers in Liverpool's Cabinet eight were peers, but of these only two had titles which went back for more than a generation, and only these two, Westmorland and Bathurst, belonged to the old landed aristocracy. Eldon, Wellington, Sidmouth, and Bexley had raised themselves to the peerage by their own efforts, and the fathers of Liverpool, Melville, and Harrowby had been the first peers in their respective families. The distinguishing characteristic of these ministers was not birth but training and environment; they lived in their own circle of society, and this was the circle of neither Whig nor Tory aristocrats.

To this generalisation there was one exception: that of the Grenvilles, for they did form an aristocratic family "connection", and attained office as a "connection". But the attitude of contemporaries to the Grenvilles shows how much the idea of government by connection belonged to the past. After Grenville's retirement the group was led by the Marquis of Buckingham who controlled six boroughs and some fifteen members of the House of Commons. Other peers had equal influence, but only Buckingham tried to use this influence as a qualification for political office. In 1821 the Grenvilles joined the Government and Buckingham expected office; but Liverpool and the King were both agreed that he was quite unqualified for such a position. Of the Grenvilles only Wynn, who had a certain parliamentary reputation, was given office, and even so Wellington refused to see in this a concession to the idea of "connection". "As well as I recollect what passed when Mr Wynn was appointed," he wrote to Buckingham, "you expressed a wish that Mr Wynn should have an office which would...give him a seat in the Cabinet; and Lord Liverpool, Lord Castlereagh and others who were at that time H.M. Ministers considered Mr Wynn's talents, character and station such as to render him an acquisition to the Cabinet. This I believe to be the real state of the transaction; and I don't think it ever was admitted that it was necessary that a connection of yours should as such be a member of the Cabinet."[1] Buckingham continued to complain of his exclusion, and to demand office as of right, not of grace. The usual channel for his complaints was Wellington, and Wellington always replied in the same vein. "I am certain that if Lord Sidmouth was to relinquish his seat...you would experience insurmountable difficulties in

1 Aspinall, *The Formation of Canning's Ministry*, p. 46.

being called to fill it," and "it is impossible for any man to force himself into that situation".[1] While the whole notion that this sort of influence could be exerted within a Government was erroneous: "There is another point...in which I think you are mistaken, that is the expediency or desirableness of having two members of the same family or party in the Cabinet. Whether it is a fault or otherwise, I assure you that such confederacy in the existing Cabinet does not exist, and if it did it would be useless. I have never known two members of the existing Cabinet go into the Council determined to be of the same opinion, and it is a mistake to suppose that the relationship which existed between Lord Sidmouth and others, or between the late Lord Londonderry and Robinson, gave either more weight or more facility in the Cabinet than they would have had otherwise. I do not think that my position in the Cabinet is altered by the relinquishment by my brother of his seat there."[2]

These remarks are emphasised by a calculation which Croker made in 1827.[3] He found, to his surprise, that of the 116 members returned to Parliament by the great Tory borough owners, only eighteen held office, and of this eighteen no less than twelve had been given their seats at the request of the Government. Beyond this 116 thirty peers returned one member each, two commoners returned four each, sixteen two each, and seventeen two each. Some

---

1 Wellington, I, 132 and 145.   2 *Ibid.* p. 132.
3 Croker, I, 371. Other principal sources for the composition of the House of Commons are: Oldfield, *History of Representation*; *Biographical Guide to the House of Commons* (1808); *The Assembled Commons* (1838); *The Black Book of* 1820; *The Pamphleteer* (1822); H. S. Smith, *Register of Contested Elections.*

of the borough owners among the commoners belonged to the commercial rather than the landed interest, but, with these exceptions, it may be said that about two hundred Tory members represented the interest of the great land-owners, and on the Whig side there were some seventy more. Yet it is a paradox of the time that the Government was not dominated by this interest, and that it chose to pursue a foreign and an economic policy which was little to the liking of the Tory landowners. Lord Redesdale, an acute High Tory lawyer, lamented that "If landed pro-perty had not a predominant influence, the British consti-tution which is founded on the predominance of landed property, cannot stand. We are rapidly becoming—if we are not become—a nation of shopkeepers";[1] and "Trade, manufacturers, and money are everything. The landed proprietors are mere ciphers, they are of no consequence, either with ministers or with Opposition."[2]

The country gentlemen—most of them members for English counties—were always considered the most in-dependent men in the House. Their temper was the barometer of the House, it was necessary at all times for the Government to pay particular attention to their de-mands, and the stoutest Tory amongst them might turn against the Government on some particular question. In 1816 T. S. Gooch, the member for Suffolk, who could certainly be described as a stout Tory, declared that the ministers could no longer enjoy his support unless they embarked upon a policy of retrenchment and economy;[3]

1 Pellew, *Life of Sidmouth*.   2 Colchester, III, 401.
3 Hansard, XXXIII, 461.

and in the same year many country gentlemen joined with the Whigs to defeat the Property Tax. The next spate of opposition by the country gentlemen came between 1820 and 1822, when the distresses of agriculture led them on to attack the measures of the Government, particularly the resumption of Cash Payments. "The country gentlemen treat the Government exceedingly ill;" wrote Wellington, "what I complain of is their acting in concert, and as a party independent of, and without consultation with, the Government."[1] The recognised leader of the agricultural interest was not a Tory but C. C. Western, the Whig member for Essex; and Tory gentlemen were quite capable of joining hands across the House with their Whig brethren when agriculture was threatened. During 1822 thirty were consistent supporters of the Government, twenty-eight voted against on certain questions, and ten voted for on certain questions. The opposition of the country gentlemen was dangerous because they could claim, with some show of reason, that their demands were "completely free from party feeling and had nothing in view but the good of the country".[2] Yet the Government was saved by the fact that Tory rule was the first essential for the good of the country, and, as Thomas Grenville wrote to the Duke of Buckingham, "these blockheads all profess that they do not wish to change the Government, though they are doing all they can to annihilate them".[3]

After the aristocratic and landed interests the most im-

1 Buckingham, *George IV*, 1, 292.
2 T. S. Gooch during the debate on Western's motion for a Committee of Enquiry into Agriculture, 7 March 1816.
3 Buckingham, *George IV*, 1, 291.

portant section of Parliament was the commercial, under which vague term can be included all those engaged in banking, commerce, and manufacture. This "interest" had not the solidity of the agriculturalists, and their various demands frequently conflicted; it is, nevertheless, of great importance that there were nearly one hundred members of the House of Commons intimately connected with commerce.[1] Their numbers in the unreformed House of Commons are not generally realised: of bankers and financiers there were thirty-three, of general merchants twenty-two, the great and often hostile interests of the East and West Indies claimed nine each; finally there were six brewers and six manufacturers. Innumerable difficulties confront anyone who attempts to make an exact classification, for complex blending of classes has always been a characteristic of English social life. Two mercantile families had entered the ranks of the political aristocracy: two Alexanders, cousins of the Earl of Caledon, sat for Old Sarum, while the banking house of Smith, Payne, and Smith, whose head was the Earl of Carrington, owned two boroughs. At Bridgnorth a Whitmore had filled one seat with very few breaks since 1621; in 1820 two Whitmores sat for this borough, and they might certainly be counted as landed gentry, yet one, T. Whitmore, was a Governor of the Bank of England, and the other, W. W. Whitmore, was a director of the East India Company and a free trader. A large number of the "merchants" had bought their way into Parliament; once there they could make exactly the same claims to independence and to freedom from influence. So perplexed was Southey

1 Appendix A.

by this species of corruption, which gave the House some of the "most independent men...as the mob representatives are undoubtedly the least so", that he proposed a novel piece of parliamentary reform; why should not "the illegality be done away with; and the purchase of a certain number of seats authorised and regulated, and the money appropriated to a fund for public works of local and general utility"?[1]

To the party manager it was more important that these men could not be controlled. About forty-five of them were professed Tories, but twenty of these might be considered as doubtful and a number of them did in fact desert over the Property Tax. The standard of information and argument on commercial questions was certainly higher than it had ever been before, and on certain questions, such as the defence of cash resumption, the Government could enlist the support of men who were Radical rather than Whig. Such a one was the great Ricardo, whose defence of the Government came with an authority more in accordance with the Treasury Bench than with the Radical back benches. The Government could gain as much as it lost from the independence of mercantile men, and, after 1820, it began to play for their support.

From these two sections of Parliament which exercised the largest measure of independence, the Tory party managers could estimate a possible maximum of something over a hundred, but they had to allow for a possible defection of about fifty. In addition there was the possibility of some great magnate deserting on some question or re-

1 *Essays.*

leasing his members from their party allegiance. There were also members who might be called away on military or naval business, members who showed a reluctance ever to appear at Westminster, and members who were liable to grow tired as the night advanced and to slip off for late supper before the vital division had been taken. It is these difficulties which account for the frequent weakness of the Government in the House, and for Treasury miscalculations such as the estimate that the Property Tax, defeated by thirty-seven, would pass by forty.

The greatest source of Government weakness was that there was not a ministerial group sufficiently large to guarantee safe divisions. In 1822 a Committee of the House of Commons reported that eighty-nine members of the House of Commons were in places of profit under the crown. This figure and the list compiled was seized upon by Radical writers as the "Treasury Phalanx". It seems incredible that the list can have passed the most casual scrutiny of those who were seeking the sinister hand of corruption, for it included such "places of profit" as King's Counsel, and one of these was a consistent Whig! On the other hand the list does contain the names of a fair number of those belonging to the ministerial "interest". The word "interest" is used advisedly, for the "official men" in the House of Commons may be said to form an interest as distinct as those of the landed and commercial classes. The solid core of this interest was composed of those who held active office under the Government; these were regular in attendance and could be relied upon for departmental business. The Household Officers were expected to vote with the Government, but their attendance was less regular. The sinecurists were now few in number, most of them were superannuated servants of the crown, and few were prepared to play an active part in the day-to-day work of the session. The ministerial interest was recruited by a number of men whose family connections bound them to the ministry, or who owed their seats solely to Government influence, and there were, of course, a number of hangers-on and careerists who were looking for particular favours or political employment. But these were fewer than there have been in many Parliaments; the Liverpool ministry was in office for nearly fifteen years and during that time there were remarkably few changes even in the subordinate Government offices; it followed that the young man looking for quick advance found the opportunities meagre and the competition severe. Particularly noticeable is the absence of lawyers making their way quickly to the front; the careers of Thurlow, Dundas, and Wedderburn did not find counterparts in Tory politics of the early nineteenth century.

The Government could count on the unconditional support of about a hundred, and the regular attendance of rather less. This was useful, but it was not enough, and, to be safe, the Government had to rely on the support of a hundred or even a hundred and fifty more members. There were certainly enough Tories to fill this need, but many of them laid claims to an independence which they were not afraid to exercise. The time of trial came when the Government felt bound to press measures which it deemed necessary but which public opinion found distasteful.

Besides the uncertainty of divisions upon such topics, the decline of the patronage system left the Government very weak in debate. Most Government officials were immersed in the business of their departments, and there were no great sinecurists ready to defend the Government on any question. In 1826 Canning wrote to Liverpool: "I think it due to myself and to the Government to represent to you the state in which we are left in the House in respect of official support. The offices of Treasurer of the Navy, and Master of the Mint, can never henceforth be looked to as other than accessory situations to be held by persons whose hands are otherwise full of business—they never again can stand alone as available for the general business of the Government. The second Paymastership is already absorbed in the same manner. The remaining Paymastership is the single office of rank now remaining from which any aid, beyond departmental duty, can be derived. In this state of things it behoves us to take care that other offices—usually Parliamentary—are not lost to us by our own fault. There are three to which I particularly allude, which have for the first time been allowed to go out of Parliament by the present Government.... I mean the Master of the Rolls, the Judge Advocate, and the King's Advocate: all important, in the highest degree to the well carrying on of the King's business in the House of Commons; all within my memory, and till of very late years, useful and efficient supporters of the Administration."[1]

The Government of Lord Liverpool was working in some respects under the conditions of a modern Govern-

[1] Add. MSS. 38193, f. 239.

ment, for there was not enough patronage to provide a certain majority. But a modern Government has the advantage of a strict and efficient party machine, and this advantage Liverpool's Government did not possess. It got the worst of both worlds, the importance of the independent member was greater than it had been or has been in later years, and public opinion, once it had passed through the narrow doors of the representative system into the open forum of Parliament, could have a considerable effect upon the course of policy. The character of Lord Liverpool did not make the problem any easier, though his failure in this respect was entirely honourable to himself and, in the long run, probably established the personal esteem with which he was regarded. For Liverpool's honesty always precluded him from promising that which he could not give; "I believe", he wrote to an applicant, "that there is no individual in a public situation who has been more cautious on the subject of making promises than I have. In most cases in which I have made one either directly or implicated I have desired the individual to write to me in order that he might have an answer which should state beyond the power of future misconceptions what the nature of the promise was and what qualifications or exceptions were connected with it."[1] How this strictness might affect the business of party management may be gathered from another letter: "I do not see how it is possible for me to hold out the expectation suggested to Lord Charleville. I could have had *four seats* from Sir L. Holmes and *three* from Sir W. Manners if I could have promised them that they should

1 Add. MSS. 38572, f. 141.

have been made peers upon the first creation, I have *lost* them and I would rather lose them than make an engagement, and though it has been intimated to me that, without making an engagement, I might have held out the expectation...I have always felt that such a course of proceeding was either a virtual engagement or an act of deception."[1] Liverpool believed that these principles would ultimately strengthen rather than weaken the Government; to Peel he wrote: "Do not suppose me too Romantic...but (independent of my indifference to office unless I can hold it creditably) I am satisfied that a disposition to contract engagements of this description will in the end rather weaken than strengthen any government."[2] In the long run he was probably right, but he shut off from the party managers some of their time-honoured devices, and the immediate effect was inevitably to lose support in the House of Commons.

This strict attitude towards the administration of patronage was dictated in part by the diminishing resources of the spoils system. Burke's Economic Reform and subsequent Acts of the same type had abolished large numbers of ancient offices; yet still the House of Commons clamoured against sinecures, it was necessary to administer patronage with the utmost discrimination, and finally, in 1817, to pass an Act which abolished further offices. Some idea of these difficulties may be gained from a correspondence between Liverpool and Masterton Ure, the Parliamentary manager for Weymouth and Melcombe

1 Add. MSS. 40181, f. 23. The names are omitted from Parker, I, 43.
2 Parker, I, 43.

Regis: Ure pointed out that in the past few years he had returned nine loyal Government supporters, including himself, and that he was now anxious for some office tenable with a seat in Parliament, "the duties of which can be performed in London, or, if a situation elsewhere, which does not require personal attendance".[1] Liverpool replied that "situations tenable with a seat in Parliament having official duties annexed to them are few in point of number and are subjected to so many strong claims of an official as well as a political nature, that I must confess I see no prospect of any opportunity being afforded of me having the pleasure of promoting your views in this respect. In regard to situations of another description alluded to in your letter—viz. such as are tenable with Parl^t and have no official duties to require personal attendance—there are scarcely any of that nature now existing and such as may exist are subject by late acts of Parliament to regulations in the event of their becoming vacant as will dispense them hereafter of the character of sinecures."[2] It was indeed becoming difficult to find suitable rewards for faithful servants, and Liverpool said in the House of Lords that "there was no country where the salaries of great offices are so small, or have been so little augmented as in this country. Let anyone look at the last fifty years, and compare the increase of salary with the increase in price of every article, and he will be convinced that the rise in official salaries had been less than any other rise. There had been many instances of persons totally ruined in fortune by the public service; and indeed such must be the case, unless the officer

1 Add. MSS. 38262, f. 352.   2 Add. MSS. 38283, f. 121.

had a reasonable private fortune."[1] On another occasion he was writing, "The Pension Fund is so limited, as to be scarcely able to meet the just claims which are daily made upon it for the distressed nobility, and for the persons and families of those who have long laboured in the public service", and he replied to solicitations for a pension by saying, "I could on no account make such a grant to a connection of my own, who has been some years in a similar situation, and is the father of a numerous family."[2]

Nor could the deficiencies of the pension fund be supplemented by the provision of posts in the civil service. These required constant attendance and undivided attention, which hardly fitted them for the gentlemanly friends of "friends". To one applicant Liverpool wrote: "The prospects of a young man in an official department in this country are very limited. There are few persons who have ever risen in this way to any distinction, and even in the higher situations in the Office to which they may expect to come in very slow succession, the emoluments...are barely sufficient to cover the expenses of a Gentleman."[3] Moreover about 1820 Liverpool initiated some reforms in the most important of civil service departments, the Treasury, which on the one hand removed it entirely from the political sphere, and on the other hand increased the chances within the service for a really able man. This reform has been little noticed by constitutional historians, but it seems to mark the definite acceptance of the civil service as a non-political

1 Hansard, xxxiv, 812.
2 Add. MSS. 37310, f. 233: Liverpool to Wellesley, who had applied for a pension to his Private Secretary.
3 Add. MSS. 38275, f. 173.

sphere in which rewards were given to ability alone.[1] There were some valuable appointments in India, but here again the Government could offer very little, and Liverpool had to confess to an applicant that "the influence of Government at this time over the East India Company as a body is positively none. So far from the Court as a body having any disposition to comply with our wishes on any point, which is within their own discretion, I really believe, and in more instances than one I have found, that they have a satisfaction in mortifying the Government by opposing what they desire."[2]

In the past the Church had often been used as an aid to parliamentary management; but in the early nineteenth century the Church was receding from politics. This was due in no small measure to the conscientious manner in which Liverpool administered his Church patronage. The improvement in the manners of the clergy was much remarked upon, and Liverpool, when writing to Wilberforce,

1 *Report upon the Re-organisation of the Civil Service*, 1854–5. Evidence of G. Arbuthnot, Auditor of the Civil List, explains that about 1820 "Lord Liverpool, with a patriotism for which he has never received due credit, voluntarily surrendered the influence obtained by the power of making direct appointments to the superior offices of the Customs Department...from that time all collectorships and other offices of importance were filled by the advancement of officers already in the service, instead of by the appointment of strangers to it on a political recommendation". See also the Treasury Minute of 10 August 1821. The salaries of all officers were regulated and every office was restored to its condition in 1797 unless adequate cause could be shown for acting otherwise. Useless offices were abolished; promotions were to be by merit at the discretion of the departmental head, and there was to be a regular superannuation scheme consisting of a 5 per cent charge on all salaries and an additional charge on salaries which had been excessive.

2 Add. MSS. 38474, f. 69.

could not forbear from laying some claim to a share in this improvement: "It is never pleasant to speak of oneself, but I must begin by setting myself so far right, that I believe I can safely say that no minister ever made so little use of the patronage of the Church for political or family purposes, as myself, nor ever given so much preferment solely on the score of merit without any connection with, or personal knowledge of many of the individuals to whom it has been given."[1] Insistence upon the necessity for preserving or improving the purity of the Church was a constantly recurring theme in his correspondence. At the very beginning of his premiership he wrote to the Lord Lieutenant of Ireland that "it is a lamentable circumstance to reflect how little eminence there is on the Bench of either country—and I am satisfied that unless this can be corrected the Church will not long be able to hold up its head against the Dissenters and Sectaries which are opposed to it. I am far from thinking that all bishops should be learned men, or that it does not often happen that those who are not are as decent and correct in the exercise of their Episcopal duties as the most eminent members of the Church. But it is indispensibly necessary that there should be a proportion of learned men upon the Bench in both countries. When I say learned men, I mean of men who are known to be learned by their works, and by their zeal and activity in propagating thro' their works the Doctrines of Religion. We have in England lost within these few years Morley, Markham, Douglas, Porteus, and their places, I must say, have been most miserably supplied."[2] In the same letter

1 Add. MSS. 38287, f. 272.   2 Add. MSS. 38252, f. 310.

he set the tone of his policy towards the Church by recommending Dr Magee for an Irish bishopric, in spite of objections as to his political opinions. He was anxious that
men appointed by him should perform their duties effi-
ciently: to a prospective Dean of St Paul's he wrote: "I feel
it however an imperious duty upon me to offer it condi-
tionally. I know of no situation in the Church where
residence is of more importance and I have long determined therefore if this preferment should be vacant whilst
I was minister not to recommend any person for it who
would not promise to reside six months in the year at least
at the Deanery."[1] And when his own family was honoured
by the appointment of John Jenkinson to the See of St
David's, he wrote to another brother: "It only remains
that you impress upon him not to be singular in anything,
and where he is in doubt, to take the advice of those of his
Brethren on the Bench whose characters stand highest for
Piety, learning, combined with a due proportion of Prudence and Moderation. His proceedings will be more
watched than those of an ordinary bishop."[2] Nor did he
cease to criticise Eldon for what he conceived to be a
scandalous misuse of his patronage: "The Chancellor", he
complained to Peel, "has nine livings to the Minister's one.
With respect to these he does occasionally attend to local
claims, but he has besides four Cathedrals, and to no one of
these Cathedrals has any man of distinguished learning or
intellect been promoted."[3]

Modern party discipline depends largely upon a rigid

1 Add. MSS. 38286, f. 120.   2 Add. MSS. 38300, f. 55.
3 Add. MSS. 38298, f. 279.

control over the electoral machine; in the early nineteenth century this control could only be exerted through the local government patronage. In a few boroughs only was the Government patronage so considerable that it could decide elections alone, and even those which were considered the safest ministerial seats might give trouble at times. Such a one was Harwich, where the Customs House, the Port Administration, the Mail Pacquet, and the Revenue cutter had long been considered the deciding factors in elections; yet in 1822 Vansittart, who had been ten years member for this borough, wrote to Liverpool that "Harwich will require some attention. I have acquired some weight there and should probably have no difficulty in a re-election unless there is time for a previous cabal: but the second seat is not at all secure. If Canning went down there, the Corporation would be flattered and I believe there would be no difficulty, but they must have a man either of patronage, éclat, or else a man who resides near enough to pay them a good deal of personal attention."[1] "Patronage, éclat, or personal attention": these might well be taken as the key-words of the old representative system. In a borough such as Harwich patronage might suffice, but even there a "previous cabal" might succeed. Elsewhere patronage might play a very subsidiary part.

In 1820 Lord John Russell wrote: "A class of offices which is more important perhaps than all the rest, is that of persons employed in the collection of the revenue; upwards of four millions a year are spent in this necessary service.... The offices of the excise are generally given by

1 Add. MSS. 38191, f. 214.

the commissioners of excise appointed by the government, a few being reserved for the patronage of the Treasury; i.e. in other words for members of the House of Commons. The offices of the customs are entirely at the disposal of the Treasury; the offices of the stamp and post-offices are given by the Treasury at the recommendation of members of Parliament voting with the government. The receivers general of the land-tax, whose poundage alone amounts to about 78,000*l.* a year, and whose balances give as much more, are appointed at the recommendation of county members voting with the government. In the instance of one county, this office was lately divided into two, to increase the patronage. Where the members for the county both vote with the opposition, the appointment is given to the person whom the First Lord of the Treasury thinks ought to be the member for the county. Thus it is that the influence of the crown has not only been augmented, but organised, and directed in a manner never before known."[1] The accuracy of the last statement may be doubted, so may the general assumption that all this was corrupt; given a system in which these large number of offices were to be filled by nomination, they had to be filled at the recommendation of somebody, and the Government could hardly be blamed if it favoured a friend. The whole matter was argued out by Liverpool and Canning during the latter's period of Opposition in 1812–13. Canning, after his election for Liverpool, approached Lord Liverpool on the subject of local patronage: " The revenue offices, and other places at Liver-

1 *Essays and Sketches of Life and Character.* By a Gentleman who has left his Lodgings [Lord J. Russell]. London, 1820.

pool in the gift of the Treasury and of its subordinate boards, have, so I understand, uniformly been given to applications from the principal individuals and interests of the town: and such applications have been uniformly made through the Members. I have of course received and expect to receive, in common with my colleague, many such applications to forward. In forwarding them, I wish you to understand two things: the first that I can have no personal wish to gratify, and no personal interest of my own to consult, on such occasions; my only concern will be to endeavour to decide between rival claims...with impartiality:—the second, that as I shall never make such applications with any personal views of my own, so I shall not consider the compliance with them in any degree as a personal obligation....Should you choose to point out another channel through which you would prefer to receive such applications for Liverpool patronage...I should not take such a declaration amiss....But if you do not think it necessary to do this, then I hope and trust I may rely upon you, that my relation to the Government will never be allowed to weigh with you in deciding upon any applications from Liverpool of which I may happen to be the channel."[1] Canning was trying to have it both ways, and Liverpool replied that "in far the greater number of instances which will arise the considerations which will govern my decision must be of a mixed nature, as there will be few offices in any such place to which there will not be several and in most cases many claimants, whose pretensions may be equal, or nearly equal, and the individual who

[1] Add. MSS. 38568, f. 33.

obtains it will receive it therefore as a mark of personal favour as well as of public confidence. I have only to add that you will find me at all times ready to attend to your recommendations but I shall often think it right to communicate with your colleague, or with other persons before I decide upon the different applications."[1]

Nor can the Tories be accused of a rigid adherence to political qualifications, for, in the highest prizes of local patronage they admitted exceptions. A letter of Lord Liverpool respecting the Lord Lieutenancies may be quoted here: "The rules respecting Lords Lieutenant of Counties have been, of course, always to give them to the friends of Government where there could be anything like fair competition. The Whigs never, I believe, would have made an exception. The Tories have." And he cited the instances of the Duke of Devonshire and the Marquis of Buckingham, made Lords Lieutenant in Derbyshire and Buckinghamshire while in opposition.[2] Great honours were also occasionally conferred outside the party bounds; in 1826 the Duke of Devonshire was given the Garter in spite of Wellington's complaint "that many of our great Tory supporters had been of late out of sorts with the Government, and he should have wished not to give them this cause of dissatisfaction".[3]

But the crucial point about the patronage system was that nothing save a salaried office could ensure the votes of a member, and such offices were relatively few in number. A Tory country gentleman might vote against a measure

1 Add. MSS. 38568, f. 34.   2 Add. MSS. 40311, f. 64.
3 Add. MSS. 38302, f. 117.

which the Government believed to be of the greatest importance, but should the Government take from him the administration of local patronage the outcry would have shamed the Government into weakness far more serious than the one lost vote. When Fitzwilliam was dismissed from the Lord Lieutenancy of the West Riding for an offence which many believed to be almost revolutionary, the Whigs raised a loud and popular cry; louder and more damaging would have been the cries of a loyal country gentleman deprived of his just rights for exercising that independence which was his prerogative. In the election of 1826 Liverpool did, indeed, refuse to give Government aid to Holme Sumner, the peculiarly difficult member for Surrey; but this was largely the outcome of local quarrels in the county, and of the fact that Liverpool himself was, to some extent, involved in these local matters. "The real cause of the contest is not political," Liverpool told Peel, "the cause of it is Sumner's personal unpopularity, he is hated by all parties except his own immediate friends, his temper and his manners are considered as offensive and overbearing."[1]

Government influence might sometimes turn the scale, but only in alliance with some powerful local interest. In rivalries between squires and territorial magnates, between corporations and local landowners, between rival parties in the boroughs, the spirit of party was kept alive; the Government profited somewhat from the spirit and vigour which these local animosities breathed into the mouldering frame of ancient political differences, but it was also at the mercy

1 Add. MSS. 40305, f. 187.

of these many small conflicts when it tackled the problem of party organisation. The Government found itself compelled to tread a tortuous path amid the contending forces of local politics, but it could seldom, after the fashion of modern party machines, reconcile all differences by providing a stranger and a safe man. The weakness of the central organisation meant that it had to combine with those who were already on the field; and the simplest and most direct form of control was precluded by the operation of Curwen's Act. This Act, passed in 1809, prohibited the purchase of parliamentary seats; it was practically a dead letter so far as private persons were concerned, but the Government was forced to observe it rather than risk scrutiny and exposure. In 1812 Liverpool instructed Peel that it "will be absolutely necessary that we should so conduct ourselves...as to be able distinctly to state that we have been no parties to any money transactions whatever between those who may have influence in boroughs and persons who may be elected to represent them".[1] To Sir William Scott, brother of the Lord Chancellor, he wrote: "You will, perhaps, be surprised when I tell you that the Treasury have only one seat free of expense, for which our friend Vansittart will be elected. I have two more which personal friends have put at my disposal; and this is the sum total of my powers free of expense. Mr Curwen's bill has put an end to all money transactions between the Government and the supposed proprietors of boroughs. Our friends, therefore, who look for the assistance of Government must be ready to start for open boroughs

1 Parker, I, 38.

where the general influence of government, combined with a reasonable expense on their own part, may afford them a fair chance of success."[1] When the Government had so little to offer, it is not surprising that its terms had to be easy, and Liverpool is found writing: "I only expect from my friends a generally favourable disposition, and I shall never attempt to interfere with his right to vote as he may think consistent with his duty upon any particular question."[2]

It will be seen that the Government was severely limited in the control which it could exert over members, yet, to a majority of members the continuance of the Tory Government was of the first importance. It is by an exploitation of this same feeling that a modern party relies for much of its discipline; a disposition to criticise is restrained by the knowledge that the Government may feel bound to resign if it is defeated even upon a snap vote; and the independent member has to rely more upon his arguments outside Parliament than upon the use of his vote within it. In the early nineteenth century there was a very strong sentiment of Toryism and this played its part in perpetuating the Tory rule even when the ministers appeared to be weakest; but there was hardly any attempt to exploit this sentiment on the part of the Tory politicians. In 1820 Castlereagh did inform office holders that their support was vital to the Government,[3] but this is exceptional and an example of the general laxity of party control rather than a sign of strict party management. On the contrary, the

1 Yonge, I, 372.   2 Parker, I, 41.
3 A. Aspinall in *E.H.R.* 1926, p. 395, quoting from Hatherton MSS.

Government seemed as a rule more anxious to pander to the independent judgment of members than to request that they should curb their criticisms for the good of the party.

There was no established convention by which the Government should resign when defeated, and on the great question of the income tax, the defeat of which altered the whole financial policy of the Government, there was no idea of resignation. The precise moment at which a Government should resign was left to the discretion of the Prime Minister, and his discretion was guided by the capacity of the Ministers to carry on the King's Government, not by the occurrence of isolated defeats. The complete difference in tone between modern and early nineteenth-century party management may be gathered from a letter written by Arbuthnot, who conducted a great deal of party business; he was asking for the vote of a member upon the Army Estimates in 1816, and he added: "I would particularly notice to you the strong line of distinction between the question of those establishments and the Property Tax; as many of our friends seem to imagine (most erroneously) that they are committing themselves upon the latter by giving a previous vote in favour of the former."[1] Nothing illustrates more clearly than this letter the plight of the Government which had to connive at the frequent adverse votes of those from whom it hoped to obtain a general support.

If the Government forbore from putting pressure upon its supporters, it might be expected that it would take steps

1 Add. MSS. 19242, f. 288, Arbuthnot to Gooch.

to see that they were well informed of the Government's intentions. But party meetings were few, and were usually held only when the Government had particularly unpopular measures to propose. Such meetings were held in 1817 and 1818, the one to disclose the Government's plans for sinecures and the other to inform members of proposals to make marriage allowances for the royal Dukes. Even at such meetings little more was said than a bald statement of fact, and Peel, who probably had a clearer idea than any other Tory of the problems of party management, declared that he was never more surprised in his life than to hear Liverpool "intimate to a very numerous assembly of the supporters of this administration its intention of proposing to Parliament allowances to the royal Dukes which there could not be a hope of Parliament acceding to...a man must be really infatuated who could flatter himself that this House of Commons, now perhaps on the eve of dissolution, which was prevailed upon with the utmost difficulty and after the most unpleasant discussions to grant 60,000 *l.* a year to the Duke of Cumberland, could now be induced to grant him...12,000 *l.* more."[1] This particular attempt at party management seems to have been singularly maladroit, for, after announcing its intentions the Government heard no statement of views, and went on to suffer an irritating defeat in the Commons.

Members frequently received letters from the party managers—Holmes,[2] Arbuthnot, or the leader of the House —but these were no more explicit than the ministerial

1 Parker, 1, 263.
2 W. Holmes, Treasurer of the Ordnance and Tory "whip".

statements at party meetings.[1] Liverpool, in requesting the attendance of members controlled by Rutland and Lonsdale, was more explanatory;[2] but this was an exceptional case. The summonses, indeed, were illustrative of the Government's difficulty in obtaining the attendance of supporters, not of efficient "management".

Very different would have been the result if party meetings had been the regular rule; many independent men could have been induced to vote with the Government; and, what is hardly less important, the Government supporters would have gone down to the House with a clear notion of the arguments for a motion instead of hearing it for the first time from the Treasury Bench. In this way the Government could have gained the initiative in debate and a safe majority. At times Liverpool held meetings of one particular "interest". Thus in 1815 he called a "very full meeting of the landed interest" to discuss the proposed Corn Law; this meeting included Whigs as well as Tories, and the Government took the extraordinary course of leaving to the meeting the decision upon the measure. The Government would have preferred a sliding scale but the meeting "almost unanimously and particularly Mr Western" preferred the prohibition of import when the price fell below 80s.[3] Occasionally meetings seem to have been used to recruit fresh support; in 1818 the Grenvilles were beginning that dalliance with the ministers which was to

1 Cf. Add. MSS. 19242, f. 269, for a typical example. Castlereagh to T. S. Gooch: "No questions of the greatest importance will come under discussion....I trust you will excuse my expressing to you the anxious wish that I feel for as full an attendance as possible at the opening of the session."   2 Add. MSS. 38262, fs. 323 ff.
3 Add. MSS. 38742, f. 4.

lead them finally to office in 1821, and one of their number, J. H. Stanhope, received a note from Liverpool asking him to call; he went and found, to his surprise, that he was in the midst of a party meeting. The use of party meetings seems to have been sporadic, and inspired by no consistent plan of party leadership.

The impression left by an examination of these details of party management is certainly not that of an efficient machine. Rather it is that of men often at their wits' end to know how to carry on the day-to-day business in the House of Commons, frequently at the mercy of a capricious independent vote, and realising but slowly that their methods were ill adapted to the needs of the time. Liverpool is found writing with pained surprise that the Government was "exposed to the most acrimonious, systematic and persevering opposition that I can ever recollect to have seen in Parliament",[1] and again that the Government "certainly hangs by a thread", for neither defeats nor concessions had had the "least effect in conciliating those who have deserted us".[2] Liverpool complained that the "spirit of the House of Commons" was worse than it ever had been; and this spirit reflected the tone of public opinion in the country at large. There was a very large body of Tory opinion in the country, but, just as it failed to instruct their parliamentary supporters, so the ministers failed to inform or encourage their supporters in the country at large.

Against the Government the Whigs ranged all the modern apparatus of propaganda and popular appeal. In 1816

1 Yonge, II, 270.   2 *Ibid.*

Brougham organised county and parish meetings against the Property Tax, and, for many nights, the House of Commons was monopolised by the Whigs as they poured forth furious eulogies of the petitions presented by these meetings. For country gentlemen the extravagance of the ministers was stressed, for commercial men the inquisitorial nature of the tax, and for everyone the shocking behaviour of the tax collectors. The result was one of the greatest victories for public opinion and one of the greatest blows to sound finance in the history of Parliament. The Whigs followed up this success with a wholesale attack upon the various items of a supposedly extravagant administration. Again they had public opinion on their side, and a motion to reduce the salary of the Secretary to the Admiralty—which Liverpool considered a direct vote of censure upon the Government—was defeated only because Brougham overstepped the mark with a personal attack upon the Prince Regent. From this Opposition offensive there resulted various measures for the reduction of expenditure and, in 1817, for the abolition of those sinecures which still remained.

The riots and agitation of 1817 had the effect of frightening the independent members, and in that year the Government becomes somewhat stronger and the direct influence of public opinion upon legislation becomes less marked. Public opinion had, however, one further victory to score in these post-war years. In 1819 the Government announced its intention of postponing cash payment for one more year, but when the irritation of the Commons and the public at this became apparent the Government changed its mind and consented to a Committee of Enquiry. Both parties were agreed that a return to the Gold Standard was desirable, but the Tories said that it was impossible to restore it until the Bank had accumulated sufficient bullion, while the Whigs insisted that it could be restored at any time if the Government and the Bank would observe the principles of the Bullion Report of 1810. The findings of the committee amounted to a complete vindication of the Whig view, the Government yielded gracefully, and even implemented its recommendations with enthusiasm. Yet this, as much as the Property Tax, was a victory for public opinion and in a far worthier cause. The adoption by the Government of Peel's committee had one important result: it meant that the Government had espoused a commercial rather than an agricultural policy. Resumption of cash payments meant a restriction in the circulation and a fall in prices, and the class which felt this most was the agricultural class with its fixed rents and long-term contracts arranged under a depreciated currency and to be paid under an appreciated currency. During 1821 and 1822 the Government faced a persistent and angry attack from the agriculturalists and this meant that, in searching for the approval of public opinion, the Government sought consciously for commercial support.

When Radical disturbance had subsided and with the great achievement of resuming cash payment to their credit it seemed that the ministers might look forward more happily to the future, but all their hopes were dissipated when George IV insisted that penal measures must be taken against his Queen. "Now that the circulation is settled on a fixed foundation, and that the annual loans are beginning to be no longer wanted," wrote Liverpool, "the Country appears, for the first time, to be settling itself into a state of peace. It is provoking under such circumstances to have such a business as that now depending before the House of Lords to keep the country in a ferment and to give so strong a handle to the disaffected of all classes and descriptions."[1] Once again it may be said that public opinion was the Queen's salvation; indeed had the Queen been a little less disreputable nothing could have saved the Government. Public enthusiasm could not clear the Queen of guilt, nor could it replace her name in the Liturgy from which it had been excluded, but it could convince a very large number of men that, whatever the Queen's crimes, it was impolitic to punish her for them. When the majority in the House of Lords on the third reading of the Bill of Pains and Penalties fell to nine, the Government took the line that the Queen's guilt had been proved and that it was inexpedient to carry the matter any further. It was another victory won by public opinion over a Government which commanded the King's favour, a majority in both Houses, and all the resources of the spoils system.

So, in the five years which followed the greatest victory in the annals of British history, the Government which had presided over that victory was repeatedly forced to bow to public opinion. At the end of these five years it was so weakened in personnel and in prestige that some change in its composition was essential; it will be seen hereafter that public opinion had its part to play in the transformation of the Government, but first it will be as well to ask on what

1 Add. MSS. 38742, f. 26.

opinion the Government could depend, what opinion had supported it through these difficult years, and what steps it took to organise and foster this opinion.

The Tory party was far stronger in sentiment than it was in organisation. The old traditions of "Church and King" were enshrined with the new administrative efficiency in the memory of Pitt. Throughout the country Pitt clubs performed for the Tories the service which Holland House and the great country mansions performed for the Whigs, and with long after-dinner speeches, well-drunk toasts, and execrable verses the Tories saluted their idol. The ministers, most of whom had been the friends or protégés of Pitt, caught some of the reflected glory; and in them the power of sentiment was substantiated by honesty and ability which did not descend to the vulgar arts of popularity. But, as strong as any sentiment and far stronger than any reasoned belief, was the simple feeling of dislike for the Whigs. In the Whigs were united aristocratic insolence and the unseemly violence of democracy; they were the men who would have surrendered weakly to Napoleon; they would even now let in Popery; and no man could trust them not to lay sacrilegious hands upon the constitution. The strength of the Tory party lay in the Church and in the smaller landed proprietors, but there was also a very considerable Tory following in the commercial classes of the large towns. There was, it is true, a Tory aristocracy; but the Tory aristocrats did not lead their party as the Whig aristocrats led theirs. The typical Tory was still the squire, and the party reflected in equal proportions his good and his bad qualities.

The ordinary Tory was not an enthusiastic politician

unless he was stirred, and, above all things, the Tories required encouragement similar to that which the Whigs gave to their country supporters. But this encouragement was not forthcoming: throughout the country Tories were hissed upon the hustings, their arguments went unheard, and even when they were accorded a hearing, they had little original to say, for their leaders did not provide them with a programme. Members of the Government seldom spoke out of Parliament, and most of them, as peers, had not even the necessity of composing election addresses. Only Canning showed any eagerness to speak outside Parliament, and he, when he persuaded Liverpool to speak in public at Bristol in 1824, wondered whether he would be accused of seducing the Prime Minister into the base courses of popularity.[1]

Nor could the Tories look for much inspiration in the press. The Tory *Courier* was a pedestrian journal to place beside *The Times* and the *Morning Chronicle*, while other Tory newspapers such as the *Sun*, were mere time-serving rags whose editors were playing for pensions.[2] For the most part the Tories had to fall back upon their own inspiration when they wished to rebut Whig arguments and upon their own initiative when they wished to call counter meetings or carry counter petitions. Their weakness is revealed by a speech of George Rose during the Property Tax agitation of 1816: "If people were told that by petitioning they would get relief, they would naturally take

1 E. J. Stapleton, I, 234.
2 Cf. Castlereagh, *Mem. and Corr.* XI, 17, Liverpool to Castlereagh: "No paper that has any character, and consequently an established sale, will accept money from Government."

the advice given to them. He recollected a meeting which he attended when it was proposed to petition against the tax. Every hand was held up in favour of the proposition, which was seconded by a friend of his who paid nearly £3000 per annum property tax. If any person had then stated that, if the tax were removed, the sum would probably then fall on individuals not so wealthy as he was, he had no doubt that some difference of opinion would have been excited."[1] The trouble was that no one did say this, the Tories were cowed, and their leaders either ignored or deplored such popular manœuvres. From 1816 to 1821 the impression formed by a study of popular agitation and of popular petitions presented in the House of Commons is that the country was solidly Whig and Radical; in truth this is testimony not so much to the strength of Whig opinion but to the weakness of Tory party organisation.

For this neglect of public opinion the Tories reaped their reward during the Radical agitation. The ministers were extremely loath to take legislative action against the Radicals, and they felt very keenly that Tory magistrates throughout the country were not doing their duty. In 1817 Sidmouth told the Nottinghamshire magistrates that "The prevailing impression certainly was that there was a want of vigilance and activity in the magistracy. Government could do no more than give the impulse, and all the aid that could be afforded, to the execution of the laws."[2] And Liverpool told a Yorkshire Tory that "The Property of the country must be taught to protect itself. The active disaffected in any quarter are not numerous. The majority

1 Hansard, XXXII.   2 Pellew, III, 152.

go with the tide, and if they see all the zeal and activity on one side, and only apathy on the other, their choice cannot be expected to be doubtful."[1] This was written in 1819, and it shows that by this time the ministers were aware of the true state of affairs; indeed, throughout the debatable events which followed Peterloo, the dominating motive of the Government was the necessity of encouraging Tories throughout the country.

To Canning the rights or wrongs of the magistrates' action at Peterloo was almost irrelevant. "To let down the magistrates", he wrote, "would be to invite their resignation, and to lose all gratuitous service in the counties liable to disturbance for ever. It is, to be sure, very provoking that the magistrates, right as they were in principle, and nearly right in practice, should have spoilt the completeness of their case by half an hour's precipitation."[2] In the months which followed Peterloo the Whigs tried to repeat the tactics which had proved so successful against the Property Tax: they called large county meetings and petitioned for enquiry. Lawrence Dundas appeared and spoke at a meeting in York, and shortly afterwards Earl Fitzwilliam signed a requisition for a county meeting in Yorkshire and spoke at it in favour of petition. Earl Fitzwilliam was Lord Lieutenant of the West Riding, and the reaction of the Government was to dismiss him from his post. This was not a mere manifestation of party spite but a sign that the Government did not intend to repeat the mistake of 1816. Liverpool was convinced that strong measures would have the desired moral effect: "Our forbearance", he

1 Add. MSS. 38280, f. 205.   2 Add. MSS. 38741, f. 314.

wrote, "would be ascribed to nothing but timidity, and would discourage our best friends."[1] The decided line taken by the ministers had its effect in heartening the sadly perplexed Tories. The Bishop of Lincoln had heard from a friend with connections in Lancashire and Yorkshire that "everybody rejoices in the dismissal of Lord Fitzwilliam and in the vigour of ministers".[2] The action of the magistrates at Peterloo, whether justified or not, had given the Whigs a great opening; left to themselves, as they had been left in previous years, they would probably have been able to bring the whole force of a well-directed stream of public opinion to play upon the Government; but the action of the Government turned the tables and robbed them of their advantage. From York the President of the "King and Constitution Club" reported that many of the respectable Whigs were against the meeting;[3] the Grenvilles condemned the meeting for "childish folly and imbecility"; Sir Robert Heron was unable to call meetings in Lincolnshire and Northants "such were the fears of some and the apathy of others";[4] and the ministers found, to their surprise, that they were able to pass all their remedial measures with relative ease before Christmas. Success came to them now because they had at last realised the necessity for leading and encouraging Tory opinion.

The same idea determined the principle of the new laws, the notorious gag acts. "The encouragement which has been given to the seditions and blasphemies by meetings in other counties... has aggravated all the evils ten fold,

1 Bathurst, pp. 479–80. 2 Add. MSS. 38280, f. 80.
3 Add. MSS. 38280, f. 80. 4 Heron's *Notes*, p. 107.

and makes me seriously doubt whether in some parts of Lancashire and Cheshire we should soon find magistrates to execute their duty unless the law is in some degree strengthened,"[1] wrote Liverpool, and he thought that "the alarm in the country is now considerable and we ought to take advantage of it".[2]

The Government encouraged its followers by its example, but the Government was far from initiating a "publicity campaign". It saw that Tories must be given a lead, and that the very large reserve of Tory sentiment should be utilised; but Canning was the first Tory to view public opinion in the way that Brougham or the other Whig organisers did, and Canning did not make conscious use of public opinion as an instrument of policy until after 1822. The characteristic attitude of the Tories can be judged from the remarks which usually preceded the presentation of a petition in the House of Commons: the highest recommendation was that the petitioners were "numerous and respectable", failing that respectability was a far higher recommendation than mere numbers, and the enemies of a petition would usually attempt to prove that it was signed by a numerous rabble. In Tory eyes the political part of the nation began with the educated middle class, below that people had, or ought to have, no politics but merely loyalty and industry. Nor was this view merely reactionary, for it was reinforced by the most modern and most humane theories alike. The new doctrines of *laissez-faire*, to which the Prime Minister was a convert, taught that economic ills had nothing to do with political grievances and could be

1 Add. MSS. 38280, f. 121.   2 Add. MSS. 38280, f. 146.

remedied only by the free interaction of economic causes; while the Evangelicals, under whose influence most of the ministers had fallen, taught the duty of obedience to Christian governors. The deduction which the ministers were not slow to make was that the whole alliance of distress with political agitation was not only foolish but also immoral.

It followed that the principal aim of the Government was to break the alliance between politics and social distress, and the last method to which they would resort was that of counter agitation among the working classes. In defending the suspension of the Habeas Corpus Act in 1817 Liverpool said that in 1812 "the manufacturing parts of the country were in a disturbed and dangerous state, in consequences of which certain papers were laid before both Houses of Parliament. Those papers were referred to a secret committee and upon the report of that committee some new laws were formed to meet the evil; but it never was in contemplation of Government to adopt any measures similar to the present, because it was the firm conviction of that committee that political opinions were not the foundation of the evils that then existed. There might indeed have been some remote connection but it was so remote as not to call for the kind of proceeding which it was now proposed to adopt."[1] During the Radical agitation the most frequent phrases in Tory mouths was "the deluded people", and it was the aim of Tory legislators to prevent the access to the people of those who deluded them. It was this theory and not mere panic which dictated the much

1 Hansard, xxxv, 568.

criticised acts limiting the right of public meeting and the freedom of the press.[1] The first restriction manifested what may be called the "parochial" element in Tory thought. Liverpool could conceive "nothing more outrageous than that bodies of men at a distance should take upon themselves to exercise this judgment upon the conduct of magistrates placed in a critical and difficult situation".[2] Every man was concerned with the affairs of his own parish and might meet with others to discuss local affairs, but men had not the right to assemble in large congregate meetings to discuss things which did not directly concern them. The Tories did not wish to interfere with county meetings legally convened by the constituted authorities, though they might deplore the use which Whigs might make of these meetings, but the mass meeting convened at the discretion of a Radical orator was ruled out by the new restriction of meetings other than county meetings to the inhabitants of the parish in which it was held, or, in certain large parishes, to specified districts containing a population of 10,000. In the same way they took from the agitators the weapon of the press. "An effectual and permanent remedy for these monstrous evils is the thing to be found if possible," wrote Canning, "the root of them is the Press; and who is prepared to go to that root directly"?[3] and the press was, in

---

1 The correspondence of the Whig leaders shows that they too were disturbed by the phenomenon of large mass meetings. Lambton, who expressed also Grey's opinion, wrote to Wilson: "The only thing we did not quite approve of was your welcome of Hunt.... Keep clear of him as you would of infection": Add. MSS. 30109, f. 78. Brougham and Erskine both expressed their doubts of the legality of such meetings, and Mackintosh, Scarlett, and the two Lambs condemned them even while they censured the magistrates.
2 Add. MSS. 38277, f. 363. 3 Add. MSS. 38741, f. 314.

Liverpool's opinion, the "real source of the evil—but one more subject to embarrassment as a source of legislation, than any of the other evils of the day".[1] The result of these considerations was two Acts, one punishing blasphemous and seditious libels, the other bringing political pamphlets under the same licensing and stamping regulations as newspapers.

In judging the reaction of the Government to the great Radical agitation of 1819 it is necessary to remember that it acted under the immediate apprehension of revolution, and that its remedies certainly did achieve their object in divorcing political agitation from social evils. Bootle Wilbraham, a Tory magistrate and member of Parliament, wrote of the disaffection in Lancashire which had become "open hostility, not only to the Government but to all the higher classes, whose landed property is in this County (I understand) actually parcelled out for future distribution".[2] Lambton wrote that "The Tories in Yorkshire are greatly alarmed at the state of things. They fully expect a revolution, and in my opinion nothing can prevent its taking place but the removal of the ministers";[3] and Grey, in rebuking Wilson for his dalliance with the Radicals, wrote: "Look at the men themselves who lead in this cause. Is there one among them with whom you would trust yourself in the dark? Can you have, I will not say, any confidence in their opinions and principles, but any doubt of the wickedness of their intentions? Look at them, at their characters, at their conduct. What is there more base, and more detestable, more at variance with all tact and decency, as well as all

1 Add. MSS. 38741, f. 314.   2 Add. MSS. 38280, f. 19.
3 Add. MSS. 30109, f. 79.

morality, truth, and honour? A cause so supported cannot
be a good cause. They may use Burdett as an instrument for
a time, and you also if you place yourself in their trammels,
but depend upon it, if a convulsion follows their attempt to
work upon the minds of the people, inflamed as they now
are by distress, for which your reform will afford a very
inadequate remedy, I shall not precede you many months
on the scaffold, which you will have assisted in preparing
for us both."[1] It requires an effort to realise that the writer
of this passage was the Whig leader, and, when men were
writing openly in this vein, it is hard to censure the ministers
for measures which, with all their faults, were successful.
The Radicals were not able to make the Queen's trial the
occasion for a rebellion, and, what is more striking, in 1825
the great distress of that year was not accompanied by any
political agitation.

The Government had, with some reluctance, taken
strong measures and encouraged the Tories by example.
By the beginning of 1820 Tory opinion had rallied after the
threat to its very existence as an articulate force in 1816;
with the Queen's "trial" Tory opinion was once more
eclipsed, but general belief that the Queen had been more
sinful than sinned against, the operation of the Six Acts,
and the fact that the ministers did not push the case to a
decision, enabled the Tories to revive in the following year.
During 1821 the Tories still demanded signs and portents

1 Add. MSS. 30109, fs. 56ff. Other examples of the predominant fear
are found in Dropmore MSS. x, e.g. p. 449: "If the history of all
ages did not shew how constantly the moderates have in all revolu-
tions been made first the tools and then the victims of the most
furious agitators." And in Add. MSS. 38280, f. 168, Bootle Wilbraham to Liverpool. There was enough evidence to "satisfy anybody
but a Whig that a plot of the most serious nature exists".

that their cause was good. The Government was deplorably weak in the House of Commons and, to add to its other difficulties, there was a revolt of the landed interest against the operation of Peel's Act. Liverpool responded to the obvious need of his party for stimulus, and initiated a considerable change in the personnel and the tone of his Government. During the next two years Sidmouth was replaced by Peel, the Grenvilles and Wellesley joined the Government, Canning took Castlereagh's place, Robinson succeeded Vansittart, and Huskisson entered the Cabinet. These changes meant not only a strengthening of the Government's debating power, but they meant that the Government had consciously begun to cultivate the good opinion of the commercial classes. In 1825 Liverpool, speaking at Bristol, said: "If there be any merit on my part in the course of the administration of public affairs, with which I have been trusted, that merit consists in good intentions. I certainly have used my best endeavours to further the good of the country, but neither those good intentions nor those best endeavours would have been successful, if they had not received the valuable support, and been aided by the talents, of my excellent and able colleagues, and, above all if they had not received the support of the great commercial interests of the country."[1] It was this conscious union of the Government with commercial opinion which produced the brilliant last period of Liverpool's administration, the period of Canning, of Huskisson, and of young Peel, the period which may be called that of Liberal Toryism.

1 Speech transcribed in the *Morning Chronicle*, 16 January 1825, from the *Bristol Gazette*.

CHAPTER V

THE TRANSFORMATION OF
THE GOVERNMENT

IN December 1820 Huskisson told Canning that he still thought the ministers would "break down, or be broken down before Easter".[1] He thought so notwithstanding "all the reliance which may be placed on the blunders, the intemperance and the dissensions of their opponents and on the alarms and fears of the squirearchy". These prophecies were echoed by Croker—"a government cannot go on without the gift of the gab"[2]—and Peel looked upon their obvious weakness as the outward and visible sign of an inward failing: "Do you not think", he asked Croker, "that the tone of England—of that great compound of folly, weakness, prejudice, wrong feeling, right feeling, obstinacy, and newspaper paragraphs, which is called public opinion —is more liberal—to use an odious but intelligible phrase —than the policy of the Government?... Will the Government act on the principles on which, without being very certain, I suppose they have hitherto professed to act? Or will they carry into execution moderate Whig measures of reform? Or will they give up the government to the Whigs, and let them carry those measures into effect? Or will they coalesce with the Whigs, and oppose the united phalanx to the Hobhouses, and Burdetts, and Radicalism?"[3] At the end of 1820 men were sure of one thing: the Government must gain new strength or it must fall. It was one of those

1 Add. MSS. 38742, f. 156.   2 Croker, I, 184.   3 *Ibid.*

rare times at which men feel that they have seen the end of an epoch and that the future will demand new men and new ideas.

The immediate threat to the existence of the Government came from the King. On 16 November he had prepared, though he had not sent, a paper stating to the Cabinet that "he considers himself under the necessity of taking measures for the formation of a new administration".[1] At the same time he set in motion the whole machinery of backstairs negotiation in order to discover the dispositions of the various political groups. He had resolved "to proceed upon the road of negotiation if possible with Lord Grey",[2] but Grey, as was his wont, had retired to Howick so soon as parliamentary business was over.[3] The King's intimate adviser throughout was Sir William Knighton, who now first enjoyed the full light of the King's favour, and the first emissary was Lord Dacre, who had to discover whether the Opposition had "any settled plan of conduct for future difficulties",[4] in other words whether they had any plan for dealing with the Queen. Dacre saw Tierney, but his report was not very encouraging.[5] Lauderdale, now hovering between his former Whig allegiance and a Tory conversion, was also consulted; he advised against the expediency of changing the Government before the Queen's business was settled, and told the King that "a middle government" would be hard to find.[6] For Knighton the King summed up his

1 *George IV*, No. 867.   2 *Ibid.* No. 878.
3 *Ibid.*   4 *Ibid.*
5 *Ibid.*   6 *Ibid.* No. 877.

views: the Queen would have to agree to anything proposed by the Opposition, since she could not have recourse to the old ministers and the Radicals were too few; and by a change of Government "the publick mind would probably be diverted", and proposals coming from new ministers would "be more likely to suit the temper of the times, than anything coming from the old government". On the other hand the known principles of the Opposition "may be designated under the term Liberaux", suppose they wished to release Bonaparte, to change the system and spirit of foreign policy, to emancipate the Catholics, and to reduce the army; the Government had frequently failed to consult his feelings, but "they have been a good government for the country"; and above all was the fear of the day when he might "be shut out on all sides from any set of men, as servants, that could make my life tolerable".[1] Other friends of the King made enquiries among the Opposition leaders. Lord Donoughmore saw Lansdowne, who was sympathetic but thought that no government could be formed under the circumstances. Lord Hutchinson saw Tierney, who gave the same advice and added: "Let them proceed taking full responsibility upon themselves, and if beat it would be very fortunate"; the Whigs were naturally unwilling to come in as the King's nominees, but should the Government be beaten in the House of Commons, then it would be a very different matter. Leach, the Vice-Chancellor, saw Holland, who would say or do nothing without Grey. Bloomfield saw Buckingham, who condemned the Government, "but thought it would be complete ruin to me were

1 *George IV*, Nos. 879, 880.

I reduced to hold any communication, or to throw myself in any shape upon Holland House". Faced with the results of this unofficial negotiation, the King decided that he must "continue without yielding and with trust in providence".[1]

The Tories were still in possession of the field but rumours of the King's negotiations had been widely circulated, and it was known that the Government did not possess the confidence of the King. This made the position of the Government peculiarly awkward; they were weak, but without the promise of stability implied in the King's confidence none would join them. No one realised this more clearly than Liverpool. In December 1820 he requested Bragge Bathurst, Chancellor of the Duchy of Lancaster, to undertake the duties of the Board of Control, which Canning had relinquished: "In the state in which the business now stands," he wrote, "it cannot be surprising that persons not connected with the Government should be unwilling to take responsible offices"; if Bathurst would take temporary charge of the Board of Control it would avoid encountering any refusals, and would give an opportunity of strengthening the Government at a future date, for "if the Government is to remain, something must be done sooner or later to strengthen it, and it appeared to be inexpedient to put out of our power so important an office as that now vacant".[2] Nor was Liverpool entirely unaware of that change in the tone of the country upon which Peel had commented, though he attributed it to that natural recovery from post-war troubles which he always foretold. In September 1820 he had seen the country "for

1 *George IV*, No. 881.   2 Add. MSS. 38288, f. 386.

the first time to be settling itself into a state of peace".[1]
The Queen's business had prevented him taking any advantage of this during the closing months of 1820, but during 1821 his course was plain, he would attempt to strengthen his Government, and he would attempt to give the country a Government suitable to a "state of peace".

The first to whom Liverpool looked was Canning; he had not seen the necessity of Canning's resignation over the Queen's trial, and he took the first opportunity to negotiate for his return. There was no political difference which might hinder this object, but, on the other hand, the Tories if they accepted Canning did not accept him gladly; they recognised his abilities and they realised that their Prime Minister had set his heart upon restoring Canning to the Cabinet, but they still harboured a suspicion that his talents were not balanced by honour, that his ambition was not countered by loyalty, and that he was a charlatan without an acre of land in the country. For this reputation Canning had himself to blame, and a Tory unable to appreciate the greatness of the man might look with justifiable reprobation upon his past record.

The apparent turning point in Canning's career was the year 1812. Before that he had made many enemies, but Brother Bragge and Brother Hiley might forgive and Castlereagh showed himself ready to forget. In the negotiations which led to the formation of Liverpool's ministry he had played a part to which not much exception could be taken, and it was after the establishment of that ministry that he made his fatal error. In August Liverpool made to Canning

1 Add. MSS. 38742, f. 26.

an offer which Canning himself described as "perhaps the handsomest that ever was made to an individual". Canning was to have the Foreign Office, Wellesley was to have Ireland, and most of the Canningites were to have subordinate office. There was but one condition: that Castlereagh was to retain the leadership of the House. In an evil hour some of Canning's friends suggested that he should demand this too, and in an evil hour Canning agreed to do so. Of all demands it was the most unwise to make and the most impossible to concede. Castlereagh was already acting as leader of the House, and he had already made a great concession to Canning by yielding the Foreign Office and contenting himself with the Chancellorship of the Exchequer. Nor would the leadership give Canning much more real power than he would possess as Secretary of State; as leader Castlereagh would have to arrange the business of the House, speak for the Government when the minister concerned was in the House of Lords, and share in the distribution of Government patronage, though his influence so acquired would scarcely recompense him for the great patronage of the Foreign Office which he relinquished voluntarily. Castlereagh was, in fact, acting a disinterested and generous part; it was Canning who was being arrogant and unreasonable. Canning soon realised his mistake: "With regard to what is called the lead in the House of Commons," he told Liverpool, "I heartily wish that it had never been mentioned at all." But the trouble was that, once the subject had been mentioned, neither could yield without a sense of self-humiliation, and Liverpool was certainly not going to put pressure upon Castlereagh in order to make him yield to an unjust demand. Canning, on the other hand, stated his case as: "While I beg, on the one hand, that I may be considered as not claiming it for myself, I cannot, on the other hand, submit to the claim of it for Lord Castlereagh."[1] There was, however, no suitable person under whom both could serve, and on that note the negotiation ended.

Canning had put himself thoroughly in the wrong. He had put personal jealousies before national advantage, he had tried to dictate terms to a Government which was already treating him with extraordinary generosity, and, from an entirely selfish point of view, he had allowed a momentary consideration to hinder his political advance. Throughout the Canningite correspondence of the next ten years there hangs an air of melancholy and a sense of lost opportunity. In 1815 Canning was writing, "My 'abdication' took place in 1812. I felt it so then and never for a moment since...have altered that opinion."[2] Huskisson was "as fully convinced as Canning himself that the decision of 1812 was irretrievable by any subsequent negotiation";[3] and in 1821 Canning wrote in gloomy retrospect, "Wellesley is now just where he might have been—by my doing—in 1812. No other person...is ever likely to regain what they then lost."[4]

To Liverpool it was due that Canning did not ruin his career by the decision of 1812, and but for Liverpool the career of Canning would be simply one of disappointed ambition. In 1814 Canning, with a somewhat specious

1 Yonge, I, 405–6.   2 Add. MSS. 38740, f. 109.
3 Add. MSS. 38740, f. 198.   4 Add. MSS. 38743, f. 129.

gesture, disbanded his "party", or, in other words, told his friends that they might fend for themselves. The result was that Huskisson, Sturges Bourne, and Ellis took office, and Canning himself accepted a splendid and pointless embassy to Lisbon. Canning was peculiarly gratified with Liverpool's action at this time—probably on account of the generous provision made for his friends—and this year marks the resumption of really intimate relations between the two men. "I cannot wait", wrote Canning to Liverpool, "to express to you, not from politician to politician, but with the genuine warmth of old Christ Church feelings, the exceeding satisfaction which I have derived from the fairness and friendliness of your whole conduct in these discussions."[1] The result of the arrangement of 1814 was that the Canningites had shyed off any flirtation with the Whigs,[2] that they had identified themselves with the Government, and that Liverpool would bring Canning into the Cabinet when the occasion arose.

Canning professed no great anxiety to get back into office: the succession of a Whig Government was perhaps the only circumstance "in which I should ever *wish* to resume my place in the House of Commons",[3] and in 1816 "nothing is further from my wish than that *any* opening should occur at this moment and I would not on any account have one *made*".[4] These professions may, however, be

1 Add. MSS. 38193, f. 25.
2 Add. MSS. 38739, f. 271, Canning to Huskisson: "It is a satisfaction to me that those most inclined to them among my friends must now see...that the hatred of the Whigs to me is tenfold greater than that of any part of the Opposition to the Government or than any part of the Government to us."   3 Add. MSS. 38739, f. 271.
4 Add. MSS. 38739, f. 278.

attributed to the grapes which were sour; Canning had been assured of Liverpool's "friendly and cordial feeling", Huskisson held a watching brief on his behalf,[1] and, on the death of Buckinghamshire, Canning immediately accepted Liverpool's offer of the Board of Control.

Canning had now humbled himself and had taken an office not of the first rank in the ministry which he had aspired to dominate. In this situation he continued for four years, not without looking to the prospect of promotion when one of the older ministers should retire, yet doing so without ostentation. In August 1819 he had an interview with Liverpool, which, he told Huskisson, "was an intimation in the most amicable tone that on *any* opening I should expect to be consulted as to the whole. Not however seeking or wishing for any; but not thinking that any could arise which must not affect me far otherwise than the only one which had arisen since my succession.[2] . . . The answer was 'Certainly'—accompanied with an assurance that nothing of any sort was at present in contemplation or in prospect—except as to what Ld Sidmouth might meditate for himself, and he appeared now to have given up entirely the notion of retreat which he occasionally professed to entertain. I said not one word as to his particular situation —or as to any other, except incidentally as to my own, to which I reminded L. that your wishes, and mine for you, were entirely directed. The whole conversation did not

1 Immediately the death of Buckinghamshire was announced Huskisson wrote to Liverpool with a specific reminder that Canning would expect the offer. Add. MSS. 38741, f. 4.
2 Lord Mulgrave had retired from the Mastership of the Ordnance to give Wellington a Cabinet office. Mulgrave was, however, still attending the Cabinet in 1820.

take up more time than it will cost you to read this account of it. The acquiescence was so prompt, that I had nothing to combat or to stimulate, and I wished to say what I had to say with as little emphasis as possible, lest the exposition of my expectation as to an eventual contingency might be misconstrued into a design to hasten the event."[1]

So, in 1819, Liverpool was looking forward to a reconstruction of his ministry, and in that reconstruction Canning would have played an important part. The retirement of Sidmouth was the anticipated occasion for Cabinet changes, but Liverpool was also thinking of a junction with the Grenvilles[2] and Peel was an obvious candidate for Cabinet office; so it may be assumed, with some show of probability, that the changes which were finally completed in 1823 were being considered by Liverpool four years earlier. But whatever plans he was forming at this time were rendered void by the insistence of George IV to be rid of his Queen. Canning had been a friend of the Queen, and he felt that he could not now be party to proceedings against her.[3] Nor, at the end of the year,

1 Add. MSS. 38741, f. 314.
2 Add. MSS. 38272, f. 104: R. P. Ward to Liverpool, 9 June 1818, shows how the Grenvilles and the Government were sending out feelers to ascertain views as to a possible alliance. Ward reported that Buckingham was "clearly and distinctly satisfied...as to your Lordship's conduct...of the Government at large", and he elicited the important fact that "the Catholic question might not produce so vital a difference as to be fatal to a connection with the Grenvilles".
3 Liverpool did not think that Canning's scruples need have taken him to the step of resignation. The inference is that Canning may have known the Queen better than is usually imagined—there is a hint in Dorothy Marshall's *Rise of George Canning* which seems to point that way—but there is no need to draw from that the inference drawn by George IV, that the Queen had been Canning's mistress.

could Peel be persuaded to join, and any attempt to recon-
struct the ministry had to be postponed until the last
echoes of that dismal affair had died away.

Liverpool had, however, taken such steps as he could
to leave open the way for Canning's restoration to the
Cabinet as soon as the Queen's business was over. The
editor of a volume of Canning's papers[1] went to some
lengths to show that Canning's real reason for resignation
was his disapproval of the Government's social and foreign
policy. But Canning had been looking for promotion in the
previous year, and nothing had happened since to change
the Government's policy; he had been a convinced supporter of the ministerial policy after Peterloo, and Foreign
Policy was now nearer to his views than it had been at any
other time since the war. The true state of the case seems
to be quite the contrary, for Canning was at pains to show
that the Queen's business alone necessitated his retirement,
and, at Liverpool's suggestion, he took the unusual course
of circulating an explanatory memorandum to the Cabinet
stating that he "separates from them with unfeigned reluctance, that he bears them collectively and individually the
sincerest good-will; and that it is a deep mortification to
him that one unfortunate question should, from circumstances over which he has no control, prevent him at a
moment like the present from continuing to take his full
share in upholding in conjunction with them those principles of policy external and internal, upon which they have
been acting cordially together". One of the replies which
he received was from his old enemy Sidmouth, which

1 E. J. Stapleton, *Some Official Correspondence of George Canning.*

shows how very much Canning had been on his best behaviour during the past four years: "Your kind, cordial, and honourable conduct has made a strong and lasting impression on my mind."[1] These things point not to a deep dissatisfaction with the course of Government, but, on the contrary, to a desire for early reunion with it. There is also the attitude of his friends towards his resignation. At the end of 1820 one of them wrote: "Had I resigned at the same time, and if I do not, I can assure you that it is from no strong attachment to my office, I should have been acting very unfairly by Mr Canning in giving to his retirement a character which does not belong to it."[2]

1 A. G. Stapleton, *Life and Times of Canning*, p. 318.
2 Add. MSS. 38742, f. 159. This letter, which is found among the Huskisson papers, is signed G. W. The author may be Sir George Warrender. Stapleton also asserted that Canning hung back from office in 1821 for the same reasons; in support of this he uses an argument which is largely hypothetical, but produces as proof a letter from Canning to Chateaubriand explaining why he had not joined the Cabinet during the year: "Le Roi a bien voulu s'opposer à outrance à ma rentrée dans le ministère....Ce que je sais bien, c'est que si j'avais risquer cette question, quoiqu'il est possible que j'aurais été la cause de la chute du Ministère ou, au moins, de la démission de Lord Liverpool." Stapleton comments: "Why should Canning's acceptance have upset the ministry, or at least the dismissal of Lord Liverpool? The only explanation is that Canning himself would feel bound, once in the ministry, to protest against and obstruct High Tory policy." But it is obvious that Canning refers only to the question of his admission, not to the consequences of that admission. In any case Canning would be unlikely to give to a foreign statesman an impression which he carefully avoided giving to anyone at home. In view of his expressed opinions in Parliament, in private letters, and in the circular to the Cabinet, this attempt to plant in Canning's mind the Liberal disapproval of Liverpool's Government before 1822 would make him out to be the most consummate of charlatans. Canning suffered enough in his lifetime from suspicions of disloyalty and insincerity; enough is now known of his character to say that, had this been the real motive for his actions, he would have said so; at least he would not have denied it.

Canning was Liverpool's first object, but beyond that he looked to Peel, to Wellesley, and to the Grenvilles; in short to his favourite plan, the reunion of the old Pitt party. Peel was a "Protestant", and the favourite of the older High Tories; he had also been one of Liverpool's most successful promotions in 1812. But in 1821 Liverpool was less well disposed towards him than he had been in former years; in 1818 he had resigned from the Chief Secretaryship of Ireland for private reasons, at the end of 1820 he had refused the Board of Control for private and public reasons. Either he had a genuine desire to retire from politics, or he was playing some deep game; in neither case were his actions likely to recommend themselves to a Prime Minister sorely pressed by weakness in the House of Commons; in no case would Liverpool consider Peel an equal rival with Canning. No two men had displayed more personal bitterness than Liverpool and Wellesley in 1812, but Liverpool was always ready to forgive, and Wellesley was mellowed by near ten years without power and without friends. But past history would still preclude him from joining in a cabinet with the ministers whom he had formerly offended; on the other hand he required some place of dignity and authority. Ireland seemed to answer these necessities. Wellesley was a "Catholic", and his appointment to Ireland would raise many qualms in High Tory hearts; but it would quiet the scruples of the Grenvilles, who had, for the past two years, been hovering between Whig and Tory, and whose only real difference with the Government was upon the Catholic question. Any attempt to strengthen the Government would mean a strengthening of the "Catholic" element, but this Liverpool was quite prepared to do. More Catholic sympathisers might be found in high places, but this would not alter the voting strength of the two parties, and, so long as the Catholic question could be kept "open", the opinions of individual ministers would count for no more, perhaps for less, than their opinions as independent members. But whatever the claims of other aspirants to office, Liverpool would consider those of Canning first; Canning was Liverpool's friend, he was the greatest orator in the House of Commons, and he must be given a good office—he was not above sinecures, but he would not re-enter the Government unless he was given a post of influence. Liverpool looked for the first opportunity to bring in Canning, and that opportunity seemed to occur immediately; for, at the beginning of 1821, Sidmouth signified his wish to retire from the Home Office.

On 23 April Liverpool saw Canning, and the latter wrote to Huskisson: "I had a long talk with Liverpool...in the course of which we opened our minds fully to each other and I touched upon every point which I had reserved in our first conference. I should not like to *write* all that passed: and I am persuaded it will be more satisfactory to us both, that we should be able to say that we have not repeated anything personal to anyone." Canning went on to ask what changes other than the most desirable—Huskisson's known aim was the Board of Control—would be welcome: "Would Treasurership of the Navy?—I suppose it would. Would Mint?—I doubt it. Would Ireland?—I doubt it still more. Is there anything else?"[1] The plan of campaign arranged by Liverpool and Canning had no out-

1 Add. MSS. 38742, f. 202.

ward effect until far on in May; on the 31st Croker noted that "Lord Melville tells me that he is about to be kicked upstairs (his expression) from the Admiralty to the Home Office".[1] It was expected that the King might object to Canning at the Home Office, for the Home Secretary was the minister, apart from the Prime Minister, who saw most of the King; he was also the minister who would have to carry through any arrangement for the Queen. Melville therefore would be put in Sidmouth's place, Canning would take the Admiralty, and something would be done for the other Canningites.

The High Tory objection and alternative was obvious: if the Queen's business was sufficiently a matter of the past to allow Canning to rejoin the ministry, surely it would no longer be considered a bar to office by Peel; why should not Peel have the Home Office, and Lord Melville remain where he was most useful and most satisfied? Accordingly Liverpool approached Peel, but his desire to bring in Canning made him less straightforward than was his usual custom. On 2 June he offered Peel Cabinet office "in a strange shuffling hesitating sort of way", and from expressions used Peel understood that he meant the Board of Control. On 6 June Peel gave an explicit refusal to the Board of Control; "Lord Liverpool said hastily, 'And anything else I should offer?' Peel begged to say that, when anything else was offered it would be time enough to decide on it." Peel would probably have given a general refusal had he not suspected that Liverpool wanted one, which "piqued him a little". Croker's explanation of these

1 Croker, I, 186.

manœuvres is plausible; Liverpool wished to be able to tell Melville that Peel would not enter the Cabinet and that he alone could succeed Sidmouth.[1] In spite of this small rebuff—or rebuff not large enough—Liverpool proceeded with his plan and persuaded Melville to concur.

But while this negotiation was being pushed forward behind the scenes, Liverpool was shocked to find the extent of the King's objection to Canning. Brooding over the fiasco of the Bill of Pains and Penalties the King had magnified Canning's retirement into a great betrayal; he lent a ready ear to a rumour that the Queen had been Canning's mistress, and the action of Canning's friends in the House of Lords, in voting against the bill, confirmed his suspicions. "Canning has been misused by his friends in the Lords," Arbuthnot told Huskisson, "they have followed precisely that conduct which is calculated to do Canning harm."[2] But it was not dislike of Canning alone which influenced the King; in addition to his other complaints against the Government, he now had a personal grudge against Liverpool. Early in April the King had requested that Sumner, the tutor of the Conyngham children, might be given a vacant canonry at Windsor. Sumner was young and obscure, the canonries of Windsor were among the most prized positions in the Church, and Liverpool refused to comply with the King's wishes. After sending a protest which enumerated all the misdeeds of the Government, the King gave way; but he did not forgive. Later in the year Wellington told Liverpool that "the King has never forgiven your opposition to his wishes in the case

1 Croker, I, 188.   2 *Ibid*. p. 187.

of Mr Sumner. This feeling has influenced every action of his life in relation to his government from that moment; and I believe to more than one of us he avowed that his objection to Mr Canning was that his accession to the government was peculiarly desirable to you."[1] These embittered feelings were hardly auspicious beginnings to a difficult political negotiation.

On 10 June Liverpool laid his arrangements before the King; Canning was to go to the Admiralty, and Wynn, the most prominent parliamentarian of the Grenvilles, was to have the Board of Control. The King replied with indignant objections to Canning, and on 16 June Liverpool, his spirits dragged down by this unexpected vehemence and by the death of his wife four days before, unburdened himself to Arbuthnot: "It is idle to say that the question respecting Canning is not one of *proscription*. What King or what individual can ever say that he *proscribes another* for *ever*? Excluding a man at the time his services are wanted, and when there is an opening for him, is to all intents and purposes *proscription*—and upon such a principle I cannot agree to remain at the head of the Government. Recollect the question is not whether Canning should be forced into an office of constant personal intercourse with the Sovereign. Such a step I should never press, but the office which I have proposed is one of those in the whole Government in which there is least necessity even for personal communication between the Sovereign and the individual who holds it. The considerations I have already stated are sufficient, but you know as well as I do,

1 Wellington, I, 195.

what has been passing behind the scenes. The Objection to Canning, if it really exists, is one of *personal* pique and *resentment*. These qualities unfortunately existing where they do exist have been the source of all our past Errors and Calamities. I doubt however whether on the present occasion they would have led to what appears now to be the determination if there had not been a secret scheme, not to destroy the government at present, but to have the means of destroying it whenever the opportunity may be more convenient. I look upon the principle of the present arrangement as the test whether we are or are not the government."[1]

Politics were becoming exceedingly intricate. Liverpool would have Canning, looked upon this as a test whether the Government was to continue or whether it waited only upon the King's whim, and was prepared to go if his point was not granted. The King would not have Canning and he would be pleased to see Liverpool go; but on the other hand his experiments in November 1820 had proved to him that he could form no government to his liking, so he wished to keep the Tory Government, if possible without Liverpool. To Croker "he began to complain of Lord Liverpool. He says he cannot go on with him and will not; that he likes all the rest of his cabinet, nobody for instance better than Castlereagh; that if the Cabinet chose to stand or fall with Lord Liverpool, they must fall; if not he does not wish for any further change.... He asked how it could be suspected that he wished to get rid of his Ministers, he who had made them himself. But Lord Liverpool was

1 Yonge, III, 146.

captious, jealous, and impracticable; he objects to every-thing, and even when he does give way, which is nine times in ten, he does it with so bad a grace that it is worse than an absolute refusal.... He is rex Dei gratia, and Dei gratia rex he would be."[1] Between these two were the other ministers, who now found themselves in a peculiarly difficult position; torn between loyalty to their leader, the traditional respect of Tories for the Sovereign, and their personal indifference to Canning, their only hope was for a compromise. All knew the disruption which the resignation of Liverpool would bring about, and all looked upon the Whigs as irresponsible and impossible; it is not, then, surprising that every member of the Cabinet who was aware of the serious nature of the crisis, and every subordinate minister with a taste for intrigue, should have begun to conciliate, to argue, and to hope that one or other of the two contestants would find himself able to yield with honour. All were with Liverpool when he complained that the King was not giving the Government his full confidence, but when he made Canning the test of the King's intentions they were less happy. "The refusal of the King to allow the Government to be strengthened would occasion a necessity to break it up," Wellington wrote to Bathurst, "but the refusal of the King to receive Mr Canning into his Government at this moment does not amount to a refusal to strengthen the Government, particularly as such a refusal is accompanied by an offer to allow Lord Liverpool to make any other arrangement he pleases."[2]

In spite of this Liverpool, on 21 June, deliberately re-

1 Croker, I, 199.   2 Wellington, I, 176.

jected an easy way out which was offered to him. Canning wrote: "I entreat you not to let any consideration for me endanger the stability of the Administration, and least of all your own situation in it. If I have myself felt (as you know I have) the impossibility of my succeeding to the office of Home Secretary of State, so long as the recollections and perhaps some of the practical difficulties belonging to the conflict with the Queen should be still alive, I have no right to be surprised if the same considerations should appear to the King to extend further."[1] Liverpool communicated the substance of this letter to the King, but he added that it "could make no difference to the advice he must humbly submit". Liverpool wished to strengthen his Government, but he wanted Canning for himself alone, and he believed that no Government would be possible in which the "personal pique and resentment" of the King was allowed to determine the composition of the cabinet. "A King should be most cautious of acting upon such a principle, for the effect of it will generally be to exalt the individual and lower the King.... I was the person in 1806 to advise the late King to waive his exclusion to Mr Fox."[2]

Wellington had his doubts, but no one can accuse him of failing in loyalty to Liverpool; he could, perhaps, see both points of view, but he inclined to Liverpool's view of the constitution, and was prepared, in private, to use much the same arguments as Liverpool. In an interview with Bloomfield, at which Arbuthnot was also present, he endeavoured

1 E. J. Stapleton, I, 24.
2 Hist. MSS. Comm. Bathurst, p. 449.

to put the Prime Minister's case in a reasonable and acceptable way: "What I lament is this: the King is proving by
various of his acts that we have not His confidence, and is
proving it also by the unwillingness he has manifested to
allow us to strengthen ourselves. His Majesty cannot suppose that we are not sensible that Mr Canning's conduct
was not very advantageous to us. But viewing the state of
the Government, we were convinced that he was the person
most likely from his Parliamentary talents to assist the
Government if in office, and on the other hand to be
elevated to a situation in which he would have the power of
being most mischievous if *left out*. That *being left out* he
would immediately be surrounded by the discontented of
all descriptions, and by the young Philosophers who would
look to him as their rallying point; and that in short he
would have the means of collecting round him such members as would put the Government really in his hands. The
only mode therefore of preventing him from attaining this
power, and of rendering him really useful was to bring him
into the Cabinet."[1]

For four months, from July to November, affairs remained in a state of suspended crisis. At the King's
request Sidmouth remained in office during the coronation
and the state visit to Ireland, but he was old and tired and
his retirement could not be long postponed. A further delay
was caused by the King's visit to Hanover; in spite of
efforts by the ministers to settle matters one way or the

1 From the "Substance of a conversation between the Duke of Wellington, Sir Benjamin Bloomfield, and Mr Arbuthnot". This was
sent to Liverpool by Arbuthnot on 21 July: Add. MSS. 38370,
f. 25.

other, the King sailed for Germany and left his Government to await his pleasure when he should have done with his progresses. During this long delay two minor matters added to the general bad feeling between King and Prime Minister. After the coronation Lord Hertford wished to retire from the office of Lord Chamberlain, and the question of his successor became a problem. Liverpool professed that he had "no personal or political wishes on the subject, and he is earnestly desirous upon this occasion, as upon all others of a similar nature, to meet the personal feelings of the King as far as he can do so consistently with the responsibility which necessarily belongs to his situation as His Majesty's First Minister".[1] The King replied that he wished Lord Liverpool "distinctly to understand that whatever appointments the King may think proper to make in his own family are to be considered as quite independent of the controul of any minister whatever",[2] and further, it was his pleasure that the new chamberlain should be Lord Conyngham. But Liverpool suspected that Lady Conyngham was largely responsible for the "secret scheme", and the appointment of her husband to the head of the Household would be a public humiliation for the ministers. And in any case, if the Prime Minister could not advance his friend who was a distinguished statesman, why should the King be allowed to advance the husband of his mistress who was a nonentity? The other event which kept bad feeling alive was the funeral of the Queen, who died on 7 August. The funeral was mismanaged and caused some rioting, and a few weeks later Liverpool was complaining

1 *George IV*, No. 945.   2 *Ibid.* No. 946.

that this was "the *great sin* of which the King now accused the ministers".[1]

The King was employing his favourite strategy, a waiting game. He knew that Liverpool's colleagues were not so friendly towards Canning that they would risk all for him. He hoped that either Liverpool would weaken or that there would be a revolt against his authority; and of the two he would prefer the latter. Nor did the King fail to drop broad hints in private conversation; Croker, by his own account, received a large share of these hints, and Croker, who was a gossip and easily flattered, passed on the confidences of the King to those who would think most deeply upon them. To Sidmouth the King hinted that political worry might induce in him his father's madness.[2]

Slowly the seeds of compromise grew. On 9 September Croker "hinted that Lord Liverpool had perhaps some personal excuses to make on one or two points", and tried to persuade him to meet the King "not argumentatively, but kindly and frankly". Liverpool compared himself to the lamb and the King to the wolf in the fable, but seems to have decided to make a conciliatory move. On 16 September he called at Carlton House, but found himself subjected to the astounding insult of being refused an audience. At the same time the King saw Eldon, Londonderry, and Bathurst. It was, said Croker, "a mortification to which I wonder Lord Liverpool can submit". It may be hazarded that it was the King's object to make Liverpool come to the same decision; if Liverpool could be impelled into offering his resignation, the other ministers could hardly

1 Croker, I, 209.   2 Add. MSS. 38370, f. 57.

go with him on such a personal question. On 24 September the King sailed for Hanover, and during the next month it would be necessary for him to make up his mind.

Meanwhile another prospect had opened before Canning. Moira, become the Marquis of Hastings, might retire from the Indian Vice-Royalty, and Canning, discouraged by the prejudices against him at home, flattered with the approaches which the Court of Directors made to him, and sorely embarrassed in his finances, might take the splendid exile. This seemed to settle every man's problem: the King would not have to accept him as a Cabinet minister, the ministers would be relieved from the fear of Canning at large in the House of Commons, and the way would be open for an honourable retreat by Liverpool. The idea was sufficiently attractive to the King to allow him to make the barren concession, in a letter to Londonderry during his Hanover visit, that he would admit Canning to the Cabinet were he in a position far removed from personal intercourse and if he would take India when vacant.[1] Londonderry had gone to Hanover with the King, and he now began to use his influence to soften the King's prejudice against Liverpool. To his brother he described the fruit of his labours: the King put the whole matter in his hands, "and he sent me to Liverpool to hold confidential intercourse before matters came into formal discussion. After much negotiation I brought matters to bear."[2]

Londonderry's way had been made smooth by the advice

1 *George IV*, No. 958.
2 Quoted by Aspinall, *George IV*, ii, 471, note 1.

of Liverpool's friends and colleagues at home. "I im-
plored him", said Arbuthnot, "not to take any decision in
consequence of the King's persevering repugnance to admit
Mr Canning into the Cabinet, and...told him that those of
his colleagues with whom I had conversed considered him
as the Pivot upon which the whole machine turned. That
were he to abandon the Government the whole country
would be thrown into confusion, and that without him the
other members of the Cabinet would not under such circumstances have a hope of remaining together."[1]   This
advice was reinforced by a long and important letter from
Wellington: he began by saying that he was still anxious for
Canning to be brought into the Cabinet, but he went on:
"I don't believe you will find your colleagues ready to incur
all risks for this object, although I believe they were all
sincerely desirous of having Mr Canning in the Cabinet;
some, like myself, thinking it desirable on the ground of the
services he can render to the Government and on his own
account, and others out of deference to you. But I don't
think that you will find many of them disposed to resign
the government from their hands if they should not attain
that object. Neither...do I believe you will find the party
in general disposed to approve your resignation on this
ground. There is no doubt that Mr Canning is not very
popular with them....I would recommend you to propose
him to the King, then, not in the spirit of hostility, not as an
alternative to be taken between Mr Canning and us, or
anything else the King can find as a government, but...as
an arrangement calculated for the strength of the Govern-

[1] Add. MSS. 38370, f. 57.

ment, the benefit of the country, and the honour of the King."[1] As to the new Lord Chamberlain, Wellington said: "Why should *we* look for a quarrel? Is it not rather our duty to settle this petty question?...I don't mean to depreciate the importance of a point of honour to a government; but I would observe that the prevention of this particular appointment became a point of honour after the rejection of Canning in June, the question of the Irish peerages, and of the Green Ribands, and all the follies of the Coronation." The Duke went on to say that the Government could not resign with a clear conscience for in doing so it would hand over the country to Whigs, Radicals, and irretrievable ruin. "The result may be that we shall break down; but we shall have the satisfaction of reflecting that this misfortune is the effect of the circumstances in which we are placed, and of the character of the person with whom we have to deal, and not our own act."

The result of this pressure upon the two chief disputants made both ready for some compromise at the end of the Hanover visit. "One thing seems certain," wrote Croker on 12 November, "that the King and Lord Liverpool will come to an understanding."[2] The formal reconciliation took place on the following day, and by the 21st Londonderry was able to tell his brother that "Liverpool is now very well received", and on the 24th that "complete harmony has been restored between the King and his Government, and he has received Liverpool with cordiality".[3] By the beginning of the new year the King was asking Liver-

1 Wellington, I, 192.   2 Croker, I, 127.
3 Londonderry MSS. Quoted by Aspinall, *George IV*, II, 471, note 1.

pool for personal advice and underlining the words "as my friend".[1]

The terms of the reconciliation appeared as a victory for the royal right to exclude, but they were also a victory for the idea that the King must give his confidence to a government supported by Parliamentary majorities. Canning was to remain out of the Cabinet and to be offered India when the vacancy occurred, but, on the other hand, there were to be no more "flirtations with the Whigs". Had the ministers, other than Liverpool, been whole-hearted in their advocacy of Canning, compromise would have been impossible; but, even beyond the indifference or dislike which some of them felt towards Canning, there was the traditional Tory dislike of forcing the King's hand. Wellington knew well the deficiencies of their royal master, but his loyalty and his theory of the constitution made him regard a certain freedom of action by the King as an essential; the King might do wrong but the ministers must be able to show that they had treated him fairly. In the long run it was probably of more importance that the King was forced to give his confidence to ministers whom he had wished to turn out than that he maintained his right to exclude undesirable ministers; henceforth backstairs intrigue and communications with the Opposition would be not only wrongheaded but also unconstitutional.

Canning took his exclusion with philosophic resignation; he too was a Tory, and he too had shown his unwillingness to force the hand of the King. He looked back upon his political career, upon his great mistake of 1812, upon the

1 *George IV*, No. 982.

thwarting of his ambitions, upon his subordination in a ministry which he had hoped to command, which he had at first despised, and whose continuance he now thought to be of more importance than his own ambitions. To Huskisson he wrote: "Enough of retrospect which can now do no good—not even as experience so far as I am concerned—since I foresee no imaginable combination of things through which I can ever again be engaged upon a political negotiation."[1] Moreover, with all his disappointments, there was still India, with its opportunities for putting large ideas into practice and for recouping a shattered fortune. But, in spite of his protestation to Huskisson, he still cast his eyes longingly upon office at home, and there remains one curious letter written to Liverpool in January 1822, and when Liverpool had already offered the Home Office to Peel: "Here are a few remarks with which I threatened you yesterday. When you say that 'it would be easier to persuade P. to remain *out of office altogether for the present* than to induce him to change the one office for the other':—do you mean to use *that* expression only as an illustration of great difficulty as when one says 'I would rather cut off my right hand than do so and so'? Or does it imply that there would be a chance of obtaining the decision which you speak of as 'easier'? The words 'for the present' seem to countenance the latter construction; and the proposition so construed tallies with rumours which have been current (I understand) for the last two or three months of a delay in P.'s acceptance of office.

"Now, supposing Peel (for *any* reason) inclined to post-

[1] Add. MSS. 38743, f. 129.

pone his accession to the Government, and supposing the Home Office vacant, I confess I do not see the difficulty relating to that office in the light which it appears to strike you—though you know how little I like it. I think the natural course would be to propose me for *that* office to the King. I think if H.M. consented at all it would be in a spirit of grace and oblivion, and I have a strong feeling that a month's intercourse in business would do more to efface unpleasant retrospects and recollections, than years of occasional and unwilling communication. I would not therefore that, in such case, Melville should be troubled with any proposition on your part or wish on mine. If the *King* insisted upon the one great arrangement, it would be for H.M. to press it, not for you.

"But, as on my part, the death of the Queen has removed all publick and stateable objection to the Home Office— so, on the other hand, I can hardly believe that (the getting rid of me in the H. of C. once out of the question) the King would think it right, or expedient, to make me the single exception to that general amnesty which (if I am not mis-informed) he is proclaiming or allowing to be proclaimed.

"You say that the entire relinquishment of India must necessarily precede office. Be it so. You say that 'time' is requisite for the subsiding of what has passed upon this subject. To that proposition there is one objection—that, if during that 'time', P. becomes Sec. of State—the door is closed against me for ever. The question is, therefore, would a declaration of the final relinquishment of India on my part enable you to re-cast this part of your arrange-ment? Whether now, or some time hence, matters not;

provided no insuperable impediment grows up during the interval."[1]

This letter is interesting only as proof that Canning still hankered after office, that Liverpool was still looking forward to a time when Canning might be brought in, and as a clue to the hesitations and changes of mind in which Canning was indulging over India; nothing was done upon the lines suggested by Canning, and it was but a few days later that Peel received the seals of the Home Office. The door seemed to close against Canning for ever.

At the end of November Liverpool was able to state that "there was now no question of the government's continuance or of the King's confidence". This new-found stability enabled him to turn his mind to those other changes, which he had contemplated formerly, but which he had considered as secondary to the accession of Canning. On 28 November he offered the Home Office to Peel, who promptly accepted. With no further difficulty Wellesley was offered and accepted Ireland; his appointment was valuable in itself and it would facilitate the next move—negotiations with the Grenvilles—by satisfying some of their scruples over the Catholic question. This idea, of a union with the Grenvilles, had been in the air for some time; Liverpool had mentioned it to the King in June, and the Grenvilles, with their final separation from the Whigs and the attempt to form—for bargaining purposes—a "third party", had shown themselves ready to treat.[2] Within the ministry the idea was strongly favoured by

1 Add. MSS. 38568, f. 112.
2 Hist. MSS. Comm. Fortescue, vol. x *passim*.

Londonderry, "I attach so much importance to the Grenville connection not being left loose in the House of Commons for obvious reasons," he had written to Liverpool, "that, although ready to try our strength without them, I cannot too strongly urge their acquisition."[1] Throughout 1821 the Board of Control—with its valuable patronage—had been kept open as a bait to the Grenvilles, and, at the end of the year, negotiations began. In the early nineteenth-century world the Grenvilles retained the ideas and methods of an eighteenth-century connection; they had a certain uniformity of political creed, but this creed was of sufficient flexibility to allow them, in normal times, to work with either political party; upon their Whig allies they had acted as a dead weight, combating every proposal which savoured of Radicalism, and emphasising always the division between the patrician Whigs and their plebeian associates; they had broken with the Whigs over the social questions and supported the coercive measures of the Government; they now found nothing, save a few doubts upon the Catholic question, to divide them from the Government, and, whatever other consideration should arise, they were heartily sick of opposition. But they were prepared to exact a pound of flesh as the price of their adherence, and it seemed at first that Liverpool's extraordinarily generous terms—a dukedom for the Marquis of Buckingham, the Board of Control for Wynn, a post at the embassy in Switzerland for H. Wynn, a seat at one of the principal Boards for Fremantle, and possibly the Attorney Generalship of Ireland for Plunket—would not satisfy

1 Yonge, III, 162.

them. The aim of the Marquis of Buckingham was Cabinet office, but he had no political experience, he was personally unpopular, his appointment would bring the odium of a "job" upon a Government which had preserved a relatively high standard of political morality, and the days were past when the hereditary leader of a "connection" could claim office as a matter of right. Fortunately Lord Grenville, still the sage and the most able member of the group though living in retirement, approved of the ministerial terms— "there was *no possible objection* to the proposed arrangement"[1]—and faced with this emphatic approval Buckingham was bound to accede to Liverpool's proposals, and to accept the Dukedom of Buckingham and Chandos as a sufficient share of the spoils.

The accession of the Grenvilles meant more than the addition of some dozen votes, of one great orator in Plunket, and of one somewhat ineffective President of the Board of Control in Wynn; by crossing the floor of the House this small group passed an emphatic vote of confidence in the Government, and their crossing signified that the Government's difficulties from the King and from doubtful supporters, were at an end. There was still more: the Grenvilles had been members of Pitt's party, and their reunion with the parent stem completed the last stage in that project which Liverpool had accepted as a chief part of his political mission, the restoration of the old Pitt party. But the winning of the Grenvilles had undoubtedly been expensive, and it could hardly be accomplished without the mortification of some junior members of the ministry, who now saw

1 Buckingham, I, 241.

the Grenvillites stepping easily into positions for which those in the lower ranks of government had striven long and faithfully. No man was more bitterly offended than William Huskisson.

Huskisson's ambition was the Board of Control, and already, in June of 1821, he had shown his chagrin at the prospect of being left out in a possible rearrangement. Now, with Wynn appointed to the coveted office, his resentment boiled over; he spoke of his "mortification", he thought he had been "most unfairly and unkindly used", he lamented "the injury and injustice with which his zealous and unrelenting exertions to make himself useful to the Government had been requited".[1] Liverpool offered Huskisson a place in Ireland, or to make Palmerston an English peer if he would vacate the Secretaryship at War in Huskisson's favour. Huskisson refused the one, Palmerston refused the other, and Huskisson had perforce to remain First Commissioner of Woods and Forests—an office of which he was heartily sick—and to continue his complaints of injustice. His letter to Binning explaining why he did not resign is interesting, for it shows the feelings of a Tory upon the reunion of the Pitt party, the feelings of a Canningite upon the relationship between his leader and the Prime Minister, and the feelings of a typical member of the "official" class toward the Grenville ideas of an aristocratic right to rule: "The considerations on which they lay so much stress are these—that I could not go out now without appearing to invite a comparison of personal pretensions, a thing in itself too invidious not to be avoided if

1 Add. MSS. 38742, f. 255.

possible—that it is an arrangement which brings together so many of Mr Pitt's friends and followers, it will not be pleasant to be held out as detracting either from its harmony or its value as an accession of strength—and further I could not go out now (when S[turges] B[ourne] is also retiring) without creating a surmise that there existed or was likely to exist a want of cordiality between L[iverpool] and C[anning]. This I own has most weight with me.... If the arrangement was of more worth I might the less repine: but I own I cannot bring myself to believe that the numbers of the Grenvilles in our House, backed by all their talents, are sufficient to outweigh their want of popularity, their sinecures, their lofty and greedy pretensions, and the sore feelings at the expense of which their pretensions are to be gratified in other and more faithful friends of the present Government."[1]

The result of the negotiations of 1821 was to give the ministry, which, at the beginning of the year, had seemed ready to die of weakness, a new lease of life. It was now certain that there would be no change of government so long as a party split could be averted. Taken with the more settled and prosperous state of the country, this seemed to be a fair augury for the future, and such men as Peel—perhaps Liverpool himself—would not be content to ride passively upon the crest of the wave, they would take the opportunity to effect some long-needed improvements. Peel made clear that he would treat the question of penal reform as one to be decided upon its merits, not as an attack on the constitution to be resisted to the last;[2] Liver-

1 Add. MSS. 38743, f. 59.   2 Yonge, III, 216.

pool had already told a Free Trade deputation that he had
long been convinced of the truth of their theories,[1] and,
with great and characteristic caution, he was considering
the whole question of economic reform; at the Board of
Trade the Vice-President, Wallace, was earning much
praise for the first tentative steps in the same direction.
The Bank had found itself able to renew cash payments
before the prescribed time, and Government spokesmen
were already being forced into some solid economic thought
and argument in order to resist the attacks of the agriculturalists upon Peel's Act; and it is an omen of no small
significance that, in this resistance, they were backed at
every point by Ricardo. The great nineteenth-century
alliance of theorists and practical politicians was already at
hand. On the other hand there were still disadvantages:
Vansittart pursued his amiable and incompetent way at the
Exchequer, Huskisson was still a disappointed man, the
spirit of Eldon and Sidmouth was still strong, especially
when it could enlist the support of a man such as Wellington, and two members of the Cabinet—Bragge Bathurst
and Maryborough—did little to justify their positions. But
after the changes of 1821 little could be done; should
Liverpool attempt further changes he would risk another
battle with the King, which might mean the end of his
ministry, or he would offend faithful supporters, and
whatever happened he would seem to be in a hurry to
get rid of old friends. To a Prime Minister such as Liverpool these were weighty considerations, nor was it entirely
weak good nature and a wish to avoid difficulties, for his

1 Tooke, vol. VI, Appendix.

hold upon his ministry depended largely on a reputation for fairness and integrity, and such things would be challenged by a charge of ingratitude. So matters rested, in tranquillity and without further change, until 12 August 1822.

The exultation of Liberals at the succession of Canning has obscured the fact that the suicide of Castlereagh was one of the major tragedies of the nineteenth century. In the same way his quarrel with Canning has lent colour to the illusion that he was the blindest of reactionaries. In truth the difference between the two men was one of temperament and of method rather than of policy. Castlereagh was already moving slowly, perhaps reluctantly, along the road which Canning was to follow with spirit and enthusiasm; both realised the impossible folly of binding England unconditionally to the Allied Powers and to the existing order in Europe. But the work of Castlereagh was not confined to the business of the Foreign Office, he was also leader in the House of Commons, and commanded the respect of the whole Tory party. He spoke badly, but his stumbling sentences were dearer to Tory gentlemen than all the oratory of a Canning or a Whig. "He goes on as usual," wrote Croker in December 1821, "and like Mont Blanc continues to gather all the sunshine upon his icy head. He is *better* than ever; that is colder, steadier, more 'pocurante', and withal more amiable and respected."[1] Here was a man of business and a gentleman, far more to be trusted than any of those "damned men of genius"; yet Castlereagh knew his own deficiencies, he could command the stout Tories, but his speeches lacked the power to draw

1 Croker, I, 219.

over the doubtful or the independent votes; for this reason he had been anxious to see Canning on the Treasury bench. Canning could not be brought in, and in 1822 Castlereagh prepared himself once more for a task which was over-taxing his physical and mental strength; a task which was now rendered more difficult by the attacks of the agricul-turalists upon the Government and by the doubts which began to gather around the policy of the Concert of Europe. Few suspected that his powerful mind and his unruffled temper were breaking under the strain: according to Pro-fessor Webster he betrayed signs of strain in May when, normally an introvert, he became temporarily an extravert and burdened comparative strangers with unexpected con-fidences; but on 1 August Madame de Lieven found him in excellent spirits.[1] On 9 August he called upon the King and betrayed every symptom of mental disorder—he was a fugitive from justice, he was accused of a terrible crime, he had ordered his saddle horses and would fly to Portsmouth and from there to the ends of the earth—the King at-tempted to calm him, a doctor was sent for, and he was got away safely to his home at Cray Farm.[2] There, in the early hours of 12 August, he cut his throat, and died crying, "It is all over".

By this time the King was in Scotland, where he was making a ceremonial visit. Peel was with the King; Liver-pool, Wellington, and Bathurst were in or near London; the other ministers were out of town.[3] Liverpool imme-diately sent the news to the King and to Peel. "What a sad

1 *Letters of Princess Lieven to Metternich*, p. 187.
2 Lieven, p. 189.   3 Parker, I, 334 (from Diary of H. Hobhouse).

catastrophe this is, Publick and Private," he wrote, "What a conclusion to such a life. Pray God have mercy on his soul."

All discussion upon his successor was deferred until the King should return from Scotland. But the King foresaw the danger of Canning, and wrote that the arrangements for India must remain unchanged, and tried to enlist Peel's support by telling him what he had done. Peel, with exemplary constitutional propriety, refused to express an opinion and sent to Liverpool an account of the interview. Whoever might be qualified to take over the Foreign Office, only Canning could succeed Castlereagh in the House of Commons; this was something upon which nearly every one connected with politics was agreed. "It would be worse than nothing to attempt a Government without Canning" was the opinion of Lord Grenville, and "such seems to be the opinion of everybody, such was the language of all official men". The consequence was that Buckingham wrote to Wellington intimating that, if an offer was not made to Canning, the Grenvilles would feel themselves at liberty to withdraw from the Government. Liverpool's mind was already made up, but the action of the Grenvilles was a useful card to play against any objections from the older ministers and subsequently against the King. Liverpool "had locked himself up and declined talking to those whom he wished to avoid", but he was said to be "very cast down and depressed in the extreme"; he hinted that he expected more than simply a new secretary.

Certainly the attitude of the King did not promise an easy victory for those who favoured Canning. Croker found him "evidently averse from Canning" when he returned on 2 September, he had "made up *his* mind on that point".[1] Liverpool saw the King and recommended Canning, adding that the Cabinet majority was with him; but Sidmouth and Eldon both advised against Canning, the latter saying that he would "get rid of all his Majesty's old servants".[2] The King's immediate reaction was to express himself as "much surprised" by Liverpool's proposition, he had hoped that Liverpool would make no approach on this subject, as he had particularly desired that the arrangements regarding India should remain undisturbed. "The King cannot but regret that Lord Liverpool and those members of the Cabinet who agree with him should not have thought it due to the King's feelings to have submitted a double project; they would thus have fulfilled what they might have considered a duty to *themselves* without setting aside all delicacy towards the King, of which the King feels he has just reason to complain. The King now waits for Lord Liverpool's second project before the King will come to any decision on that already proposed. If there be no alternative the King takes for granted that Lord Liverpool and the other members of the Cabinet are prepared to break up the Government."[3] It seemed that, between the King and his Prime Minister, matters had reached a breaking point; but Liverpool was now in a far stronger position—in spite of the defection of Eldon and Sidmouth—than he had been in 1821, and the sequel to

1 Croker, I, 222.
2 Parker, I, 325 (Diary of H. Hobhouse).
3 *George IV*, No. 1042.

the King's answer was a letter from Wellington, which probably decided the King.[1] Wellington wrote that Canning's "talents and abilities are much considered and the continuance of his presence in the House of Commons is anxiously desired by many of the best friends of the government, whose support would probably be lost if advantage were not taken of this opportunity.... I am convinced that he will serve your Majesty in that situation with ability, zeal, and fidelity, and will give your Majesty satisfaction, that his principles and opinions are in all points of your Majesty's policy, domestic as well as foreign, the same as those of your other servants; and that there is no other arrangement which will not leave the government in a state of inefficiency in one or more departments.... There is no difference of principle or opinion between the Lord Chancellor and Mr Canning, which does not exist between the Lord Chancellor and others of your Majesty's servants.... The honour of your Majesty consists in acts of mercy and grace, and I am convinced that your Majesty's honour is most safe in extending your grace and favour to Mr Canning upon this occasion."[2] This, coming from the most respected man in Europe and the man whom the King wished to see at the Foreign Office, was powerful advocacy. On 8 September the King at last brought himself to swallow the "bitter pill".

An offer was to be made to Canning, and that offer could be one thing only. Huskisson had told Arbuthnot, and Arbuthnot would have told Liverpool, that "If it should be

1 According to Greville it was Bathurst who finally decided the King.
2 Wellington, I, 274.

thought right to call for his services in the House of Commons, I cannot too strongly impress on your mind, that the offer must be unaccompanied with anything which could look like a contrivance to curtail the situation now vacant".[1] In other words Canning must have the whole heritage of Castlereagh, he must be both Foreign Secretary and Leader of the House. Yet on 9 September Canning received a letter from Liverpool which Mrs Canning later described as "vague and unexplanatory and confirming a general impression that the offer would not be acceptable".[2] Canning was then at Birmingham; he arrived in London on the 11th. He was still very doubtful of the wisdom of sacrificing India; "by far the greater number of considerations public and private were against acceptance, and to the last day I hoped that the proposal made to me might be one that I could refuse".[3] But when he saw Liverpool he learnt that "the Proposal *was* that which...I could alone have accepted".[4] Even so he did not give an immediate reply, and Liverpool, seeing his hesitation, wrote to him the same evening: "I cannot refrain from declaring to you that after the severe calamity which the King and the Country have sustained and under all the circumstances of the present Crisis, a Sense of Public Duty must preclude you from making any difficulty as to taking your part in the

---

1 Melville, *Huskisson Papers*, p. 143. Huskisson said much the same thing to Croker (Croker, I, 227). And on 7 September Wellington prepared a memorandum for Lady Londonderry in which he said, " He must be leader of the House", and went on to show that he must be Foreign Secretary as well (Wellington, I, 277).
2 Temperley, "Some Letters of Joan Canning", *E.H.R.* 1930.
3 Bagot, II, 137, Canning to Bagot.
4 *Ibid.* p. 133, to Bootle Wilbraham.

Councils of the King's Government at this time."[1] Canning was certainly disposed to make difficulties, for he objected to the terms of the King's letter. The King had said that he was aware that "the brightest ornament of his crown is the power of extending grace and favour to a subject who may have incurred his displeasure". Canning saw here lavish expressions of forgiveness, where he recognised no offence; it was, he said, like being given a ticket for Almack's and finding "Admit the rogue" written on the back. For three days Canning hesitated, and Greville heard from Lady Bathurst that the ministers were "greatly surprised at the delay". But by the 14th his friends had prevailed upon him to sink these scruples, and he accepted the Foreign Secretaryship and the Leadership of the House of Commons.

A tragic accident had brought into the ministry the man for whom Liverpool had striven in 1821; it remained to be seen whether Liverpool would press on further changes in the ministry. Eldon had warned the King that Canning would get rid of all his old servants, and Arbuthnot told Huskisson that "having had a good deal to do with the discussions which preceded the offer to Canning, I am able to tell you that had not his question been an isolated one, all our efforts with the King would have failed. He expressed great fear and jealousy lest there should be a secret intention to extend the arrangements; and he most positively declared that should there be a secret intention to extend the proposal made to him to introduce into the Cabinet any other person, he would not consent to have an offer made to Canning."[2] In spite of this Canning

1 Yonge, III, 201.   2 Add. MSS. 38743, f. 200.

began to use his influence on Huskisson's behalf, and
Liverpool was prepared to promote him if possible. The
first chance was that the vacancy in India might be used to
give Huskisson the object of his ambition, the Board of
Control. Manners Sutton, the Speaker, might be made
Viceroy, and Wynn might be moved to the Speaker's chair.
But Liverpool had in mind a more extensive arrangement,
and on 3 October Canning discovered that he was thinking
of displacing Vansittart.

"I have had", he wrote to Huskisson, "a long talk with
L, a much fuller and in some respects more satisfactory
than any former one...the satisfactory part...is that Van
is not immovable. He would take the Board of Control, if
proposed to him. But what is satisfactory or unsatisfactory
to me, according as you may feel on the subject, [is that] L
is confident that Robinson would not only take the Ch. of the
Ex. if offered to him; but that he would feel himself passed
over if the offer were not made. This course of arrangement
would open to you Robinson's office." Canning gave an
account of his conversation, "I asked him whether he was
as much wedded to Van, and Van to his seals as ever? The
answer, to my infinite surprise was, Oh no! I could get him
out, and would if I saw my way to an arrangement that I was
sure would satisfy all parties; but I could not get him out
for Huskisson to succeed him, and the India Board which is
H's object would be the surest lure to Van....The trouble
is, I believe, he *still likes* Van better than anything which
could be put in his room; I believe that he would like *you*
better in V's room (if he is to have anyone) than a politician; but he thinks he could not carry that change with

Van, with the King, or his colleagues; and he would therefore perhaps have been as little inclined to make any change
now as last year, if he had not received some intimation
from Robinson of his willingness to be put forward....
I think it right to tell you, that you would do right to
acquiesce in this arrangement. The grounds of that opinion
are shortly these. First, the getting Van out of the Exchequer is so great an object, for the Publick, for the House
of Commons, and for the Government, that if it were
known or suspected that that object had been frustrated
by your adherence to the succession to Wynn instead of
Robinson, the best friends of Government and of our own
friends too (Littleton for example) would never forgive you.
...Secondly the bringing forward of Robinson would be
scarcely less popular in the H of C than the getting out
poor Van." Finally, Canning added a sentence which was
to give Huskisson much pain: "L asked me whether you
would insist upon Cabinet with the I. Bd...there would
be great objection to it. I asked if on the part of the K?
He said 'Yes and elsewhere too'."[1]

The King would see, in any attempt to place Huskisson
in the Cabinet, the first step in a plan to replace the
existing ministers by Canningites; he was prepared to
resist this, and other members of the Government would
regard it with scarcely less jealousy. The King was already
insisting that the Cabinet was too large and must be reduced; he was perhaps looking forward to the inevitable
retirements of the older ministers within a few years, and
was safeguarding himself against the promotion of an over-

[1] Add. MSS. 38743, fs. 217ff.

whelming number of Canningites; but the size of the Cabinet was then, as it has been so often, a frequent cause of complaint. It was unfortunate that the attempt to reduce the Cabinet—or to exclude Canningites—should involve Huskisson; for Huskisson felt that he had been neglected, and this feeling was made the more bitter by his over-sensitive realisation of his own social obscurity. He was quite ready to take the Board of Trade and to forgo the patronage of the Board of Control, and he agreed that the Cabinet might, with advantage, be reduced in size, "but when the attempt is made, it should be made with a younger man...and, if I may fairly state all my feelings with someone in a different (I mean a higher) sphere of life from myself...I cannot be what Robinson now is in office and remain excluded from the Cabinet".[1]

The prospects of this negotiation were blighted at the outset by the attitude of the Grenvilles. Canning succeeded in winning the support of Lord Grenville, who agreed to press Wynn to take the Speakership.[2] But Wynn was very unwilling to leave the Cabinet, and Buckingham delivered an ultimatum: if Wynn left the Cabinet, the Grenvilles would leave the Government, unless Buckingham himself was given office. This was typical "connection" politics, but for the moment they seemed to promise success, and Liverpool even proposed Buckingham to the King as a minister without portfolio. Showing sound political sense the King refused to consider this, and, even Huskisson, who would have benefited immediately, admitted that the

1 Add. MSS. 38743, f. 223.
2 Add. MSS. 38743, f. 215: "Nothing could be fairer or kinder than L⁴ G. He wrote to C. W., and I brought the letter back to town."

admission of Buckingham would be against the public interest. All attempts to move Wynn, without losing the lately won allegiance of the Grenvilles, having failed, Huskisson wrote bitterly: "I must make up my mind to remain as I am till that chance which Liverpool pointed out before Londonderry's death—the millennium when Bragge Bathurst will discover that his retirement might be an accommodation to the Government."[1]

It was precisely this possibility, the hastening of this millennium, which now occupied Liverpool's mind. If Bathurst could be persuaded to retire, Vansittart might consent to take his office, the Chancellorship of the Duchy of Lancaster; Robinson could then succeed Vansittart, and Huskisson take Robinson's place. The first condition was that Huskisson should withdraw his claim to Cabinet rank before the negotiations commenced, since Canning was sure that Liverpool would not begin if he felt that it would entail a battle with the King.[2] Huskisson does not seem to have abandoned his claim, and he certainly returned to it later with added force and resentment; but Liverpool decided to go forward nevertheless.

Bragge Bathurst had been Chancellor of the Duchy of Lancaster since 1812, and during the year 1821 he had taken charge of the Board of Control; apart from this service he had played little active part in the business of Government. But he was related both to Sidmouth and to Bathurst, and beyond these useful connections he seems to have had certain real qualities; his speeches in the Commons were infrequent, but Liverpool paid tribute to his disinterestedness and to his accommodating temper, and

1 Add. MSS. 38743, f. 230.   2 Add. MSS. 38743, f. 248.

Wellington to his usefulness at the Council table; but whatever qualities might have originally supported his claim to Cabinet rank, he was now grown old and was no longer able to fulfil even those small duties which had been demanded of him. It now seemed time to hint that his retirement might be more useful than his services; and it is interesting to note that it was to Sidmouth that Liverpool saw fit to make his explanations. "Connection" was no longer a vital force in politics, but men still observed some of its conventions. Liverpool's letter to Sidmouth is an excellent example of his tactful approach to such difficult personal matters: "You well know my sincere regard for Mr Bathurst and that there is no man living whom I should be more unwilling to wound or distress in any matter.... I should never therefore have thought of saying what I did say... to you, if I had not understood that his health had been on various occasions much affected, and tho' it improved always in the country, he had for some time invariably suffered by a continued residence in London. If I could hope that for any reasonable period he could continue to go thro' the fatigue of the House of Commons in an official situation, and at times like the present, I never could have contemplated that which actually did present itself to my mind. But if circumstances should arise to make him wish to retire at no distant period it might happen at a moment when the vacancy of his office, so far from being any convenience or advantage to Govt in other respects, might on the contrary be the cause of considerable embarrassment."[1]

On 14 December Liverpool wrote "a letter of dismissal"

1 Add. MSS. 38291, f. 150.

to Vansittart, which, in spite of rumours to the contrary,[1] was expressed in the kindest terms and written in his own hand. Whatever were Vansittart's private feelings he showed no resentment in his reply: "I shall consider your proposal in the same spirit of kindness in which I am convinced it has been made. . . . In what you suggest with respect to Robinson and Huskisson, I see much prospect of public advantage and nothing could be more satisfactory to me than to have Robinson for my successor in respect of private feeling. I have long felt myself growing unequal to the labor of the House of Commons, and, as I told Arbuthnot lately, I think nothing could reconcile me to enter upon another Parliament. My inclination would rather lean to a total retreat, if it could be managed without the appearance of public or private difference; but this might not be easy to avoid."[2] This seemed very satisfactory, but the reference to the "labor of the House of Commons" contained an obvious hint, which Liverpool either ignored or failed to perceive; it was not until Arbuthnot pointed out the obvious recompense which Vansittart expected, that Liverpool recommended him for a peerage.[3] He retired to obscurity and the Upper House as Lord Bexley.

With Bathurst out of the Cabinet, and Vansittart out of the Exchequer, there remained only the question of Huskisson and Cabinet rank. At the end of December he was still protesting that exclusion from the Cabinet was a positive dishonour and an insuperable objection to his succeeding Robinson.[4] Canning and Arbuthnot both used their

1 Colchester, III, 300.   2 Add. MSS. 38291, f. 220.
3 Cf. Add. MSS. 38291, f. 237.   4 Add. MSS. 38291, f. 285.

influence to persuade him to relinquish his claims. The
King, on the other hand, consented to waive his objection,
and to sacrifice temporarily his object of reducing the
Cabinet. It was now urged upon Huskisson that it would
be graceful in him to yield, and not to force himself into a
situation where the King, in spite of his concession, would
resent his presence; such an action would avoid offending
the King, and would make "all the difference in the world
as to the tone of his future connection" with Liverpool.[1] A
compromise was finally suggested: Huskisson should enter
the Cabinet after twelve months' service at the Board of
Trade; to this he consented, though with a bad grace.

One more difficulty arose. Wallace, the able and energetic
Vice-President of the Board of Trade, was offended at
Huskisson's promotion over his head. He would have been
ready to see a peer placed over him, but he was not prepared to see himself effaced by Huskisson. No other office
could be opened for him, and, in spite of a kind and conciliatory letter from Liverpool, he insisted upon resigning.

In January 1823, in an effort to find some office for
Wallace, Liverpool suggested to Lord Maryborough that
his resignation from the Cabinet in favour of a House of
Commons man might be a great convenience to the
Government. Maryborough, formerly Wellesley Pole, was
a brother of the Duke of Wellington; since 1814 he had
been Master of the Mint with Cabinet rank, and had, if
anything, played even less part in the active business of
government than Bragge Bathurst; but he was tenacious of
his rank, and refused to resign. It was not until August
that he at last gave up the struggle for his position, and

1 Add. MSS. 38291, f. 299.

allowed himself to be "sent to the dogs"; in other words accepted the Mastership of the Buckhounds. This enabled Liverpool to offer the Mint to Wallace—"This is the greatest relief to my mind...you know how I felt for his disappointment last year, and how deeply I was impressed with the opinion that he had the strongest claims, public and personal, upon me and upon the government"[1]—and to give his place in the Cabinet to Huskisson, some months before he would otherwise have gained that honour. This occasioned one last protest from the King: he had supposed that Maryborough had been removed "for the purpose of lessening the numbers of the Cabinet this might have been, perhaps a reason, altho' a very questionable one, especially as that individual had been sitting in the same Cabinet, with the same members, for the last nine years. But there was a graver consideration, as it appears to the King, namely, the delicacy and propriety of feeling which should have been observed in relation to the Duke of Wellington. Can it be supposed that the Duke of Wellington can view with indifference and without silently feeling what must, indeed, be considered ungracious conduct towards his brother?...Mr Huskisson may be a very clever man, but he is not always a prudent one."[2] Fortunately the Duke seems to have raised no objection to the removal of his brother, and to have made no complaint, public or private.

So was completed the transformation of the Government; and already, in the spring of 1823, the effect had been felt in political life. Members of the House of Commons listened attentively while the pleasant voice of Robinson made the mysteries of finance appear as lucid as a

1 Add. MSS. 38296, f. 168.   2 *George IV*, No. 1110.

lesson in elementary mathematics. At the Foreign Office Canning had almost completed the break with the Continental Allies, and was taking the independence of nations as the key-note of English policy. At the Home Office young Peel was increasing the reputation which he had already won as Chief Secretary of Ireland; it was his good fortune to increase his experience in a happier field, to appear as an angel of reform not a demon of coercion. At the Board of Trade Huskisson and his chief assistant, Deacon Hume, had embarked upon that laborious task, the consolidation of the Customs Laws.

This reconstruction of the Cabinet had been the work of Liverpool and of no other; it was he who had had to bear the wrath of the King; it was he who had had to quell the doubts of recalcitrant colleagues; it was he who had had to bear all the personal difficulties, the reproaches of old friends, the insistent resentment of the disappointed. The letters which survive present no more than a façade, behind which the real struggle took place; every move had its pitfalls, every move might see a cry raised against the ingratitude or the rashness of the Prime Minister, and every move might raise an alarm at the direction which the changes were taking. Liverpool was a man peculiarly sensitive to the feelings of others; thus in a matter which might appear of comparatively small importance—the resignation of Wallace—he wrote: "I can assure you most sincerely that since I received your answer to my first letter, I have suffered more than I can recollect to have done on any occasion of the same nature in the course of my life." He was all anxiety to avoid offending Bragge Bathurst or Vansittart, and it is possible to detect the mental anguish which he underwent. Those nearest to him were able to realise how much these personal questions preyed upon his mind; in January 1823 Canning wrote that "Liverpool's agitation has, in some stages of this business, amounted to illness, and to him every successive stage has been an effort such as when I came into the Government. I thought it utterly hopeless that he should find nerves to undertake it."[1] Others were less sympathetic or less ready to appreciate his difficulties: "I really pity Lord Liverpool from the bottom of my heart," wrote Arbuthnot to Huskisson, "but in truth he has brought the whole upon himself by his gaucherie. He has wounded *you*, and me, and Wallace, and he contrived at first to mortify poor Van."[2] But those offended were few in comparison with those affected by the changes of these two years; in common with many men who depend upon tact and reason to accomplish their ends, he had sometimes overestimated the power of these weapons; but, on the whole, they had served him well. In the verdict upon his conduct during these lengthy and tiresome negotiations Canning may be allowed, not inappropriately, the last word; and to Huskisson Canning wrote: "I will not deny myself the opportunity of saying that I am quite satisfied with L's conduct; that he has worked honestly, perseveringly, and sincerely, with great dexterity, and (what was essential) without alarm.... I am perfectly confident that with less management or with more brusqueness the thing *could not have been done*."[3]

1 Add. MSS. 38291, f. 299. 2 Add. MSS. 38744, f. 57.
3 Add. MSS. 38743, f. 277.

CHAPTER VI

ECONOMIC LIBERALISM

THE economic condition of England in 1820 was the despair of all clear-thinking men. The finances of the country had, for eight years, been under the care of the well-meaning Nicholas Vansittart; possessed of a very wide knowledge of financial affairs, he was more adept at demonstrating the curiosities of financial history than at deducing any coherent system of finance; not entirely ignorant of the principles of liberal economics, he was quite incapable of explaining in a lucid manner even the few praiseworthy points in his policy; himself greatly impressed with the intricacy of his task, he asked no more of the House of Commons than a blind faith in the mystic rites of which he was the attendant priest. Yet from post-war finance it was possible, for those with sufficient patience, to discover a system not altogether unsound; the commercial legislation of the country presented, on the contrary, the picturesque confusion of a garden, once well ordered, now overgrown with weeds. The ideas of Adam Smith had been for some time familiar to the upper classes—he was quoted in Parliament more than any other author, and to prove every conceivable case—but vested interest and the diversion of public attention to other matters had left the commercial system of the country unattended for the first twenty years of the century. The one positive task of economic regulation which had been undertaken since the war was the Corn

Law, and this was open to attack from the free traders, formed a staple item of working-class agitation, and had not proved satisfactory even to the agriculturalists.

In the realm of finance the Government considered that it had followed a consistent policy, and the measures taken after 1822 were looked upon as a natural continuation of that policy. The change from Vansittart to Robinson was particularly noticeable because Robinson could talk and Vansittart could not, but it is a fact that Liverpool and Vansittart had already agreed upon the scheme of finance which was to win much praise for Robinson in his first two years as Chancellor. In commercial legislation, on the other hand, there was a complete breakaway from earlier practice: Liverpool's Government began, with all due caution though not without considerable results, that free trade policy which was to be one of the main themes of nineteenth-century history, and the beginnings of free trade legislation in England can be dated definitely in 1820. With respect to the Corn Law there was an attempt to emend its workings in 1822, but this attempt proved abortive, and it was not until 1826 that a radical change was proposed; then Liverpool undertook a measure which would have gone far to settle the vexed question by a blend of protection and free trade, but this measure was also abortive, for Liverpool's seizure wrecked its chances in the House of Lords.

The chief problem of the Government after the war was an enormous increase in public expenditure. In 1800 the Government had asked for a supply of £39,500,000, in 1813 it asked for £68,686,000, and, though the men of 1815 knew it not, it would never again be possible to reduce expenditure below £50,000,000. But increased taxation had not been able to cover the full expense of the war, and in 1815 the National Debt stood at £860,000,000. Was this debt to be a permanent feature of the financial system? The statesmen of 1815 had their answer in that most famous legacy of Pitt, the Sinking Fund. This Fund was an annual payment of £1,000,000 towards Debt redemption, but the Debt redeemed was not cancelled and its yearly interest was paid into the Sinking Fund, so the yearly interest charge of the Debt remained constant, but each year a larger proportion of the charge was available for Debt redemption. When the payment of the Sinking Fund reached one forty-fifth part of the total Debt, it would cease to accumulate, and would pay off the whole Debt in forty-five years, while stock purchased could be cancelled or its interest treated as a surplus on the Sinking Fund applicable to current expenditure. Fool-proof in operation, this scheme encountered only one difficulty: when there was no surplus of revenue over expenditure it meant that a certain sum was raised by loan and used to pay off old Debt. The Sinking Fund as originally planned contained no provision for its suspension when there was no surplus, and, though Fox added a clause authorising loans to be taken from the Sinking Fund, no Tory financier would agree either to suspend the Fund or to treat it temporarily as current supply. On the other hand the Sinking Fund was a constant temptation to hard-pressed financiers, and Vansittart, while insisting upon the sanctity of the Fund, resorted, in 1813 and 1819, to complicated accountancy and even more complicated excuses in order to take a limited sum from the Sinking Fund. The explanation of the Tory devotion to the Sinking Fund lies in its psychological effect: "This is not a mere question of profit and loss," said Liverpool in 1822, "we must look at the moral effect produced. We must look at the effect which the Sinking Fund produces on public credit. We must look at the way it multiplies and augments our re-sources; and enables us in any war, as it enabled us in the last war, to raise money with facility by way of loan, instead of being compelled to have recourse to the more burden-some, and at times scarcely practicable operation of raising the supplies within the year."[1] The Sinking Fund was considered as the pledge of national good faith; as long as it was so considered there was a justification for it.

The other great expedient of the war years was the Bank restriction. First passed in 1797 as an emergency measure to save the Bank in a time of panic, it had been continued when the value of a flexible paper currency was understood. By freeing the currency from gold the Government made possible that great expansion in credit which had taken place; without it there would have been no possibility of carrying out the financial operations—quite without pre-cedent in point of size—which had been necessary in order to provide the sinews of war for England and her allies. But, whatever these advantages, no one doubted that they were outweighed by those of a stable currency based upon gold, or that the return to cash payments was an essential part of the return to conditions of peace. The debate until 1819 lay between those who stressed the evil and those who

1 *Speech upon Agricultural Distress* (Pamphlet), London, 1822.

pleaded the necessity. Before the Bank could pay in gold, it would be essential that it should have a sufficient gold reserve; the mistake of the Bank and of the Government lay in assuming that such a reserve would accumulate in the natural course of things. In 1810 a famous committee of the House of Commons was appointed to enquire into the apparent discrepancy between the Mint price of bullion and the market price. The question was whether gold had gone up in price owing to scarcity or demand, or whether the paper currency was depreciated. The committee decided that the currency had depreciated, and that this depreciation had arisen because, in regulating their issues, the Bank paid no attention to the state of foreign exchanges or the market price of bullion. "There is at present an excess in the paper circulation of this country, of which the most unequivocal symptom is the very high price of bullion, and, next to that, the low state of the continental exchanges; that this excess is to be ascribed to the want of sufficient check and control in the issue of paper from the Bank of England, and originally, to the suspension of cash payments which removed the true and natural control."

The Government sprang to the defence of the Bank, taking as their text, "The Bank notes are equivalent to money for every common and legitimate transaction in life except for foreign exchanges". Vansittart, not yet a member of the Government but their spokesman on this question, proposed a set of counter resolutions. He went through an elaborate and well-informed survey of the other causes which might raise the price of bullion, he admitted the desirability of returning to cash payments, but thought it inexpedient to do so immediately, and, as his third resolution, moved that "the promissory notes of the Bank of England have hitherto been and are, at this time, held in public estimation to be equivalent to the legal coin of the realm, and are generally accepted as such in all pecuniary transactions to which such coin is lawfully applicable". Subsequently, with an irony which Government speakers failed to appreciate, it was necessary to pass laws forbidding the sale of guineas at more than their face value. By its rejection of the Bullion Report the Government did not, as has sometimes been implied, commit itself to an indefinite prolongation of the Bank Restriction, but they did refuse to take measures to facilitate its repeal. So long as bullion fetched a higher price in the market than at the Mint, men would not bring their gold to the Bank and they would withdraw gold from the Bank were the restriction removed. So far the argument against cash payment was sound; but this state of affairs could be remedied if the Bank restricted its issues, and this the Bank would not do, nor would the Government compel it to do so.

The Government emerged from the war with a clear plan of finance, which Liverpool outlined in a memorandum drawn up for the Committee on Cash Resumption.[1] The object of this policy was a return to normal finance and the return to cash payments in particular. Liverpool and Vansittart were quite aware that the finance of the war would not stand the test of peace-time criticism;[2] and they now

---

1 Add. MSS. 38741, f. 271: House of Lords Report upon Cash Resumption, Appendix A.
2 Add. MSS. 31231, f. 56, Vansittart to Castlereagh: "I need not remind you of the difficulties which we have had to struggle with,

hoped to reduce the funded and unfunded debt held by the Bank and so enable the Bank to buy up bullion in order to return to the gold standard. To pay off nearly £20,000,000 of Exchequer Bills held by the Bank the Government proposed to continue certain war-time taxes—the Property Tax chief among them—and this would also relieve them of the necessity of peace-time loans. The cardinal point was the retention of the Property Tax, and, as Liverpool informed a Tory deputation, "he felt the continuance of the tax as proposed to be of such essential importance to the country and that so much public inconvenience must result from the loss of it, that he was determined if the tax could not be continued that it should be the act of the House of Commons and that the Government should have nothing to reproach itself with upon that subject".[1] But the tax was wildly unpopular in the country, and the Government's plan of finance was thrown out of joint by its rejection in the House of Commons. The Government was thrown back upon the undesirable policy of peace-time loans, but it still maintained the Sinking Fund intact and it still hoped to resume cash payment by "natural" means.

In 1819 came the important change in the cash resumption policy, and at the same time there was a clarification of the Government's financial aims. Peel's committee recom-

but when I look back upon them, and particularly upon the enormous expense of the Spanish war, I cannot but feel astonished that they have been in any way surmounted. It has indeed sometimes been by expedients which only the necessity of the case could justify, but which it is now possible to supercede by more advantageous arrangements."

1 Add. MSS. 38741, f. 271. Omitted from House of Lords Report, Appendix A.

mended the return to cash payments, and, in order to achieve this, recommended the principles of the Bullion Report. It was necessary to recognise the depreciation of the paper currency and to start payment at a rate above the Mint price. At the same time issues would have to be contracted, and the currency brought back to its face value. The Government hardly looked upon these recommendations as a reversal of its former policy: it had consistently aimed at cash resumption, it had consistently claimed that immediate resumption was impossible, and the committee had now discovered the only means which would make the gradual resumption possible. Since 1814 Huskisson had been the intimate economic adviser of the Prime Minister, and early in 1819 Huskisson addressed a memorandum to Liverpool which may be considered as the result of previous consultations; in this memorandum the findings of the committee were foreshadowed and the Government's part in the great work was stressed. The memorandum recommended a gradual diminution of the circulation in order to bring the foreign exchanges to par, a large provision of bullion by the Bank by the purchases of gold at the market price, and a great reduction of the funded and unfunded debt to enable the Bank to buy bullion and contract issues without contracting mercantile discounts. If these measures had already been under discussion it is easy to see why the Government was prepared to accept the findings of Peel's committee with enthusiasm. In the House of Lords Liverpool explained the report at great length, and with great accuracy; in the years which followed he claimed cash resumption as one of the proudest achievements of his

Government. These facts show how far wide of the mark is the conventional view of cash resumption as a measure forced upon an unwilling Government; the Government did not suffer a great defeat, but in the years which followed some of its supporters among the landed gentry were to feel that, on this question, the Government had cruelly deserted them.

The other great alteration of 1819 was in the operation of the Sinking Fund. In the memorandum already quoted, Huskisson maintained that "the mystery of our financial system no longer deceives anyone in the money market; selling exchequer bills daily to redeem funded debt daily, then funding those exchequer bills once a year, or once in two years, in order to go over the same ground again; whilst the very air of mystery, and the anomaly of large annual or biennial loans in times of profound peace, create uneasiness out of the market, and in foreign countries an impression unfavourable with respect to the solidity of our resources. ...In finance, expedients and ingenious devices may answer to meet temporary difficulties; but for a permanent and peace system, the only wise course either in policy or for impression is a policy of simplicity and truth."[1] The effect of these criticisms was seen in Vansittart's budget, in which the principle that the only real Sinking Fund was a surplus of revenue over expenditure was explicitly stated, and three millions of new taxes were imposed in order to create a real Sinking Fund of £5,000,000. The taxes of 1819 were not a success, and Vansittart had one more "expedient and ingenious device" in the Dead Weight

1 Yonge, II, 383-4.

Annuity Scheme of 1822, but it may be said that from the year 1819 the Government was aiming at a sound and simple financial system. After 1820 there was a progressive improvement in the revenue, which helped forward this policy, and Robinson was able to step into the heritage of a sound financial system. How much he owed to the earlier efforts of Liverpool and Vansittart may be seen from a letter written by Liverpool to Vansittart on the eve of the latter's departure from the Exchequer. After commenting on the favourable state of the revenue, Liverpool went on: "If you are a bold man you will perhaps think me a bolder, in submitting for your consideration what I would not at present hint to anyone, whether we could not go still further than you suggest. I set out with assuming that we should go to the utmost point to which we can go, as our own act, and then make our stand. I am further impressed with the opinion that the best chance of saving our five millions surplus is giving up whatever may exceed it."[1] It was precisely this principle—the retention of a five millions Sinking Fund and the use of any further surplus for the remission of taxation—which formed the main proposal in Robinson's "Financial Statement", delivered to the House of Commons a month after his accession to the Exchequer.

The new Chancellor of the Exchequer "had always expressed a great dread of the labor and confinement of the situation",[2] and a candid friend, in congratulating him upon his appointment, added: "Though your promotion in the present instance will continually impose considerable additional labour upon you, I am not sure that it will not

1 Yonge, III, 249.   2 Add. MSS. 38291, f. 219.

be to your advantage to be placed in an office where you will be *compelled* to labour. No one is more *capable* of application than yourself, and you deserve more credit for this, as perhaps no one has a stronger *Penchant* for indolence—I am not at all sorry therefore to see you placed in a situation where *work* you must and *speak* you must."[1] But he had genuine abilities, he was attached to "liberal" principles, and no one was more popular in the Commons.[2] The Duke of Wellington indeed thought his appointment very bad indeed, he was totally unfit and would change his mind twenty times a day.[3] Not until 1828 was the truth of Wellington's estimate proven, in 1823 it seemed that the appointment had been amply justified.

Before considering the inauguration of the new commercial policy, it will be useful to digress for a moment to see what were the main currents of opinion which would influence the Government in its economic legislation. For the most striking feature of this period is the virtual abandonment of the agriculturalists by the Government and its conscious seeking after commercial support. At times during 1820, 1821 and 1822 it seemed that a new party—a "country" party—had been born. It was recruited from all parties, but its fighting strength came from the Radicals

1 Add. MSS. 40862, f. 87.
2 Add. MSS. 38743, f. 218: "The bringing forward Robinson would be scarcely less popular in the House of Commons than getting out poor Van."; Canning to Huskisson. At the end of his life it was possible to say, and to say justly, "He is a person of very delicate sensibility, accompanied with some warmth of temper; yet, in six and thirty years of political controversy he never wounded the feelings of an opponent or lost the regard of a friend." Ryall, *Portraits of Eminent Conservatives.*   3 Add. MSS. 38291, f. 244.

and the Tory country gentlemen. The Tories had something in common with Cobbett, they had nothing in common with Hume; but for a short time the independent Tories found common cause with Hume and his Radical phalanx in a demand for tax reduction and retrenchment. The Radicals demanded this on principle as a part of their political creed; the Tories demanded it because taxes and administrative extravagance seemed to be responsible for agricultural distress. Agriculture was admittedly in a shocking state, but Liverpool gave the agriculturalists cold comfort by telling them to wait for the natural self-adjustment of economic conditions. The country gentlemen cast about for their own remedies, and in 1822 the voice of rural England spoke at a county meeting in Norfolk which "consisted of persons of all parties, and many who were of no party whatever; and yet, in a meeting thus constituted, the call for retrenchment and reduction of taxation was unanimous. Both the members of the county were there, and one of them, a gentleman who had always supported the Government (Mr Wodehouse) concurred in opinion with the meeting, that a reduction of taxation was the only remedy for the existing distress."[1] Wodehouse's Whig colleague, Coke of Holkam, told the House of Commons that "unless there should be a union of both Whigs and Tories, unless the country gentlemen on both sides of the House should combine their efforts, the total destruction of the agricultural interest must ensue".[2] Country gentlemen, faced on the one side by falling rents and on the other by an unsympathetic Government, even dallied with

1 Hansard, VI, 430.   2 Ibid.

Parliamentary Reform; when a Reform proposal was put forward it was again the all too independent Wodehouse[1] who substituted for the usual uncompromising negative the conciliatory statement that "he did not know what was the nature of the reform asked for. Before he could give any opinion on the question, he must wait till it came before the House in definite shape."[2]

The agricultural revolt was a great opportunity for the Whigs. A vote-catching speech in 1822 by Brougham failed to bring over the country gentlemen, but a few days later the Salt Tax was saved by only four votes, and the Government failed to convince the House that the services of one Lord of the Admiralty and of one assistant Post-master-General were necessary parts of the administration. One Whig exclaimed triumphantly that "it was a consolation to him that gentlemen were now shaking off the dust which had been so profusely thrown in their eyes, and that the hon. members for Suffolk, Cheshire and Norfolk were beginning to take a correct view of the conduct of minis-

1 "Wodehouse is always queerish...and does not choose to commit himself till he knows what others think": Arbuthnot to Liverpool, December 1820, Add. MSS. 38574, f. 232.

2 In 1823 Cobbett carried a Reform Petition at a County Meeting in Norwich which, said the Whig Michael Angelo Taylor, "went to direct revolution in Church and State". But an amusing account by Hudson Gurney, the Norwich banker, shows that this was a freak result: "When I entered the Hall, Mr Cobbett appeared to be speaking with the most violent gesticulations from one end of the hustings; a reverend gentleman was speaking with apparently equal energy from the other; and the under-sheriff was reading a large paper in the middle; whilst from the unintermitted clamour of the circle that surrounded them, it appeared to me that not one of them knew that the others were also holding forth.... It was however a very good humoured meeting, everybody was laughing."

ters". Ministerialists lamented that "some of the country gentlemen, who represent agricultural counties, literally seemed to have run wild"; and Wellington complained that they acted as an independent party.

The Government was not broken, for the Tory country gentlemen disliked the Whigs, disliked the Radicals even more, and disliked Brougham, who led the Whigs in these matters, most of all. But in the course of their revolt the agriculturalists raised two important points: agricultural protection and the effects of cash resumption. The Corn Law of 1815 had failed, though its form had been largely dictated by the agriculturalists themselves. It did not prevent prices falling to levels which ruined the farmer, it did not prevent them from rising to levels which starved the consumer, it did not prevent a sudden inrush of foreign corn and a consequent glut on the market so soon as the price reached 80s. On 7 March 1821 at four o'clock in the morning the agriculturalists won a great victory when T. S. Gooch's motion for a committee of enquiry into the state of agriculture was carried by four votes. But the capabilities of the agriculturalists were not sufficient to lend argument to their sentiments; the hard-won committee became, in the hands of Huskisson and Ricardo, an occasion for a free trade manifesto.[1]

The agricultural discontents were aggravated by the resumption of cash payments. Contracts had been made,

---

[1] "Huskisson drew it [the report of the committee] up, and it is but justice to him to say that he is for establishing the trade on the most free and liberal foundation": Ricardo to McCulloch, p. 109. "When the Committee broke up there were very few points on which Mr Huskisson and I did not agree": Ricardo to Trower, p. 155.

money had been borrowed, and taxes assessed under the paper regime; with the return to the gold standard the value of money would rise, prices would fall, and debts contracted would have to be paid in currency of an enhanced value. Throughout 1820 gold poured into the Bank, its note issue was diminished, and a considerable rise in the value of money followed. Cobbett roused the people against fundholders who were to receive full interest in an appreciated currency; while landlords had to adjust their rents, though they lagged behind prices with consequent distress. The agriculturalists asked for a reduction in the interest and principal of the National Debt. Here, however, the country gentlemen parted company from the parliamentary Radicals and from the main body of the Whigs. The Government was resolved to stand firm; and events vindicated this determination. In 1825 Liverpool was able to say that cash resumption had been accomplished "without violating a single previous engagement which they had made with the public creditor. The task had been a Herculean one; but we had accomplished it and were now enjoying our reward—England had reached a state of prosperity greater than any other country enjoyed, nay, greater than she herself, at any antecedent period, had ever attained."[1] One concession was, however, made to the agriculturalists. The time during which £1 notes should be legal tender was extended from 1826 to 1833. This meant that some of the bullion collected by the banks was of no immediate use, and the country banks were encouraged to make very large issues of notes. For this concession, for

1 Hansard, XII, 24.

excessive optimism, for over easy advances upon credit, the country was to suffer severely in 1825 when confidence changed suddenly to panic.

The influence of the agriculturalists upon policy was negative rather than positive, but there were some whose criticism the Government would not only fear but also respect. Better informed than the country gentlemen, though often equally biased by particular interests, was the mercantile class. In political opinions they ranged from Tories to Radicals, but all alike spoke with the authority of practical men, and many were also converts to the new political economy. There was indeed one among them who might be called the High Priest of political economy; David Ricardo was in Parliament five years only, but few have built up so wholesome a reputation in so short a time. In politics he was a professed Radical, but on questions of political economy he was but seldom actuated by political feeling.[1] He was free in his criticism of Government finance, but he gave useful help in the resistance to the agriculturalists. With the country gentlemen he was indeed most unpopular; "If we were once in a position to export and import corn without restriction," he told the House, "this country, possessing the greatest skill, the best machinery, the most strenuous and enlightened industry, and every other advantage in the greatest degree, would attain to an almost inconceivable degree of prosperity and happiness."[2] This in no way convinced the country

[1] One exception is his attitude to the Sinking Fund. He criticised it not upon principle, but because the ministers could not be trusted with it.
[2] During the debate on Agricultural Distress, 30 May 1820.

gentlemen, for, as T. S. Gooch said, "the doctrine that we should buy our corn where we could get it cheapest could not be listened to; for if the manufacturer bought his bread in the foreign market, the farmer at home could not purchase his manufactures, and finally, both would suffer". Ricardo's premature death in 1823 robbed the House of one of its most useful members. The general feeling was expressed by Lord Grenville in a letter which he wrote to Liverpool: "Radical as he was I consider Ricardo's death a great loss both to the country and to Government. The extreme caution of his mind and conduct contrasted very strikingly with the extravagance of his political opinions."[1]

In the "mercantile interest" a few other names are worthy of mention. Alexander Baring, the most famous banker of his day, the "cock of the funded and paper interest", was one of the most influential men in Parliament. He was a Whig, had been untiring in his opposition to the Property Tax yet had been employed by the Government in negotiating a financial settlement with France. His ideas were not always orthodox—he advocated bimetallism as a solution of the difficulties arising from cash resumption —but he spoke frequently and with great authority. In 1825 he was called into consultation by Liverpool and Huskisson and so had considerable influence over Government decisions in the great crisis of that year. Hudson Gurney, a Norwich banker, and Pascoe Grenfell, yet another banker, were both men of influence; the former had a panacea for all ills in the reduction of the standard. W. Manning, a West India merchant and a Bank director, had taken a

1 Add. MSS. 38297, f. 63.

prominent part against the abolition of the slave trade, he was now the chief spokesman for the Bank of England. J. Marryat and A. Robertson were the acknowledged representatives of the shipping interest; Nicholas Calvert was the most forward of the brewers in the House. W. Smith was the champion of the Methodists, and represented their interests in Parliament. Except upon a few questions the names of these and other merchants appear far more frequently in Hansard than those of any agriculturalist; their presence gave to the House of Commons a leaven of practical information upon commercial topics which it had lacked in earlier times. The Government, with the exception of Huskisson, did not represent the commercial classes; but it was peculiarly sensitive to the criticism of those classes. When such criticism was made the Government tried to meet it and it was in this imperceptible modification of policy, not in spectacular revolts against the ministers, that the influence of the mercantile class lay.

The wish of the Government for commercial support was manifested in 1820 when the well-known Merchants' Petition was presented to the House of Commons. This petition had been prepared by Tooke, an economic theorist convinced of the benefits of free trade, and the petition constituted an elaborate plea for the release of commerce from the restrictions imposed upon it. In order to test the ground before presenting his petition Tooke presented it privately to Liverpool, and was agreeably surprised to find the Prime Minister as convinced a free trader as himself. "There was not a principle, not a sentiment in which he did not entirely and most cordially concur," and, though he added that "in this country, which is burthened with so heavy a debt; in which so many vested interests had grown up, and are so connected and complicated with the existing commercial system, the case is very different; and the question of any change in that system ought not to be approached but with the utmost caution," it was still, as Tooke remarked, a great step forward for the free traders to have received this authoritative blessing.[1] Liverpool followed this up with speeches in the House of Lords which embodied theoretical expositions of free trade doctrines and enunciation of those utilitarian truisms which were to be the economic dogmas of the nineteenth century.

Liverpool was unable "to hold out the prospect of any great or immediate alteration"; but during 1821 Wallace, the Vice-President of the Board of Trade, was winning golden opinions with the commercial reforms which he inaugurated. His only material legacy was the reform of the Timber Duties, but, as Chairman of the Foreign Trade Committee, he constituted a link between the Government and mercantile opinion. His considered verdict was that "we were labouring under burdens which pressed on the industry of no other country in Europe", and the remedy lay in "a full and complete revision of our commercial system. We must also get rid of that feeling of appropriation which exhibited itself in a disposition to produce everything necessary for our own consumption and to render ourselves independent of the world—no notion could be more absurd or mischievous". The influence of

[1] The account of this interview with Liverpool is given in Tooke, *History of Prices*, VI, 340.

Adam Smith—with his "sneaking arts of underling trades-men...erected into the political maxims for the conduct of a great empire"—is obvious. Liverpool had already im-plied the same thing—"if the people of the world are poor, no legislative interposition can make them do that which they would do if they were rich"—and there is no doubt that he approved the actions and statements of Wallace, for two years later he was saying that Wallace had "the strongest claim, public and personal, upon me and upon the govern-ment".[1]

With the changes of 1821–3 Liverpool was able to gather round him a group of liberal-minded men ready to take whatever opportunities were offered for economic reform. Huskisson had been his confidential adviser since 1814 and was now President of the Board of Trade; Robinson be-came Chancellor of the Exchequer; Wallace eventually became Master of the Mint, but he does not seem to have been consulted upon commercial measures; Vansittart, become Lord Bexley, was prepared to make available his tried wisdom;[2] Peel played a small part in the formulation of economic policy when he could spare time from the Home Office. As Prime Minister and as First Lord of the Treasury Liverpool was the head and the co-ordinating

1 Add. MSS. 88296, f. 168. So much did Wallace efface Robinson at the Board of Trade that the Annual Register of 1823 makes an under-standable error in referring to him as the President.

2 The inclusion of Vansittart as a liberal-minded man may seem to be merely ironic; but Vansittart, with all his incompetency, was not entirely in the outer darkness. In 1824 Robinson said: "He could confidently state that no individual in the country was more im-pressed with the principles of Free Trade than the late Chancellor of the Exchequer": Hansard, x, 1227.

agent in his "economic cabinet"; by inclination he was not likely to shirk any of the duties and the responsibilities which belonged to such a situation.

The next two years were of the greatest importance in the history of economic policy. They saw the application of the principles of free trade, the consolidation of the Customs Laws, the repeal and subsequent re-enactment in a modified form of the Combination Laws, and the launching of a new colonial policy. It is not here intended to give a history of these events, but only to trace, so far as is possible, the part which Liverpool played in them.

Liverpool did not initiate any of these policies; that was, indeed, the function of the departmental ministers concerned; but he did have to advise, to assent, and to coordinate. Huskisson had a great influence upon Robinson's budgets, but this influence must have been transmitted through Liverpool. A good example of the way in which the "economic cabinet" worked, and of the encouragement which Liverpool gave to every measure of commercial liberalism, is provided in a memorandum by Huskisson on the Reciprocity of Shipping Dues Bill: 1823. "On May 2 I requested a meeting at the Board of Trade of the following members of the Cabinet:—Lord Liverpool, Lord Bexley, Mr Canning, Mr Peel, Mr Robinson; Mr Canning, being prevented by other business, did not attend. I submitted to the other members, who did attend, three measures, which had been prepared for the consideration of this Board, and upon which it became necessary to obtain their decision." One of these measures was the Spitalfields Bill which was opposed in the House of Lords by some members of the Cabinet and lost, though Huskisson "distinctly stated to the meeting that each of the three measures...would meet with more or less of opposition, and that the fitness of moving them at all must depend not so much upon their abstract merits, of which the Board of Trade might be competent to judge, as upon other considerations not to be decided by that Board but by the King's Government". The bills had been approved by the "economic cabinet", but the question was now whether that decision bound the Government or "whether I must consider that decision as nothing more than the expression of their individual opinions". Dissentient members of the Cabinet certainly had a right to protest that they had not been consulted, and no view of the constitution could support Huskisson's contention that a decision of a few ministers could be equally binding as the decision of the whole Cabinet; but, in the existing balance of political forces, it was virtually binding.[1] Huskisson's memorandum was endorsed by Liverpool: "I think this measure of great importance in the present state of commerce, to this country," and the bill eventually passed.

The budget of 1824 was the first to contain proposals of avowed free trade. Robinson had at his disposal a surplus of £2,762,000, which he proposed to use "as a means of commencing a system of alteration in the fiscal and commercial regulations of this country". The bounties upon whale fishery, herring curing and linen export would not be

[1] The misunderstanding probably arose because Huskisson was not yet a member of the Cabinet, and so had no idea of what had passed after the decision by the "economic cabinet": E. J. Stapleton, *Correspondence*, I, 88 ff.

renewed, the duties on rum, coal, wool, and silk would be reduced. It was the proposal to touch the silk trade which aroused the most severe opposition, led by Baring, who deserted his free trade principles in this instance. The duties upon raw silk were to be reduced, the prohibition upon the import of manufactured silk was to be abolished and it was to be subject to a duty of 30 per cent. The boldness of this project lay in the fact that of all industry, silk manufacture had been most pampered by the Government, and as an exotic trade it was thought to require extreme measures of protection. Robinson and Huskisson stuck to their points, the bill was passed and, in spite of some subsequent complaints, was eminently successful in the long run.[1]

In the following year Robinson was able to report a surplus of nearly £1,000,000 more than he had estimated. The duty upon iron ore was reduced from a prohibitory level to 30s. a ton, and Robinson pointed out that England should feed her foundries and workshops with iron from whatever source. The duties upon hemp, coffee, cocoa, wines and British spirits were also reduced, and a few vexatious items among the assessed taxes were taken off.

That Liverpool continued to exercise a close supervision over the finances is shown in a letter of 19 October 1824 to Canning, which shows also the soundness of his financial ideas. Canning had written: "Are you forward in your financial plans? and can you remit us any more taxes? If so, I am for direct ones this season."[2] Liverpool replied: "The

1 Tooke, *History of Prices*, v, 414–17. But the mid-nineteenth-century prosperity of the silk trade was also proof of a proposition which no nineteenth-century economist would admit, the wisdom of fostering the trade in the first place.   2 E. J. Stapleton, I, 179.

state of the revenue is very satisfactory, and all the papers respecting it shall be ready for consideration, when we meet at the beginning of September. It is important however that you should know that we *must* make a reduction in the spirit duties of England, and we *ought* to make a reduction in those on tobacco. We shall have, I fear, no margin for any further reduction; and there really is not a pretence for any reduction in our direct taxation, except the facility which it might give us in getting through the business of the session in the House of Commons, which I do not mean to undervalue. Since our last reduction of the assessed taxes, the whole of our direct taxation does not exceed four millions per annum; less in proportion to our whole revenue than is paid by the subjects of any other country in Europe. When we made the reduction in the assessed taxes, two years ago, the distresses of the country, and particularly of the landed interest, were grounds for it; these distresses have now, in a great measure, disappeared. If we *could* do what we *ought* to do (do not be alarmed, I am not going to propose it), we should make an augmentation in our direct taxes of at least two millions; and, as a compensation, take off indirect taxes to the amount of four or five millions. By such an arrangement we should not materially reduce our revenue, and we should considerably increase the wealth and resources of the country, by the relief which might be afforded to commerce. We are already experiencing advantages from the measures adopted last session. Having said all this, I quite agree in the propriety of a careful review of the assessed taxes, particularly the house and window tax. That we should yield nothing to

13-2

clamour, and that if there is anything which we cannot maintain we should make it a matter of voluntary concession as early in the session as possible."[1] The budget as eventually presented followed very closely upon these lines, save that the surplus seems to have been a little larger than the first estimate.

Huskisson may have inspired the free trade proposals in the budgets, but he had not, meanwhile, been idle in his own department. His first attempt to remove ancient restrictions had suffered a severe set-back when the House of Lords threw out the Spitalfields Bill in 1823. The history of the Spitalfields Acts "remains a curious and untimely record of the difficulties which beset trade agreements, wage boards, and compulsory arbitration in times of rapid economic change".[2] The London silk manufacture was regulated in a way peculiar to itself, but in a way which was also the last relic of that spirit which had animated the old labour code. Wages and the minutest details of manufacture were settled by magistrates, masters could not employ weavers from other districts or employ their capital elsewhere, the same wages were paid for work well and ill done, the same rates were paid for machine and for handwork. The result was that the Spitalfield weavers had an unusually high standard of life—they played a great part in the intellectual life of London, and many famous societies originated among them—but the regulations had driven manufacturers to leave London, and large works were set up in the provinces. The most usual argument

1 Yonge, III, 311.
2 J. H. Clapham, *Economic Journal*, vol. XXVI.

against the repeal was that it would impoverish the weavers
—the philanthropist Fowell Buxton argued this very
strongly—but Huskisson's reply was that under existing
conditions there would soon be no manufacture to support
them. He succeeded in passing the measure through the
House of Commons against all manner of interested and
disinterested opposition, but in the Lords it had a rough
passage. Liverpool supported it, but Eldon and Harrowby,
the dissentient ministers who infuriated Huskisson, were
against. It remained indeed for Harrowby to find the most
ingenious argument, an argument dictated neither by
philanthropy nor by political economy but by a considerable
measure of good sense: "He considered that the residence
of a large manufacturing body in the metropolis was prima
facie a great evil... but the best description of manufacture
was that which was domestic. In plans from which domestic
machinery had been banished, the mischievous effects had
been strikingly manifest. If the present bill should pass,
thousands of weavers who now lived with their families
would be taken away from them, and stowed into enormous
buildings, where they would be exposed to every evil, and
where their excellent moral habits would be destroyed,
while half a dozen great manufacturers would amass large
fortunes."[1] Liverpool, speaking with the tongue of many a
future philosophic radical or poor-law commissioner, said:
"Whether the bill was or was not against the wishes of the
operative manufacturers, it was for their interest that it
should pass."[2] The bill was defeated in 1823, but a similar
bill introduced in 1824 by Lauderdale passed both Houses

1 Hansard, IX, 1530.   2 *Ibid.*

with little opposition; an anticlimax to a question which had threatened to become a great battle-ground of the new and the old principles.

Other bills coming from the Board of Trade had been the important Trade Duties Reciprocity Bill, authorising the King in Council to reduce duties in order to carry out reciprocal commercial negotiations with other countries; and the consolidation of the Customs. This had been carried out, under Huskisson's supervision, by a hard-working civil servant, J. D. Hume, and the Act which resulted repealed no less than three hundred ancient and obsolete statutes. A new colonial policy was launched which broke in upon the sacred terrain of the navigation laws. Henceforth the intercourse between the colonies and foreign countries would be free, but trade between the colonies and England was still confined to British ships. One innovation, which might well have aroused agricultural alarms but which passed without much comment, was the admission of Canadian wheat at a fixed duty of 5s. No one of these steps towards free trade was in itself considerable, taken together they formed an important advance in that direction; at the same time protection was limited by restricting all protective duties to 30 per cent.

The last measure of economic reform was not the work of the ministers, indeed it passed without their serious consideration. Hume, acting upon the report of a committee which he had obtained, introduced bills repealing the Combination Laws; these passed so quietly that they escaped the notice of Hansard's reporter. But the boom of 1824 brought with it labour troubles which were accentuated by the repeal of the Acts; and in 1825 a committee was appointed, with Wallace as its chairman, to reconsider the Acts. The Act which resulted made all combinations illegal except those to fix wages and hours, and magistrates were given summary powers to punish any man using force to compel membership of an association or participation in a strike.

In estimating the influence of Liverpool upon the course of legislation in these two years the scanty nature of his papers forms a considerable obstacle. It would not be fair to assume from this that he played an insignificant part, indeed the reverse would rather be true. Every measure would require the Prime Minister's sanction, and the absence of written communications leads to the assumption that all was done verbally. It is not, therefore, unreasonable to suppose that Liverpool with his "economic cabinet" passed the proposed measures under review and that correspondence was rendered unnecessary by intimate personal discussion. In two measures only is it possible to trace Liverpool's own initiative; neither of them is unimportant, but both are off the main stream of legislation. In the budget of 1824 Robinson was able to announce, in consequence of the repayment of the Austrian Loan,[1] two special grants, one of £500,000 towards the building of churches, the other of £60,000 towards the purchase of pictures for a National Gallery. Church reform and church improvement had always been a special object of Liver-

1 This was a loan made early in the war; repayment was hardly expected; but Austria offered to do so at the Congress of Verona, and negotiations were completed during 1823.

pool's ambition, and he was sympathetic to the Evangelical movement (though by Evangelical clergy he understood those who were attentive to their duties, not those who adopted the manners of a distinct sect).[1] In 1818 he had been able to make a grant of £1,000,000 towards the building of new churches in the Government's only constructive remedy for social troubles, and in 1824 it was said that these churches were all full. Liverpool was anxious that a part of the Austrian Loan repayment should be allotted to church building, and carried his point; for what better employment could be found for a godsend than a work of God? The second measure is interesting, for, in the official portrait of Liverpool by Lawrence now in the National Portrait Gallery, he is shown holding the charter of the National Gallery. Beyond this he has received little recognition for a work in which he bore the chief responsibility. The occasion was the sale of the collection of J. J. Angerstein in 1823. In that year Liverpool wrote to Baring: "In expectation of the final success of the negotiations relative to the Austrian Loan, I more than five weeks ago authorised Sir C. Long to open a negotiation with Mr Angerstein for the purchase of his collection of pictures. I had determined upon going thus far whatever was the ultimate result of the Austrian negotiation."[2]

During the year 1824 prosperity had never stood so high; in every enterprise fortune seemed to smile, the more so by contrast with what had gone before; while, in South America, a new field was opened for the employment of

1 Add. MSS. 38289, f. 117.   2 Add. MSS. 38297, f. 71.

British capital. Nothing, men felt, could hinder the success of their enterprises and 1825 opened in a mood of extravagant optimism. Every form of speculation was undertaken, money was very plentiful, and credit was given upon the slenderest securities. In the period which followed the war Liverpool might have been criticised for confident faith in a recovery which took place only after long delay, but in 1825 he was alive to danger which few men foresaw. In March 1825 "he would not say he took, he created almost an occasion of stating...what, sooner or later, would be the effect of this rash spirit of speculation",[1] and delivered this warning: "In a country like this, where extensive commercial interests are constantly at work, a great degree of speculation is unavoidable, and, if kept within certain limits, this spirit of speculation is attended with much advantage to the country. In a moment like the present, in a time of profound peace, and when the interest of money is low, it is to be expected that speculation should exist in a very considerable degree. To this I have no objection, but I wish that the public should be set to rights as to the situation in which they stand. I never knew a moment when there was a greater prospect of lasting peace than the present; but still, no man can say how long that peace may last. Now, I would ask every man to reflect what would be the situation of the public if (not to speak of actual war) any thing short of a war—any embarrassing event—were to occur?...When commercial embarrassments occurred during the late war, banks and merchants came forward and applied to Parliament for aid, which they obtained by

1 Hansard, XIV, 15.

issues of Exchequer Bills; I wish it, however, to be clearly understood, that those persons now engaged in Joint Stock Companies, or other enterprises, enter on those speculations at their own peril and risk. I think it my duty to declare, that I never will advise the introduction of any bill for their relief; on the contrary if such a measure were to be proposed, I would oppose it and I hope that parliament will resist any measure of this kind. I think that this determination cannot be too well understood at the present moment, nor made too publicly known. I have felt myself particularly called on to make this declaration, because I understand that the speculations are not confined to the metropolis, where people may have a better opportunity of judging for themselves, but that endeavours are being made, by means of country bankers, to engage people in the country to embark in speculation, the object of which they cannot know. I am one of the last men ever to interfere, by legislative provisions, with the property of individuals, or to endeavour by any means, to prevent men from spending their own money as they please. But as the consequences of the present extensive speculations might be serious, I thought, filling the situation which I do, that I should be bound to declare that I am determined not to give relief, or to listen to any claims made on account of distress, arising from such sort of speculation. In stating my opinion, it is in reference to no particular measure, but to that general spirit of speculation which is going beyond all bounds, and is likely to bring the greatest mischief on numerous individuals.''[1]

1 Hansard, XII, 1194.

Mention has already been made of the concession in 1822 to the agriculturalists whereby £1 notes continued in circulation until 1833. But by 1822 the banks had already accumulated large stores of bullion, and this encouraged them to increase their issues of notes. Under these circumstances prices rose, the value of money fell, and there was a steady drain of bullion from the country. During 1824 the Bank's reserve sank from £14,000,000 to £10,721,190; by May 1825 it had fallen to £6,131,300. At this the Bank took alarm and began to call in its notes; but at the same period the folly of many speculative ventures was being realised, and the effect of the Bank's change in policy was to increase this disquiet. Nothing could stop the drain of bullion from the Bank, and in the autumn the reserve stood at about £3,500,000. In the country depression and lack of confidence descended upon those who had taken advantage of rising prices to launch enterprises with money borrowed upon insufficient securities; many, faced with falling prices and a glutted market, could look forward only to bankruptcy.

In spite of his earlier fears Liverpool remained fairly calm. "The state of the money market has for some time occupied my attention", he wrote on 3 September, "I have no doubt it has been affected by the measures taken by the Bank (with our approbation and connivance) for reducing their circulation, in consequence of the state of the Exchanges. I am not in any alarm as to the result; provided no false step is taken, I am convinced that in a short time things will set themselves right." It is interesting to note that the Government and the Bank had been following the principles of the Bullion Report in regulating the currency with reference to the Exchanges, but in doing this insufficient attention had been paid to the psychological effects in the country. As a remedy for "the embarrassments in which we may be shortly placed" Liverpool suggested raising the interest on Exchequer Bills—"it is the plain, obvious and I may add the *honest* remedy"—which would succeed better than increasing the circulation and keeping up funds.[1]

All optimism was, however, shattered by the failure of Elford's Bank at Plymouth on 29 November. The Bank had already refused to discount bills for Payne and Smith, the Barings, Rothschild, and Harman;[2] and the news from the West Country was sufficient to spread panic in the City. On 3 December the Bank heard that the great London house of Pole, Thornton & Co. was in serious difficulties, and decided to place £300,000 at its disposal. In spite of this Pole, Thornton & Co. fought a losing battle for a week and failed on 12 December, carrying down with them many country concerns. This failure brought on the worst period of the crisis.

At the end of November Liverpool had written to Bexley: "I foresee considerable distress and commercial embarrassment, but this is the natural result of the over-speculation of the last two years, and any attempt to interfere by the authority of Government would only aggravate the evil instead of remedying it."[3] But the Government kept a close watch upon events. It was to be most intimately concerned, for, as the Bank reserve dwindled away to nothing, there came the inevitable demand for a stop upon

1 Add. MSS. 38300, f. 172.   2 Add. MSS. 38301, f. 37.
3 Add. MSS. 31232, f. 343.

cash payments. This the Government was resolved to avoid at all costs.

The two days following the failure of Pole, Thornton & Co. were the worst of the crisis; almost all the bullion had gone from the Bank, every house in the City trembled upon the brink of disaster, money could not be obtained even upon the best of securities, and men of sound fortune wandered disconsolate in the streets wondering whether the next hour would see them ruined. Liverpool called Huskisson, the Governor of the Bank, and Alexander Baring into conference;[1] the result of their deliberations was a very bold decision. There was no gold to be had, but Bank of England notes were still as good as gold; it was now decided to stem the panic by reversing the Bank's policy and putting into circulation as many notes as possible. This was on 14 December and £5,000,000 of notes were immediately printed and lent "by every possible means, and in modes never adopted before".[2] This policy was completely successful, panic was allayed in London, and on Saturday, the 17th, Richards, the Deputy Governor of the Bank, was able to go to the Cabinet, reeling with fatigue and with just sufficient strength to call out to Lord Liverpool that all was well.[3]

1 *The Financial and Commercial Crisis Considered*, by Lord Ashburton (A. Baring), London, 1847. This compares the crisis of 1847 with that of 1825. Cf. also Huskisson in the House of Commons: "The Bank throughout their prompt, efficacious and public spirited conduct, had the countenance, advice and particular recommendation of the First Lord of the Treasury and his Right Hon. friend (Robinson) to assist them" (Hansard, XIV, 231).
2 McCleod, *Theory and Practice of Central Banking*, II, 115. Quoting Harman, a bank director.
3 *Ibid.* p. 113.

The crisis was at an end in the City, but in the provinces, where it had begun earlier, it was to run in all for nearly four weeks. It was not until 24 December that conditions were once more normal, and further bank failures had only been averted by a happy accident. After the 17th there were neither notes nor gold which could be sent out to the country—or so it seemed until one of the directors remembered a case of £1,000,000 old unused notes in one of the Bank cellars—these were immediately despatched and stopped the panic.

So ended the great crisis of 1825, and there remained only the work of repair and restoration. There were many who clamoured for immediate relief, but Liverpool, adhering to his earlier resolution, was resolved against this. The first cause of the crisis had been over-confidence and ignorant speculation, but there had been contributory causes: the over-issue of paper and the irresponsibility of the country banks. By charter the Bank of England had the exclusive right of conducting a joint-stock bank in England; and the country banks were frequently in the hands of single capitalists. Liverpool disapproved wholeheartedly of this system, it was "one of the most absurd ever invented. It was in the teeth of all sound policy or common sense. It had grown up gradually and was not the result of any original plan or system."[1] And, in one of his few sentences which is frequently quoted, "any small tradesman, a cheesemonger, a butcher, or a shoemaker, might open a country bank; but a set of persons with a fortune sufficient

[1] Hansard, XIV, 17 February 1826. Not perhaps a typical Tory argument.

to carry on the concern with security were not permitted to do so".[1] In this respect Scotland differed from England; there, joint-stock banking was legal and very few failures had occurred in the past fifty years. Accordingly Liverpool and Robinson entered into correspondence with the Bank directors to persuade them to forgo their privileges. The Bank gave way with a bad grace, and on conditions; the privilege was still to be operative for a distance of fifty miles round London, and the Bank was empowered to set up branch banks in the principal cities. This last proposal was particularly pressed by Liverpool, but it cannot be said that it had the effects which he hoped, and Huskisson, who criticised the proposal, was justified.[2] The door was now open for the formation of great joint-stock banks, though it was but slowly that the country banks took advantage of these facilities.

The second remedy was to put an end to the indiscriminate issue of paper. In 1821, 1822 and 1823 the average annual value of country notes issued was £4,200,000, in 1824 it was £6,000,000, in 1825 over £8,000,000. Under the original provisions of Peel's Act £1 notes would have ceased to be currency on 1 February 1826, but in 1822, in response to pressure from the agriculturalists, the time

1 Hansard, XIV, 15.
2 *Report of Committee on Banks of Issue*, 1841, evidence of Vincent Stuckey: "Mr Huskisson said to me: 'Lord Liverpool is extremely keen upon having branch Banks of England, and I do not see any objection to them; but I very much doubt whether it will answer in the long run; it appears to me that the Bank Directors have now as much or more than they can do in London, if you throw them upon the country circulation they will soon get into considerable difficulties; therefore I should rather confine their business to London.'"

limit had been postponed to 1833. It was now necessary to reverse this decision, and it was this proposal which was likely to meet with most opposition in the Commons. "We expect great difficulties...from a combination of country bankers and city merchants, with no small sprinkling of country gentlemen connected with the former class, which threatens to run very hard Robinson's one pound note proposition."[1] The measure survived this ordeal in the Commons, but only because the Opposition supported the Government. "It is but just to the opposition," wrote Canning, "to Brougham especially, as well as to Tierney, Wilson, and others, to say that their cordial support helped very much to discourage a combination of our *friends*; which, if formed upon the basis of an adverse attack from our usual opponents, might, in the present state of suffering and consequent discontent, have been very formidable."[2] Unpopular as this measure was in England, in Scotland it was completely unacceptable. The Scots, with their stable banking system, had long been attached to their £1 notes and fully realised the advantages, when security was assured, of a paper currency. That wholehearted Tory Sir Walter Scott made his first and last appearance upon the political stage as an anti-Government pamphleteer, and his friend Croker took up the Government's defence; but in spite of Croker, and in spite of the Government's determination, the Scots won the day, and Scotland was excluded from the measure.

1 Wellington, III, 97. Canning to Wellington, who was at this time on a mission to Petersburg; from Canning, Peel, and Croker he received letters upon happenings at home.
2 *Ibid.*

There was, however, one measure demanded by the country; this was the issue of Exchequer Bills upon the security of goods to distressed merchants. Canning doubted "whether we should get through the crisis without an issue of exchequer bills, which, objectionable as it may be, and is, in principle, appears to be the only remedy to which the moneyed world will look with confidence".[1] In March Liverpool had given his specific warning that the Government would give no relief to speculators; but the general opinion was that "as soon as the whole mercantile body, as soon as Tierney at the head of the opposition, as soon as every man of the old Pitt party expressed a unanimous concurrence in that measure, we all thought it would do us no great harm to adopt it as a special remedy in a special case".[2] Every man of the old Pitt party counted without their leader's adherence to the principles of *laissez-faire*. Throughout the year he had deprecated any proposals for Government interference, now he refused completely to concur in any measure which would teach men the habit of relying upon Government when their own efforts failed. "I know that if I studied my own ease or popularity, I could not do so more effectively than by coming down to Parliament with such a proposition. If I have not adopted that course, I trust the House will give me credit for abstaining from it, from a thorough conviction that it was not likely to be attended with beneficial results. I have always thought that the precedent of 1793, in that respect, was not a favourable one and therefore ought not to be followed. But there is a great difference between that period and the

1 Wellington, III, 116.   2 Croker, I, 314.

present; for it cannot now be pretended that the commercial distress which now existed has any connection with political events....What would be the effects of such a measure? Not to leave the people to rely upon themselves. What is that but the very evil I have deprecated; namely, looking to government for aid, to relieve them from the consequence of their own extravagance. It is now three or four years since the landed interest was suffering great distress: and not a month passed at that time, that I was not beset with the most urgent applications for relief by the issue of Exchequer Bills...the applications, however, were rejected."[1] Accordingly, when a petition for the issue of Exchequer Bills was about to be presented in the House, Liverpool sent for Canning and told him that he would resign if such a measure was forced upon the Administration, and authorised Canning to say this in the House. Canning felt he could not "leave Lord Liverpool in the lurch" and announced to the House "in a very bold and uncompromising tone, that if the House chose to adopt the proposed measure they must also be prepared to find Ministers to execute it, for that they *would not*; and this he repeated very steadily, and to the ears of some country gentlemen offensively".[2]

Liverpool felt keenly his personal responsibility, and even went so far as to suggest that "the best mode of solving the difficulty was for him to retire from office, the rest of the members of the Government retaining their offices". This stirred Peel to remonstrate: "I went to him when he was alone, and told him I thought him very wrong in using that

1 Hansard, xv, 450.   2 Croker, I, 324-5.

language, that if he resigned when the country was in a crisis of financial difficulty—he, the minister who presided over the finances of the country—he would lose all the credit he had gained by long and successful service; that the country would right itself in two or three months; that the man who might succeed him would get all the credit and he personally all the blame. I added also, that what he proposed to do, to retire singly, should not take place; that I should feel it dishonourable to allow one member of the Government—and that member the head of it—to make himself a sacrifice; and if he retired...I could not but consider that his retirement under such circumstances would be a dissolution of the government."[1] A compromise was then discovered which satisfied both Liverpool's scruples and the demands for relief; by a clause in the Bank's Charter it was empowered to issue notes upon the deposit of goods. The Government requested the Bank to do this, and also to purchase Exchequer Bills in the open market; this the Bank consented to do, but only when the Government agreed to repay some of the debt to the Bank. "If", said Liverpool, "the Bank chose to go into the market, and purchase a limited quantity of Exchequer Bills for the purpose of affording relief to the public, the government would pay them part of the six million which they owed them, to prevent them from experiencing any inconvenience in so doing." But this transaction was upon a different principle than that of direct relief by the Government.[2]

The incident had come near to causing a revolt in the

1 Peel to Wellington: Parker, I, 397.   2 Hansard, xv, 450.

party, many had "whispered about that we were acting quite in a different manner from that in which Mr Pitt did act, and would have acted had he been alive";[1] and Croker thought it "altogether the most ridiculous political intrigue, if it may be so called, I ever saw". But Peel gave it as his firm opinion "that we were right in refusing, and that had we consented we should have defeated our other measures and not impossibly have had to answer for another Bank Restriction". Liverpool based his defence in the House of Lords largely upon moral argument—that men should not depend upon the Government—but Peel gives some account of the practical considerations as they were brought forward in the Cabinet. "There are thirty million of Exchequer Bills outstanding. The purchases lately made by the Bank can hardly maintain them at par. If there were a new issue to such an amount as contemplated—viz. five million—there would be a great danger that the whole mass of Exchequer Bills would be at a discount and would be paid into the revenue. If the new Exchequer Bills were to be issued at a different rate of interest from the outstanding ones—say bearing an interest of five per cent—the old ones would be immediately at a great discount unless the interest were raised. If the interest were raised the charge on the revenue would be of course proportionate to the increase of the rate of interest."[2]

From outside the Government the economist Tooke advanced more reasons in support, in a pamphlet which, said Huskisson, would "check a great deal of nonsense which, without some preliminary discussions to direct and guide

1 Wellington, III, 143 ff.   2 *Ibid.* p. 143.

the thoughts of those who do not think much for themselves, would probably find vent in the House of Commons".[1] Tooke argued that the characteristics of commercial distress were lack of lenders and lack of buyers,
since it is no profits and no loans which mean ruin for the
individual. The issue of Exchequer Bills would supply
neither of these wants. Since they went straight to persons
in distress, the number of lenders or buyers would not be
increased; an individual would, indeed, be able to exchange Exchequer Bills for cash, but, since the amount of
money had not been increased, some less fortunate person
would have to go without a loan. The issue of Exchequer
Bills would benefit certain people, it would direct capital
into certain channels, but it would not be a measure of
general relief. If the Bank bought up Exchequer Bills and
issued notes in excess of the natural limit imposed by the
state of the Exchanges, then, "the temporary relief would
be dearly bought at the expense of the alternative of suspension or of such a degree of subsequent contraction as
might renew the distress in an aggravated form".[2] In a
private letter to Huskisson, Tooke added another argument: the issue of Exchequer Bills might have the effect of
bringing out hoarded money, but the same argument—
that bills would not add to the amount of money available
—would still apply; for the Bank, seeing money to be more
abundant, would again reduce its note issue.[3]

From the great crisis England emerged sadder but saner;

1 Add. MSS. 38747, f. 194.
2 *Considerations on the State of the Currency*, 2nd ed. Postscript.
3 Add. MSS. 38747, f. 217.

and henceforth caution would restrain the hands of the speculator. The real prosperity of the country, the progress of its industry and commerce, was touched only upon the surface, and soon returned to a healthy condition. One valuable result of the crisis was the reform of the country banking system, and a result which was welcomed by many was the substitution of gold coin for small notes. In England, though not in Scotland, the Government was able to carry all its measures; but in order to do so it had to rely upon Whig support. Thus one effect of the crisis was to strengthen the bonds of sympathy between Liberal Tories and Whigs, and to emphasise the division between the former and "those who do not think much for themselves".

During the session of 1825 W. W. Whitmore, the member for Bridgnorth and a persistent advocate of Corn Law reform, spoke in favour of a fixed corn duty of 10s. During the debate which followed Huskisson promised to consider the whole question during the next session. The agriculturalists had been loud in their complaints of the Corn Law, but now that a change was threatened by the suspect Huskisson they rallied to its defence. The change they desired was more adequate protection, the change they foresaw was some measure of free trade.

The corn question had been one of constant difficulty for the Liverpool Government, and the attempt to reconcile the persistent demand of the farmers for a closed market with the equally forcible demand of the consumers for cheap bread, had not so far proved very successful. The agitation of the question had begun as early as 1813 and it had continued—under changing circumstances—ever since. In 1808 the price of wheat was 80s. per quarter, it rose to over 100s. in 1810, and after a slight drop in 1811, to 126s. in 1812; it was still over 110s. in August 1813, but between August and December it dropped to 73s. The downward trend continued until it reached the abysmal depth of 48s. in February 1816. In 1816 the expectation of a bad harvest brought the price back to 103s., but it dropped in 1817 to 78s., and was at 80s. during the greater part of 1818 until it fell at the end of the year to 78s. From these figures it will be seen that both producers and consumers had much cause for complaint; the former suffered a great set-back in 1814 and never recovered their war-time position, the latter had to pay starvation prices before 1814, in 1817, and in 1818; both alike were victims of sudden fluctuations in price, both would gain from the Government's policy of ensuring a steady supply without fluctuations in price. Had the Government been successful in that policy it would have solved one of the perennial problems which face modern governments.

Under the Corn Law of 1804 a prohibitory duty of 24s. 3d. was imposed when the price was less than 63s., there was a duty of 2s. 6d. between 63s. and 65s., and of 6d. when over 65s.; there was also a bounty of 5s. upon export when the price was less than 48s. and a prohibition of export when it was over 54s. But since that date prices had been generally over 65s., foreign corn could come in at a nominal duty, and export was forbidden. Under these circumstances it might be asked why in March 1813 there began an agitation for a change in the law. The answer is that it began not with the English but with the Irish producers, and it was aimed not at altering the import regulations but at freeing the export trade. Ireland ate potatoes and exported wheat; the first aim of Irish landowners was to sell their wheat on the continent, and it was with this object that Sir Henry Parnell moved for a committee to enquire into the Corn Trade of Ireland. But a return had just been published showing that, in the last twenty-one years, £753,634,135 of foreign corn had been imported, even while prices had risen to famine level. Under the stimulus of this return the words "United Kingdom" were substituted for "Ireland", and a few English members were added to the committee as originally named by Parnell. The obvious comment was that home supply should be increased and that prices should be lowered; but during the discussion of the committee a very fair prospect opened before the Irish members. If foreign corn was subjected to a virtual prohibition, Irish corn would have the run of the English market. In presenting the committee's report Parnell argued that importation did not lower prices—he could point to the last few years as proof—it discouraged home farmers, and so restricted produce and raised the price. He recommended a duty of 24s. 3d. when the price was less than 105s. 2d., of 20s. between 105s. 2d. and 135s. 2d. and of 6d. over that price. Export should be free at all times.

These were proposals which no Government could consider, and Parnell seemed to have failed. In 1814, however, the discussion was resumed under very different circumstances. Prices had fallen suddenly upon the prospect of peace, and "steady prices" had become the catch-

word of the agriculturalists. Though prices were now 74s.
imports were still admitted under the old law, and the high
wages and rents of former years remained constant. Parnell
now proposed 84s. as the price at which the prohibitory
duty of 24s. 3d. was to apply, and 87s. was the price at
which the nominal duty should come into force.[1] These
proposals created great alarm among the commercial and
labouring classes; many petitions were presented, and it
was decided to postpone the discussion until 1815 while
setting up a committee to examine these petitions.

The attitude of the Government to this demand was one
of modified approval: it would not admit the propositions
of the extreme protectionists, but it would admit the necessity for some new measure. Liverpool gave to the question
his particular attention. "I have", he said, "for the last
three years been revolving the subject in my mind....I
have read with all the attention in my power, all the evidence
which has been given upon the question and all the publica-
tions which have been given to the world....If there ever
was a question on which my mind was free from all undue
bias towards one particular view of it rather than another,
that is this question....My decided opinion is that the
commercial interests of this country ought not to be sacrificed to the agricultural; but with all due regard to the
commercial interest—and I have been educated in a school
where I was taught highly to value the commercial interest
—I must also say that the agricultural interest ought not to
be sacrificed to the commercial....The general principle,
supposing all nations to act upon it, is that in these cases the

[1] Hansard, xxvii, 663: 5 May 1814.

legislature ought not to interfere, but leave everything to find its own level. In such a state of the world it is perfectly clear that every nation ought to be left to prosecute without interference that particular species of industry for which by its nature and condition it was in all respect best adapted. But unfortunately the period is not yet arrived when nations would have the wisdom to act upon such a system."[1]

The measure which would have found most favour in the eyes of the Government would have been an adoption of the sliding scale principle of 1804. In 1814 Huskisson countered Parnell's proposals by a scheme which would make 63s. the price at which the prohibitory duty of 24s. 3d. should apply and diminish the duty by 1s. for every 1s. increase in price until at 86s. the duty would expire.[2] The committee appointed in 1814 ignored the many petitions against the measure and suggested 80s. as the lowest possible "regulating price". The Government would still have preferred Huskisson's proposals, but it was also anxious to produce a measure acceptable to the agriculturalists; to ascertain the feelings upon the measure Liverpool called "a very full meeting of the landed interest" which "almost unanimously and particularly Mr Western" preferred the alternative measure.[3] As there did not seem to be much to choose between the two measures, the Government accepted this ruling, and Robinson introduced a simple measure which prohibited import when the price was less than 80s. and allowed free import above that

1 Hansard, xxx, 175 ff.: 15 March 1815.
2 Hansard, xxvii, 663 ff.   3 Add. MSS. 38742, f. 4.

price. In spite of many protests from the manufacturing districts the bill passed by 218 to 56.

In supporting this measure the Government was extremely anxious to avoid any imputation of class legislation. "Were the measure one which stood upon the narrow ground of affording relief to a particular class", said Liverpool, "I would not support it...not from any want of feeling towards the sufferings of any particular body of men, nor from any indisposition to alleviate these sufferings but because from long experience I have come to the conclusion that you cannot relieve one class of people without injuring some other class more or less. Upon that subject there is a great deal of mistaken legislation in our statute books; but with regard to the present measure, it is so far from being one which looks only to the relief of a particular class, that it embraces the interests of all, and of the poor above all."[1] These arguments were expanded by Huskisson in a letter to his constituents at Chichester. "My sole object is to prevent...corn from ever again reaching the late extravagant prices. But if we wish to cure an evil of this alarming magnitude we must first trace it to its source. What is that source? Obviously this, that, until now, we did not, even in good years, grow enough corn for our own consumption...in order to ensure a continuance of cheapness and sufficiency, we must ensure to our own growers that protection against foreign import which has produced these blessings."[2] If corn were admitted free "the small farmer would be ruined, improvements would everywhere stand still, inferior land now producing corn could be given

[1] Hansard, xxx, 147.   [2] Add. MSS. 38739, f. 198.

up and return to a state of waste...to protect the small farmer is ultimately to protect the people". "Let the bread we eat be the produce of corn grown among ourselves, and I for one care not how cheap it is; the cheaper the better." And Liverpool proclaimed that "the great object is the interest of the consumer, and this, I contend, will be effectually promoted by the present measure the object of which will be to render grain cheaper instead of dearer. The important point to obtain is a steady and moderate price....it has been argued most fallaciously that this import price of 80s. would be a *minimum* price... instead of being a minimum the import price has been more generally the *maximum* in the market."[1]

The chief benefit of the law was psychological in that it did bolster up, to some extent, the confidence of the farmer. The Government was, for this reason, anxious to pass some measure without delay. "If the Bill is passed", said Liverpool, "and any inconvenience is found to arise from it, a remedy may be immediately applied, but if the measure is rejected, and capital in consequence withdrawn from agriculture, fifty years might be necessary to replace us in our present situation."[2] It might, on the other hand, be argued in retrospect that the hopes of the farmers were bound to be false hopes and that they would have done better to restrict their production immediately. The law probably did something to smooth over the brutal transition from war to peace, but nothing so important as its authors had foreseen, and whatever its merits they were largely negative. The depression of 1816 struck a blow at

1 Hansard, xxx, 175 ff.   2 *Ibid.*

English farming from which it would not recover for many years. Cultivation on the "new lands" ceased to be remunerative, the Banks pressed for repayment of loans made in order to open up these lands, the tithes pressed heavily upon the farmers, and as conditions became worse the burden of the Poor Rate became proportionately greater. In 1816 Agricultural Distress was a great item of debate in the House of Commons, and the agriculturalists demanded the reduction of taxation or, at least and with some show of justice, that a part of the burden of taxation should be transferred to the manufacturers.

The Corn Law proved very unsatisfactory in operation. It could not guarantee to the farmer a fair and steady price, and the market was liable to be flooded so soon as the price reached 80s. and large stores of foreign corn were released from bond. On the other hand prices could rise to starvation level in times of scarcity before distress could be alleviated by introduction of foreign corn. These considerations led to a revision of the law in 1822: 70s. was now taken as the price at which corn should be admitted, and above that price a graduated duty was imposed.[1] But this law was not to come into operation until the price reached 80s., and during the years which followed prices never reached this level. But though the price was low by the standard of the immediate post-war years it was steady, and, after the difficulties of transition, agriculture had been able to adjust itself and was, by 1825, in a most flourishing condition. Yet in these years there emerged another doubt:

[1] Between 70s. and 80s. the duty was 12s.; over 80s. and under 85s., 5s.; over 85s., 1s.

was there really enough corn in the country to feed the urban populations at all times? Complaints of scarcity were frequent, and in 1826 the artisans of the industrial districts attributed their distresses directly to the Corn Laws. The prosperity of agriculture was in itself an argument that something might be done to increase the supplies—by the admission of foreign corn at a duty—without injuring the interest of the farmer.

Huskisson's promise in 1825 was inconvenient to the Government, which was not anxious to agitate this difficult question in the last session of an expiring Parliament and before there seemed to be any pressing need to do so. In the summer, when Canning was pressing Liverpool to postpone the dissolution until 1826 when the heat of "No Popery" might have died away, Liverpool made it one of his conditions that the corn question should not be brought forward in the old Parliament. But, by the spring of 1826, the condition of England had changed very much for the worse, and it was Liverpool himself who first tampered with the Corn Law.

The financial crisis of 1825 was followed by severe distress in the manufacturing districts, and there were many complaints of the dearness of bread. Under these circumstances Liverpool proposed two measures of immediate relief and committed himself to some wholesale changes in the Corn Law. The two temporary measures—which Liverpool avowed were his own proposals and for which he was especially responsible—were the admission of warehoused corn at a reduced duty, and the grant to ministers of a discretionary power to admit more corn at a low duty.[1] He also announced that he would introduce a new Corn Law in the new Parliament, and that the choice would lie between the principle of the existing law with an alteration in the limiting price, and the imposition of protective duties.

For this proposed alteration in the law Liverpool was peculiarly responsible. He told Canning that "You and I ought to take the lead in the whole business both in Cabinet and Parliament. It will obviate much jealousy and prejudice, and will give an authority to our measure, which would not equally belong to it if it could be considered a Department question. God knows this is not a pleasant undertaking for either of us."[2] This was particularly so as the Department concerned was the Board of Trade, and Huskisson had been stirring a hornets' nest over this very question. During his election campaign at Liverpool a local paper reported Huskisson as saying that "the whole question was settled and the trade in corn is to be free, and that corn is hereafter to be admitted upon a duty to the great benefit of the ship owners and the trading part of the community in general".[3] Wellington immediately wrote a furious letter to Liverpool, and Canning told Huskisson that it was difficult to describe the *sensation* which the report had created among their colleagues.[4] Huskisson complained that he had been incorrectly reported, that

1 Yonge, III, 272: "They only desired to be prepared to use it if adverse circumstances should render the exercise of it necessary to preserve the country from famine. It was a power which ought to be entrusted to any ministry."
2 Add. MSS. 38748, f. 151.   3 Wellington, III, 342.
4 Add. MSS. 38748, f. 128.

"I studiously endeavoured not to go one tittle beyond what the head of the Government had gone in the House of Lords. I am very confident that I did not",[1] and wished that he had been given the opportunity of explaining. Indeed the Press was notoriously unreliable and any other minister would have been given the benefit of the doubt; it was simply "the unjust prejudice which prevailed respecting him".[2] This trivial incident was painful to Liverpool for it showed the spirit in which some of his colleagues would approach any discussion of the Corn Laws and, even if Liverpool took the lead himself, Huskisson would have to be the chief adviser of the policy.

In October Huskisson prepared a lengthy memorandum on the corn question, but Liverpool doubted "the prudence of circulating it amongst our colleagues". Writing from Walmer, "in the midst of agriculturalists with land of high farming and expensive living amongst the farmers", Liverpool had found the gentlemen "dreadfully alarmed; but would be satisfied with protection up to 60s.". He went on: "I do not anticipate any very material difficulty as to the duty not exceeding 5s. when wheat reaches 70s. the quarter, and expiring altogether (or becoming merely nominal) when the price reaches 75s. But I think the country gentlemen will expect a protection of 25s. up to 55s. the quarter, or even to 60s. If this however should be pressed there could, I conceive, be no difficulty in still adhering to your principle and only providing that between 60s. and 90s. the duty shall decrease at the rate of 1s. 6d. or even 2s. for every

1 Add. MSS. 38748, f. 131.
2 The phrase is Liverpool's. Yonge, III, 431.

shilling addition in the price, instead of the reduction of one shilling as proposed by you.... I think the *main points* are these, that 60*s*. is, as matters now stand, a *remunerating price*, and that beyond 60*s*. the monopoly ought to cease, and foreign corn flow into the country with a moderate duty."[1] The scale ultimately agreed upon conformed very closely to these proposals: at 60*s*. the duty was 20*s*., it decreased 2*s*. for every shilling increase in price, and increased 2*s*. for every shilling decrease in price. At 70*s*. the duty expired, at 55*s*. it reached the prohibitive figure of 30*s*.

Liverpool devoted all the energy which he could command to forwarding the measure. The new Parliament met in November, and, though there was no hope of bringing the Corn Law before Parliament until the new year, Liverpool pressed forward a decision upon the principle of the Corn Law. He wished the subject to be settled "for it will be impossible...to avoid daily debates in which sentiments may be elicited which may prove very inconvenient if the Cabinet are not agreed substantially upon the whole question".[2] He laboured to impress upon his reluctant colleagues that "it was as fair an arrangement between the great interests as could be made",[3] and that it would render any temporary measure or special expedient unnecessary in the future.[4] When it is remembered that of the ministers Wellington, Eldon, Bathurst, Melville and Westmorland

1 Yonge, III, 429 ff.
2 Add. MSS. 38748, f. 151, Liverpool to Canning. Also Add. MSS. 38302, f. 80, Liverpool to Bathurst.
3 Add. MSS. 38302, f. 105.
4 Add. MSS. 40305, f. 318.

voted, after Liverpool's retirement, for a crippling amendment in the House of Lords, the difficulties which faced Liverpool can be imagined.[1] He could only overcome them, he could only obtain a united cabinet, and he could only ensure that the measure would pass in the House of Lords, by an adroit exploitation of his own authority and reputation. He devoted himself "heart and soul" to the measure, and "it was so understood by many who would have made almost any sacrifice of their own opinions to have kept him at the head of the Government".[2]

Every detail was arranged when Parliament met on 8 February; even the tactful intimation to Huskisson that, though Canning was too ill to speak, it would be better for Peel to conduct the question through the Commons, than for Huskisson to attempt it. Above all there must be no *partial* explanations, "we must expose our whole system at once",[3] and so, on 8 February Liverpool announced that on Monday se'nnight he would introduce the new Corn Law. So, with interest, with alarm, or with hope, the country awaited for Monday se'nnight; but before that time an entirely unexpected misfortune had come upon English political life. On 17 February Liverpool collapsed

---

1 The feeling among the Tories may be judged from a letter by the Duke of Rutland to Lady Shelley. "Lord Liverpool feels convinced he could never carry his projected measure of an alteration in the Corn Laws during the last session of a Parliament, with the feelings of the country strongly against him; and he therefore takes the chance of being enabled to carry it with a Parliament just formed.... I trust the landed interest will not only show their teeth but *bite*, if he proposes anything which is likely to disturb the prosperous breeze under which the agricultural interests are at present gliding down a smooth stream": *Diary of Frances, Lady Shelley*, II, 129.

2 Huskisson, *Papers*, p. 217.   3 Add. MSS. 40305, f. 318.

over the breakfast table, and was found lying unconscious and paralysed upon the floor.

Liverpool's stroke was to be of fatal consequence to the party which he had held together; it was of immediate consequence to the measure which should have crowned his career as an economic reformer. Huskisson was in despair; and Canning's only hope was to introduce it "under the shadow of Liverpool's authority though in abeyance".[1] But, with Canning still upon the sick bed, it was necessary to postpone discussion, and when it was finally introduced Robinson, become Viscount Goderich, had to steer it through the Lords. On 8 March, partly through a desire to limit the action of the bill, partly through misunderstanding, Wellington carried a hostile amendment to prevent the admission of warehoused corn until the price reached 66s. This robbed the bill of its effect as an immediate measure of relief, and the ministers gave up the bill. So, after Liverpool's fatal seizure, after a vain attempt to carry the bill intact, it was defeated by that section of the Tories whom his authority alone had kept in check.

1 Add. MSS. 38749, f. 99; Aspinall, *The Formation of Canning's Ministry*, p. 8.

CHAPTER VII

LIVERPOOL AND CANNING

FROM the moment of his re-entry into the ministry, from the moment that he became Foreign Secretary, the personality of George Canning dominated the Government. Whether in leading England on to some bold stroke of diplomacy, or whether in driving the "Ultras" to indiscreet fury, that domination was evident. But the least discriminating of Canning's panegyrists have not denied his debt to Liverpool, though they may have underestimated it. Without Liverpool Canning would not have entered the ministry; without Liverpool he could not have overcome the hostility of the King, of foreign powers, and of dissentient colleagues; without Liverpool he would have had no Government behind him. The events of 1821 and 1822 had certainly not diminished the affection, they had probably increased the respect with which Canning regarded Liverpool; and the two men entered immediately into the most intimate and cordial relationship. They differed upon the Catholic question, but by tacit consent they avoided dispute upon it; apart from this there was, in four and a half years, but one hint of a disagreement. Canning was certainly the senior partner in foreign policy, though Liverpool was by no means negligible as a consultant; in economic policy Canning played very little part; in the business of keeping the Government together, of closing the ragged gaps left in the administration by Canning's progress, the work was all Liverpool's. In that precarious balance upon which the fate of the Government depended—"liberalism" on the one side, "Protestantism" on the other—only Liverpool could hold the scales. As the life of the ministry lengthened, both parties among the ministers realised this fact even more clearly: and both sides were ready to forgo treasured objects of policy, both were ready to use every entreaty, in order to keep Liverpool at the head of affairs.

It will be well to ask here what was the real cause of the division in the Cabinet, and what were the great sins of Canning. The root of the conflict lay far back: perhaps in the fact that Pitt had changed his policy and Burke had changed his mind; perhaps, ultimately, in the endemic difference between two types of English mind. The party of Mr Pitt had been a coalition; subsequent events had never quite robbed it of that character, and it was to be once more evident in its last years. In a situation in which there were many elements of discord, yet in which remarkable harmony had been maintained, Canning was a catalyst. With a force which he himself hardly realised, Canning drove on events towards the dissolution of that party to which he owed allegiance. Yet who would deny that, in so doing, he gave to England a policy and a tradition which she would do ill without?

Whether the destruction of the Tory party was of God or of man, no better agent could have been chosen than Canning. Everything in his history, his method, and his manner was calculated to inspire distrust in those who could not realise that he might also be great. The duel with Castlereagh, the calculating refusal of 1812, the desertion

of 1820, were not things that honest, faithful supporters of
the Government would readily forget. Yet, until 1822, the
difference was personal rather than political; and in 1821
Wellington reminded Liverpool that "there is no doubt
that Mr Canning is not very popular" with the party in
general.[1] The Tories were prepared to overlook accidents
of social origin—was not Eldon the son of a Newcastle coal
merchant?—but Canning retained many of the characteristics of the parvenu. He was self-assured, he was not
slow to expose the failings of his seniors, and he could
seldom resist mixing a cruel wit with such criticism. Yet,
by 1822, the Tories were prepared to believe that Canning
had learnt wisdom and restraint; at this very time he
attained office, and embarked immediately upon the course
of "liberalism". It is hard indeed to define the meaning,
to Tory ears, of this terrible word. Peel called it "odious
but intelligible"; yet "liberal" had been a favourite word
of Burke, and there was no question of confounding
"liberal" with "jacobin". The word had acquired a new
significance from the appearance of "liberales" as the
popular party in Naples, in Spain, and in South America.
Liberalism had hardly become nationalism, but it had
become the policy of the people in defiance of established
systems. His opponents called Canning a liberal; yet it was
not his acceptance of any heterodox theory which made
them do so; it was not his approval of popular revolts, for
even they knew how guarded that approval was, nor was it
simply his break with the continental allies; primarily it
was because he brought in popular opinion as his ally, both

1 Wellington, I, 192.

George Canning

BY SIR THOMAS LAWRENCE

National Portrait Gallery

in the councils of England and the councils of Europe; it was his oratory, and his publication, when it suited him, of diplomatic correspondence which a more timid—or, his opponents would add, a more gentlemanly—minister would have regarded as secret.

The High Tories in the Cabinet were Wellington, Eldon, Sidmouth so long as he remained, Bathurst, Westmorland, and Melville in all but the Catholic question. The King was frequently behind them, the Duke of York was always behind them. Outside the immediate circle of government was the imponderable mass of the Tory aristocracy, surrounded with its honours and its boroughs, the Dukes of Rutland, Beaufort and Marlborough, the Marquis of Hertford, and the Earl of Lonsdale. It was a power which could not be gainsaid, and, though few of these great peers played much part in politics, their goodwill could make or break a government. To all these Canning and his system was anathema: "political theorists without a foot of land of their own in the country", grumbled Rutland; and the lawyer Redesdale spoke for them all when he said: "I am persuaded it has become necessary to cry aloud and spare not. *Liberality* is the word of the day...it is seriously threatening the British Empire with the overthrow of all its ancient institutions by which it has been nourished."[1] The liberals were Canning, Robinson and Huskisson. If the High Tories could call up the support of the borough mongers, the liberals had the good opinion of many in the House, particularly of the commercial interest; their support in Parliament did not

1 Colchester, III, 300.

measure accurately the much larger body of support outside; and they had the Press. All sources of power suspect
to High Tories, but all very valuable in spite of that. In an
intermediate position was Peel; though he belonged by
choice to the party of Eldon and Wellington, he was always
open to conviction, and he always looked upon the continuance of the Government as a first essential. He had
studiously avoided setting himself up, or being set up, as
the High Tory trump to take Canning's ace, and though,
when the time of choice came, he chose Wellington rather
than Canning, his first desire was to avoid that choice.
Harrowby, Wynn and Bexley belonged to neither party,
and the position of each was analogous to that of Peel. The
High Tories could command six, the "liberals" three with
a probable three more, and the votes of Peel and Liverpool
were crucial. Liverpool was always with Canning, and the
authority of a Prime Minister, coupled with the impossibility of replacing him, provided the essential strategic
point, the point which produced a united Cabinet in place
of a deadlock.

The unalterable basis of England's foreign policy had
been stated by Castlereagh in his State Paper of 5 May
1820: "We shall be found in our place when actual danger
menaces the system of Europe, but this country cannot and
will not act upon abstract and speculative Principles of
Precaution." It was this principle which had gradually
emerged during the five years which followed the war, it
was accepted by Canning as the text for his policy. "I
found", he said, "in the records of my office a state paper,
laying down the principle of non-interference with all the

qualification properly belonging to it." The difference in policy, as distinct from difference in method, between the two men was, that Castlereagh wished to maintain the conference system for known and limited objects while Canning considered that England could do no good at such conferences, that she would be tricked into the acknowledgment of principles which she should not acknowledge, that her protests would be ignored, and that she would be dragged at the chariot wheels of the continental allies. When in the famous Troppau Protocol the sovereigns of Austria, Russia and Prussia demanded "the right of maintaining peace, of delivering Europe from the scourge of revolution, of diverting or checking, according to their means, the evils resulting from the violation of all principles of order and morality", it seemed that England could indeed go no more with them. But in October 1821 Castlereagh took the opportunity of the King's visit to Hanover to arrange a meeting with Metternich. The great matter in dispute was Turkey and the Greek revolt: on this specific question Castlereagh agreed to attend another Congress.[1]

The drift away from the continental powers was by no means unpleasing to Liverpool. He had been a loyal supporter of Castlereagh's policy because he saw it as a peace policy, and "I am convinced that, for all our interests, but especially for those of France, every effort must be made to prevent the sword being drawn in Europe under any pretence for a few years to come". Any war following upon

---

[1] Professor Temperley believed that Canning objected to this decision, though not publicly: *Foreign Policy of Canning*, p. 47 and p. 48, note 1.

the recent war would mean that "the revolutionary spirit would break forth again in full force, and the continent would be plunged into all the evils under which it has groaned for the last twenty years". But he was as convinced as Canning that the interests of England in Europe should be strictly limited. In 1815 he was writing to Wellington criticising Castlereagh's conduct of the Polish dispute: "We are very much dissatisfied at the last accounts we received from Vienna. The course which the negotiation has taken is particularly embarrassing. Lord Castlereagh has been substantially right in all his points; but I wish we had not been made so much *principals* in the Polish question." And in 1818 he conveyed the views of the Cabinet to Castlereagh at Aix, after the latter had written that there might be "a protocol, or declaration, to be made public, in which any sentiments arising from the present conference might find their place, and in which the allied sovereigns might announce their indissoluble union, maintenance of engagements, etc., and proceed to declare their friendly sentiments towards France". Liverpool replied: "We cannot but express the great doubts we entertain whether it would in any way be advisable by any new act to proclaim to Europe that it was the intention of the four powers to hold continual meetings at stipulated periods. ... The notion of such meetings would create a great degree of jealousy amongst the other powers of Europe." Castlereagh was already moving towards the position of Canning, though he would not glory in flaunting the continental powers as Canning did. Liverpool was able to work with either Foreign Secretary at the period when both were most useful, but he had none of Castlereagh's "European" outlook, and, by the time of Castlereagh's death, he was very ready to fall in with the more "liberal" and more insular policy of Canning.

In particular he had an appreciation of the great change wrought by the war, the emergence of nationalism. The best he could do for Poland, after stating that the restoration of Polish independence would be a "measure most just in itself and most satisfactory to the people of this country", was to hope that "there should be . . . some record of our having expressed our opinion how desirable it would be to restore Poland"; but he was aware of the new force of nationalism which Castlereagh tended to ignore or to deplore. At the end of 1813 he was speaking of the war in a thoroughly "liberal" manner: "We have seen during the last twenty years coalitions whose size promised strength crushed by the power of the enemy. What then, we may ask, is this new life which has given an irresistible impulse to the present confederacy of northern nations? The feeling of national independence, that sentiment which impels all men to stand before the liberties of their countries! This feeling, which first arose in the nations of the Peninsula, gave the war a new character, and afforded grounds to hope not only for the deliverance of those nations, but also of the rest of Europe." The man who placed this faith in the principle of national independence would feel far more at ease with the policy of Canning than he had done with the policy of Castlereagh. Canning took the lead, but Liverpool was a most willing partner; between them there was the most perfect union of ideas.

When Canning came to the Foreign Office, Wellington had already received his instructions as Castlereagh's successor at the Congress. These instructions had been drawn up while Canning had no connection with the Government, but they could hardly be attacked save on the general ground of disapproving of all congresses. Greece and the South American colonies were two chief items, and Castlereagh thought that it might be necessary to recognise the Greeks as belligerents, while the recognition of the revolted Spanish colonies was a question of time, not principle. But the question which was to dominate the Congress was that of the Spanish revolution.

The rule of Ferdinand, the Bourbon King of Spain, had mixed the worst features of an inefficient despotism with the worst of a corrupt anarchy. In 1820 a revolution, with hardly more recommendation to the admiration of posterity, had forced the King to accept a constitution. It had been a military revolution and Spain now lived under a King who had no intention of observing his oath to the constitution, and a government which blended militarism and extreme democracy. Alexander, now in his last most mystical and most monarchical phase, had proposed joint intervention to restore the King to his former power. It was this proposal which had called forth the State Paper of 8 May 1820. By 1820 the situation had not eased: democratic revolution was still in command of Spain; but now France, not Russia, was most materially concerned. In the autumn of 1822 the French proposed to advance upon Madrid to deliver the King from his enemies, and to do so, if possible, with the sanction of the Holy Alliance. France did not ask for active help, indeed the policy she wished to pursue was avowedly French and French alone,.but she would welcome the moral support of Europe signified by the withdrawal of ambassadors from Madrid. Under these circumstances Canning sent to Wellington a new set of instructions: should the allies project interference "by force or by menace", England would not join such interference "*come what may*". Wellington obeyed his instructions to the letter, declaring that "interference appeared to be an unnecessary assumption of responsibility". His action precluded any idea of a united Congress action against Spain, but there remained the question of France's intentions and France showed every intention of invading Spain in spite of England's attitude. Wellington remonstrated with the French, urged them to keep the peace, and returned to England under the impression that he had succeeded.

The English Parliament met on 4 February, and in the debate upon the Address Liverpool opened the new era of English foreign policy with a speech "intended to encourage the revolutionaries" which had a "very bad effect".[1] "The policy of the British Government is distinctly declared, and it rests on the principle of the law of nations, which allows every country to be judge of how it can be best governed, and what ought to be its institutions; and, if exceptions to that rule may arise out of self-defence, they are to be considered as exceptions, and are to stand on their own peculiar merits. His Majesty's Government, I have no hesitation in declaring, views the question of Spain as one clearly and purely Spanish."

[1] Lieven, p. 247.

Wellington may have been sincerely desirous of peace, but it is certain that his indiscreet expressions, together with those of the King and other Cabinet ministers, encouraged France in the correct belief that she could undertake the invasion of Spain without interference.[1] On 28 January the French King had made a most famous and spectacular speech to his Parliament: a hundred thousand French were ready to march to the aid of a brother Bourbon, and the arguments were not merely those of expediency, for "let Ferdinand be free to give to his people the institutions they cannot hold but from him". This speech had a startling effect in England, and Liverpool omitted the word "neutrality" from those passages in the King's Speech dealing with France and Spain. But the Cabinet were, for once, united upon a question of foreign policy: no one thought of war as either desirable or practicable. In a Cabinet memorandum the well-known difficulties of conducting a defensive war in Spain, the uselessness of a naval war for achieving the present object, the possibility of a rupture with other European powers, were stressed. But a significant qualification was added; France, if successful, might "attempt to carry into execution, what she had already held out, the measure of putting at the command of Spain her fleets and armies to assist the Spanish operations in South America", but "we have the means of easily and effectually preventing any such projects".[2]

From Verona Wellington returned vaguely dissatisfied

1 Temperley, *Foreign Policy*, p. 82.
2 Yonge, III, 231–3; E. J. Stapleton, I, 35–8. The authorship of this memorandum is uncertain; it is unsigned and undated. Yonge claims it for Liverpool, but it is probably by Canning.

with the part he had played; he had broken with the allies, he had failed to preserve peace, and he attributed both developments to Canning. Immediately after his return began the complaints which were to be a constant theme of his politics until 1827; he "complained of the haste with which Canning formed his decisions...he does not think that Canning is to be depended upon...he has a less high opinion of him as an able statesman than he had before, and he thinks he often decides in haste and then writes in haste, and that what he does write has better sounding phrases than good solid sense".[1] The Duke now bethought himself of the part which he had played in placing Canning at the Foreign Office, and he remembered the King's admonition at the time, "Thus ends this last calamity; my reliance is upon you my friend".[2] Incomparably the greatest figure in England, the part he played upon the European stage was hardly less, and he himself was the last person to underestimate it; honoured by every sovereign, he was not prepared to sink the saviour of Europe in the minister of state, nor was he prepared to observe strictly the conventions which might regulate lesser men. He began to conceive that he had a mission, a mission to watch over the indiscretions of Canning and to bring back England into the allied fold. To Madame Lieven he said that "he quite understood that his visit to Verona had had worse results than those which had at first appeared; that every day the separation of England from the great Alliance became...

1 Add. MSS. 38291, fs. 241 ff., Arbuthnot to Liverpool, 23 December 1822.
2 Wellington, I, 284.

more noticeable; that it was certainly a misfortune for England; and that he did not know to what to ascribe it".[1]

Encouraged by this confidence, Madame Lieven began to tempt Wellington with that blend of personal attraction and political intrigue of which she alone was mistress. Wellington showed her some letters—"Damme, I'll show you what I wrote about Spain; and you'll see if M. de Metternich ever said anything stronger"—and Madame Lieven suggested that he should show them to her husband and Esterhazy, the ambassadors of Russia and Austria. This Wellington refused "without permission of my cabinet", but Madame Lieven proved too subtle in argument. "Do you approve", she asked, "of your Cabinet making itself out worse than it is? Frankly no one places any confidence in Mr Canning....If personal relations with you were valuable, even at a time when our confidence in Lord Londonderry was everything we could desire, how much more precious those relations must be now with a minister who inspires mistrust? You can do good, a great deal of good; don't lose your chance!" In the middle of February she wrote again to Metternich: "It seems to me that they are paying very dearly for the satisfaction of seeing Mr Canning in an odour of sanctity among the Liberals....The poor Duke does his best; he feels, both for the Government and for himself, the necessity of getting back in our good books—hence his confidences. He tries them first of all on me. When I point out to him that to do any good he must extend them to our two

1 Mme Lieven to Metternich, 26 January 1823.

ambassadors, he begins by resisting; then lets himself be persuaded."[1]

But there was also a greater than Madame Lieven drawing Wellington from the paths of constitutional rectitude. To his intimates George IV was expressing himself very freely about Canning: "I do not like him any better than I did," he told Madame Lieven, "I recognise his talent, and I believe we need him in the House of Commons; but he is no more capable of conducting foreign affairs than your baby." On 19 March he ordered the Duke "not to let a day pass without seeing Canning, and finding out what he is up to in his office".[2] Wellington was bound to refuse this—there were some lengths to which no minister could go—but by the spring of 1823 Wellington was in close communication with the ambassadors, and he knew in his conscience that this was a breach of loyalty to his colleagues.

Against this conspiracy to circumvent Canning's policy, there was the close union between Liverpool and Canning, and there were also the constitutional conventions which had grown up in the last fifty years. The Duke found that his weight in the Cabinet was impaired by the suspicion that he spoke as the "King's favourite", and some who were with him in spirit told him that "as the leaders in the two houses had taken a different view, they had thought it best to acquiesce".[3] His confidant Arbuthnot knew him to be "so conscious of honourable intentions that this idea sours his mind, and may lead to the very worst conse-

1 Lieven, p. 237. She adds: "Now these documents are in complete contradiction to the official language of Mr Canning, and above all to the Parliamentary language of Lord Liverpool."
2 Lieven, p. 243.   3 Cf. p. 68 above.

quences".[1] If the Duke found himself losing weight in the Cabinet, there are also signs that he was being excluded from those intimate discussions which were really more important than cabinets. In June 1823 Madame Lieven saw him every day, and was every day more convinced that "he counts for nothing in affairs. For some weeks he has known nothing about them. He feels it, though he tries to put a good face on it."[2]

The great occasion of dispute was to be the Spanish-American question. England's consistent attitude had been that these republics were either actually independent, or were likely to become so; if they were independent, English interests would be placed in an intolerable position if they had still to defer to the nominal authority of Spain; therefore, sooner or later, the South American states must be recognised. Two considerations retarded the final decision: the uncertain and precarious nature of the republican governments, and the desirability of avoiding all conflict by making Spain take the first step in recognition. The crisis was brought on by the French invasion of Spain, for there was the danger that France might recompense herself for her expenses and her slight material gains in Spain by taking over some of the Spanish colonies. The prospect of a French army, backed by all the moral support of the Holy Alliance, was not altogether remote. The continental powers tried to push forward the idea of a Congress on South America. Canning resolved to act separately with France; and, in conference with Polignac the French ambassador, he extracted an admission that the South American states were virtually independent and a renunciation of any desire on the part of France for territorial gains or for any exclusive advantages in South America. On England's part, she would recognise the colonies if any trade restrictions were enforced against her by Spain, she would not tolerate any French interference in America, and she would not attend a Congress unless the United States was also a member. On 30 January 1824, the United States having expressed their isolation by the Monroe Doctrine, Canning expressed his by refusing to join a Congress.

Canning had not been half-hearted in his attempt to mediate between Spain and the republics. He offered to guarantee Cuba if Spain would recognise the independence of her colonies; this offer was refused. At the same time Canning was gathering information on the state of the South American republics. In July 1824 the consul-general at Buenos Aires was empowered to make a commercial treaty with that state. Completion of such a treaty would amount to recognition, but the step was not made public, and the general question of recognition was undecided.

Meanwhile the storm against Canning had been blowing up in high places. The occasion for the first protest by the King was Canning's attendance at the Lord Mayor's banquet on Easter Monday, for the Lord Mayor on this occasion was Waithman, an extreme Whig and former protagonist of the Queen. The incident is also interesting in that it illustrates Canning's attitude to popularity. Personal and public motives were strangely mixed in the King's mind: "The public life of the individual filling the office of

Chief Magistrate of the City of London has been marked by a continued series of insults to the Government, to the monarchy and above all, personally to the king himself"; and "The king will never consent that his Government shall be degraded by such attempts to acquire popularity". He also thought that "Mr Canning could not be ignorant of this, and has long known that his visit to the Mansion House would in the highest degree be offensive and personally disagreeable".[1] Liverpool had now to find some means of soothing the King's feelings.[2] From Canning he received a long letter of explanation, and sent it to the King with a letter composed by Wellington and himself. Liverpool recalled his own attendance at a similar dinner during the impeachment of Melville in 1805, which certainly prevented the expression of public sentiments "which would indubitably have been manifested in the absence of any of the king's ministers".[3] Canning offered the same defence: his presence had curbed expressions which might have been highly embarrassing to the Government and very unfavourably received abroad. "I am, I own, decidedly of opinion that the Government should not, on such occasions, leave a clear stage to their opponents. *The City* may be a very inconvenient power in the state. But

---

1 Yonge, III, 280.
2 Canning had tried to persuade Liverpool himself to attend (E. J. Stapleton, I, 147–8) and Liverpool told the King that "he should have had no objection to have been present at the Mansion House if he had happened to be in town that week" (Yonge, *ibid.*). That unexceptionable man Lord Bexley had also written to Liverpool: "I really think it desirable that some members of the Government should attend the Lord Mayor's dinner" (Add. MSS. 38298, f. 257).
3 Yonge, III, 282. The last and most humble part of the original draft is in Wellington's handwriting.

there it is. . . . I flatter myself that I have as good right as any publick man of the present day not to be suspected of courting popularity by a compromise with Jacobinism. I have passed near thirty years in fighting the battle with it. I have incurred as much unpopularity at various times, in that contest, as any man, and have braved that unpopularity as fearlessly. But I think that the battle is now fought. I think we have gained the victory. And I think it would be something like a dereliction of publick duty not to reap the full advantages of the present position of the Government."[1] This argument was no mere afterthought, for he had written to Liverpool when announcing his intention of attending the dinner. "I think our business is to admit the extinction of party feeling, rather than show a determination to keep it alive."[2] That his attendance would be "in the highest degree offensive and personally disagreeable", he had no suspicion; and that the King's wishes had been intimated to him, as the King seemed to imagine, by Lord Francis Conyngham, he denied.[3] Those explanations sufficed to allay the storm, but the suspicion with which every step of the Foreign Secretary would be watched had been amply demonstrated.

The next occasion for disquiet was Canning's disposition to travel in the autumn of 1824. In September Canning proposed to visit Wellesley in Ireland, and the High Tories immediately scented a "Catholic" plot. Liverpool seems to have doubted Canning's discretion if faced with an enthusiastic Irish audience, and it was only with promises of

---

1 *George IV*, No. 1163. 2 E. J. Stapleton, II, 148.
3 *George IV*, No. 1163.

good behaviour that he was allowed to go. Canning seems to have accepted the doubts of his colleagues in good humour: "Depend upon my not getting into difficulties," he wrote to Liverpool, "I have inculcated privacy on Wellesley, and he has engaged for it; and I am determined not to go any where without him." A far more serious dispute arose when the King of France died, and Canning proposed to go himself upon a mission of condolence and respect.

The first objection came not from the King but from Liverpool. On 18 September Canning told Liverpool of a conversation which he had had with the King in expectation of this event: "For congratulation, whenever that might come, the mission of a grandee would probably be advisable ...that for condolence, I thought I might either send Granville to Paris...or, that as soon as we saw to what hands the new king entrusted his ministry, I might make it a pretext to go there myself, for the purpose of coming to an understanding with Villèle, supposing him to be the person...." The King's remark upon this suggestion was, "I think it would be your duty to do so."[1] Liverpool replied: "If the mission is to be in any degree political, I think it would be better that you should go than any other minister, but I doubt the policy of giving it this character. Diverging as our policy does on so many points, but more especially respecting South America, from that of the other great Powers, the arrival at Paris of any minister of ours, but particularly of a Secretary of State on such an occasion, would create alarm amongst all the other missions and their

1 E. J. Stapleton, II, 162.

respective Governments. And the very circumstance of the alarm might embarrass the French Government, and render them less disposed to be open and explicit with us than they might be through Granville or through any other ambassador in whom they knew you and the Government had implicit confidence."[1] Canning replied: "There may be all the objection which you state to the project, which I had meditated; and I am not quite sure that the purpose with which I conceived it may not be answered a short time hence in another way." He said that he did attach considerable importance to seeing Charles X and Villèle, but he admitted that the easiest solution of the present problem would be to send Granville, already destined for the Paris Embassy, on the dual mission of conveying condolence and succeeding Sir Charles Stuart.

Here it might seem that the matter would end. Canning's own version was that when he found Liverpool to be "*rather* against the measure I gave it up at once", but he had also hinted at some other means of accomplishing his purpose. On 4 October the Duke was astounded to hear from Lord Francis Conyngham that Canning intended to make a personal visit to Granville at Paris on the 15th or 16th; the announcement was made before some foreign ambassadors who "were put in a fever on hearing it, for they felt that he would make much confusion at Paris by his negotiations".[2] The revelation was not only indiscreet but also inaccurate, for Canning had named no date, but,

---

1 Yonge, III, 292 ff.
2 Add. MSS. 40340, f. 104, Arbuthnot to Peel, 3 November. It is here that Lord F. Conyngham is named as the informant.

according to his own profession, "when the novelty of the new reign shall be a little worn off, I thought and still think—that a visit to Granville there might be not only pleasant but useful". He told Liverpool of this project, and he mentioned it to the King. The King told Wellington, but saying that he had heard it not from Canning himself "but from some other quarter".[1] The King was, in fact, abusing the confidence of his Foreign Secretary, but did not reveal that it was a confidence. Wellington did nothing until he heard the announcement on 4 October naming a specific date less than two weeks ahead; this and the obvious displeasure of the ambassadors induced him to write to Canning on 5 October. Canning believed that this letter was concocted with the King.[2] Wellington's letter was not angry, and ended with the sentence, "I hope you will excuse me for the frankness with which I write to you on this subject, and will impute my doing so to the real motive, my conviction of the inconvenience to the public and annoyance to yourself which will result from it".[3] Canning's temper was never of the most even, and he now lost it; he saw in Wellington's letter not a private remonstrance but an "Ultra" plot. He began in his reply by practically doubting Wellington's account of the disclosure: "I recollect accurately the only persons to whom I have ever said a word upon the subject...and none of those persons *can* possibly have fallen into the blunder of

1 Bathurst, p. 574.
2 Wellington neither admitted nor denied this. The truth would seem to be that he wrote it alone, but knowing that he expressed the views of the King, with whom he had had conversations (cf. Bathurst, p. 574).   3 Wellington, II, 313.

the Equerrys' Room." A blunder there had certainly been, for Canning had never thought of the 16th as a possible date, but the scene in the Equerrys' Room is confirmed by Madame Lieven, who was there. Canning then brought out his strong point: Westmorland had recently had a conversation with Charles X in Paris, he had reported this to the King but not to Canning. Canning declared himself willing to forgo his visit to Paris if the King commanded him, but hoped that the King would lay "a similar interdiction" upon other ministers. He hinted also that the whole protest had been dictated by the influence of the Russian ambassador.[1] Wellington's two letters to Bathurst[2] practically clear Wellington of the accusation of acting in concert either with the King or with the ambassador, but he realised that his own dealings with the "Cottage Coterie" made it extremely difficult to offer any excuses which would be believed. The root of the whole unfortunate quarrel seems to have lain with the King, who offered no objection to Canning's proposal, but who tried to stimulate Wellington to object, and who allowed Wellington to believe that his information came from rumours, not from Canning's confidence. Even then the whole matter might have been settled verbally, but for Conyngham's foolish gossip in the Equerrys' Room.[3] After several exchanges of letters with Wellington, Canning laid his case before Liverpool. He would yield to "grave and substantial reasons", but he could not yield when he knew that

1 Wellington, II, 315.
2 Wellington, II, 315 and Bathurst, p. 574.
3 His gossip was, of course, accepted as truth since he was Canning's Private Secretary.

the whole truth was not told to him. "I *know* that the first letter...was written after a long conference with the king, which took place on Saturday the 2nd, two days after my interview with his Majesty upon my return from Ireland. I *know* that in that conference the king repeated to the Duke of Wellington what passed in my interview, because the Duke of Wellington repeated it to a person who repeated it to my informant. I know that the letter of the 5th was shown to the king before it was sent to me. And yet neither in that letter nor in any subsequent part of the correspondence is there any admission that the king was privy to it. Now this I hold not to be fair. I have the highest respect for the Duke of Wellington, and I do not presume to limit the confidences of the king. But when one finds that all that passes between the king and one's self is repeated as a matter of course to a third person, and that third person one who thinks himself at liberty to repeat it to others, at the same time as he conceals the fact of his knowing it from one's self, it is high time to look about one, and to beware of what Burke calls 'traps and mines'."

Liverpool refused to take sides in the matter. He reiterated his former objections to the Paris visit—the French Government would not risk its popularity by an ostensible *rapprochement* with the English Foreign Secretary, though it might come to an understanding through the usual diplomatic channels, "a failure, or even *negative success* in a Secretary of State is very different from the same result in a minister or ambassador", and the visit would be unpopular in England—and he made no comment upon Wellington's letter. He would object naturally to "secret influence", but might suspect that the whole incident was exaggerated; he did, however, forward Canning's letter to Wellington.[1] The Duke attempted no defence, and the whole matter was at an end, for Canning did abandon his visit to Paris. His reason for doing so, as given to Granville, shows how Canning, even when angry, was still generous and balanced: Wellington, he said, was "entitled to every consideration—even when one's opinion is not exactly the same, nothing could be so agreeable to the Ultras or so inconvenient to me, as the divergence of our opinions on any question or action, of real or supposed importance". Canning was the most forgiving of men once the occasion of dispute had passed, but Wellington neither forgave nor forgot.

In all these matters Liverpool was called upon to act both as a mediator and as a partisan. It was his business, as Prime Minister, to see that the Government was not dissolved; it was his business, as a convinced supporter of Canning, to see that his policy was pushed through the Cabinet. Throughout 1824 the question of South America hung like a great cloud on the horizon. By both parties in the Cabinet it was accepted as the great test of Canning's policy: if England recognised the South American republics, in defiance of France, of Spain, and of the Continental Alliance, she set her feet for all time on a path separate from Europe; if she did not recognise those states, she might once more play that part in the Councils of Europe which she had played under Castlereagh. Canning was deter-

[1] It is in the Wellington papers, and can only have come there if Liverpool gave it to Wellington.

mined to read "England" for "Europe"; Liverpool, who had never been completely at ease with Castlereagh's policy, was resolved to support him. Throughout the year the division in the Cabinet became more and more marked. The language Canning used in speaking of "the opposing and superior party in the Cabinet is quite unmeasured. 'THEY' have done this, and *they* choose to do that, is the mildest sort of phraseology he uses. Neither he nor Lord Liverpool conceals their feeling as to the preponderance."[1] Liverpool was Canning's only support, for Robinson and Huskisson could hardly pull their weight in such discussions, and Canning fully realised how much his position depended upon the goodwill of the Prime Minister.[2] Liverpool became to doubt his ability to carry on in this heated atmosphere, and in July he was pushing forward certain matters in his office "because I possibly may not be the person to settle them if delayed".[3] Wynn stated accurately the balance of power within the Cabinet: "I think Canning with Liverpool's support too powerful to allow the introduction of a foe, and I think that power is viewed with too much jealousy to admit of its being further increased."[4] But all asked how long this could continue; Liverpool's health seemed to be breaking down, and the rate of his pulse became a matter of national importance.[5]

1 Buckingham, II, 126, R. P. Ward to Buckingham.
2 Buckingham, II, 126: "His greatest ally is Lord Liverpool, who, to use the expression used to me, is 'Ultra against the Ultras'."
3 Buckingham, II, 110, R. P. Ward to Buckingham, 31 July.
4 *Ibid.* p. 113.
5 *Ibid.* p. 91, Fremantle to Buckingham: "How we shall meet again I won't pretend to say: it all depends entirely on Lord Liverpool's health." Colchester, Diary, 4 June: "Lord Liverpool, who for some

In July the King protested against the decision to negotiate a commercial treaty with Buenos Aires; he feared that it carried with it "the appearance and promise of an early recognition to the different insurrectionary States of South America...it is impossible that the Great Allied Powers can view the policy of this country, as regards South America, with indifference; and sooner or later this policy will endanger the peace of Europe". In view of "what he supposes to be the unanimous opinion of his Cabinet" he would not oppose, but he delivered a solemn warning: "When the Prince of Wales undertook the Regency of this Kingdom...[he] abandoned all those friends with whom he had lived on terms of the most unqualified friendship during the best years of his life: because the Prince, as Regent, thought their liberal and anti-monarchical sentiments unfavourable to the good government of his father's dominions; but the king now finds that the opinions of the opposition and liberals are uniformly acted upon. The king cannot be supposed to be blind to this state of things."[1]

"The cabal against Canning grows in strength", wrote Madame Lieven on 2 September. The autumn of 1824 was indeed a trying time for the nerves of all in political circles. Wellington was furious with Canning, and did not speak to Liverpool save at Cabinet meetings. The King said Canning was a scoundrel, Canning complained bitterly of Westmorland, who "continues to agree in measures and to differ in words, and to labour to bring down the state-

months past has always favoured and laid up *one* leg, now puts *both* legs upon the bench where he sits, and is evidently in worse health. His pulse was forty in March fifty four when he returned from Bath, and is now forty again."   1 *George IV*, No. 1187.

ment of measures to his own standard—that is, to the standard of his own language at Crockford's and White's".[1] Madame Lieven, in giving Canning a courtesy invitation to dinner, found herself in some difficulty; who was to be invited to meet him? "All the ministers have quarrelled with him. There is the same difficulty with members of the social world. I suggested it to several persons; they all begged me to excuse them from meeting him."[2] But for Liverpool Canning would have been isolated; even with Liverpool on his side it seemed that a split would be driven in the Government. "How this will all end I cannot guess," wrote Arbuthnot to Peel, "I do not mean this discussion with the Duke, for it is over, but I mean this general state of things. I feel sure that the Duke will never lose his temper. He will however watch Canning closely, and I am certain that he will agree to nothing which he thinks false policy and wrong."[3]

At the beginning of December Liverpool came in strongly on Canning's side, and circulated a memorandum urging immediate recognition of the South American states in the clearest and most forcible terms. The result was an offer of resignation by Wellington. "As for my part," he wrote, "I came into the Government to support yourself and the principles on which you had been acting, and for which we had struggled in the field for such length of time. I should wish to go on as I have done, and nothing makes me so unhappy as to differ in opinion from you. But as you know, I am not inclined to carry these differences further

1 E. J. Stapleton, I, 213.　　2 Lieven, p. 339.
3 Add. MSS. 40340, f. 104.

than is necessary; and I have advised, and shall invariably advise, his Majesty to follow the advice of his cabinet. But I can easily conceive that it must be equally irksome to you to have a colleague whose opinion upon any subject is so undecidedly different from yours; and I can only assure you that I am ready whenever you wish to retire from your government."[1] It seemed that the dreaded moment had arrived, that Cabinet unity could no longer be preserved, that Wellington, and doubtless others with him, would break off from the Government; yet, on the other hand, Wellington's letter was definitely conciliatory in tone, he included a personal compliment to Liverpool, he hinted that he would not press matters to a final crisis, he promised to use his influence with the King to make him accept the Cabinet's advice, and he placed the decision in Liverpool's hands. Liverpool replied in similar vein; he could only assure Wellington "most truly that nothing could give me more sincere pain, *privately* or *publicly*, than your separation, from any cause, from the Government";[2] he lamented the difference over South America, but asserted his very reasonable conviction that "if we allow these new states to consolidate their system and policy with the United States of America, it will in a very few years prove fatal to our greatness, if not endanger our safety"; he lamented also the "strong prejudices" of the King, and thought that he should be made to feel "that the opinion which he sometimes avows on the subject of legitimacy would carry him to the

1 Wellington, II, 365–6.
2 Yonge, III, 305. It must not be imagined that Canning was in any way desirous for Wellington's resignation. See p. 251 above.

full length of the principle of the Emperor of Russia and Prince Metternich". If the Duke's letter had been conciliatory in tone, Liverpool's was masterly in the way that it threw back the onus of decision upon Wellington, while bringing forward the two arguments to which Wellington was likely to be most sensitive. This exchange of letters made it fairly certain that Wellington would not resign, and that Liverpool and Canning could bring the full weight of their authority to bear upon the Cabinet minority and the King.

A lengthy memorandum upon the South American question was circulated in the Cabinet. The memorandum went far back into historical origins, and proceeded to the present problem. "Is it possible to leave so large a part of the world for any length of time in a state of *outlawry*?" The United States of America had already acknowledged the republics, England's commercial interests could not long delay her acknowledgment; the objection of the legitimists would be exactly the same twenty years hence; Austria, Russia and Prussia have "positively no national interest, not the slightest in the matter"; France had an interest, namely "first to thwart our views, and secondly, to profit by them when accomplished". "Are we to sacrifice the advantage and prosperity of the people of this country to the extravagant principles or prejudices of governments which have proved to us that in their own concerns in Europe they are not disposed to sacrifice a tittle of their views and their policy to the views and policy of the British Government, when a difference of opinion arises between us?" The existence of a French army of occupation in

Spain made the question urgent, "we should prevent the American dependencies of this Power from being involved in that same objection". The commerce of the states would foster England's naval power, it would certainly foster that of the United States if allowed exclusive rights of commerce. The naval supremacy of England might one day be threatened by a combination of France and the United States, but "the disposition of the new states is at present highly favourable to England. If we take the advantage of that disposition, we may establish through our influence with them a fair counterpoise to that combined maritime power. Let us not, then, throw the present golden opportunity away, which, once lost, may never be recovered."[1] The Cabinet considered this memorandum on 6 December and the all-important resolution—"that the question should be decided without reference to the opinions of Continental Allied Powers"—was passed with Sidmouth alone dissenting. But this left unsettled the main question of recognition, and Canning determined to force the issue. Through Granville he enquired whether France would undertake to withdraw her troops from Spain; and Villèle would not give such an assurance. With this additional argument in their favour, Canning and Liverpool prepared to force immediate recognition upon the King and the Cabinet. Liver-

---

[1] Yonge, III, 297–304. The authorship of the memorandum has been disputed. Yonge, whose discrimination is not to be relied upon, claims it for Liverpool. Professor Temperley thought (*Foreign Policy*, p. 498) that it was "technically at any rate, by Liverpool, with touches by Canning". But Canning sent it to Wellington and his covering note is quite clear: "The subject of the enclosed memorandum is that which I shall bring first before the Cabinet tomorrow. Lord L. only has seen it; but I will send another copy in circulation."

pool prepared a memorandum; Canning revised his.[1] Both then faced the Cabinet and threatened to resign if their advice was not taken. The plain alternative was offered—recognition of the South American states or the end of the Government—and Peel, the wisest of the Tories, reluctantly came round to their side. Sidmouth had resigned after the Cabinet of 6 December, though not ostensibly for that cause, and the "Ultras" were now in a minority. Liverpool and Canning won the day, and the Cabinet recommended that the King should recognise the South American republics. "The fight has been hard", wrote Canning triumphantly to Granville, "but it is won. The deed is done. The nail is driven. Spanish America is free; and if we do not mismanage our matters sadly, she is English and 'Novus saeclorum nascitur ordo'. You will see how nobly Liverpool fought with me on this occasion."[2]

After the Christmas holiday there came one last protest from the King: "The Jacobins of the world, now calling themselves the Liberals, saw the peace of Europe secured by their great measure and have therefore never ceased to vilify the Quadruple Alliance. The late policy of Great Britain has loosened these beneficial ties, by demonstrating

---

1 Canning to Liverpool, 11 December: "I return your paper. I have not changed the order of the topics, nor added any new one. The object of my scratchings and interpolations is chiefly to make the course of argument more clear by dividing into heads—of which there is one more than Hydra had" (viz. ten). Same, 14 December: "Your paper is very greatly improved by this alteration and addition. I am recasting mine" (Stapleton, pp. 212–13). An official memorandum was sent to the King with the Cabinet's advice; another is printed in Temperley's *Foreign Policy*, p. 550, from the Vansittart papers in the British Museum; this he believed might be the work of Canning.   2 Stapleton, *Life and Times*, p. 411.

a restless desire of self-interest in direct opposition to those wise and comprehensive principles, by which the peace and general interest of Europe were bound together."[1] And "the king would wish to ask Lord Liverpool whether he supposes, the great abettors of this South American question (connected with the Opposition) give their support to a recognition of the Spanish Provinces in relation to the great mercantile advantages which this measure may offer to this country, or from their love of democracy, in opposition to a monarchical aristocracy".[2] But the King was abandoned, and he had to admit defeat; though he did so with a bad grace.

Since the summer of 1821, save for the interlude between December 1821 and August 1822, the King had been consistently on bad terms with his Government. He had fallen readily into the schemes of the foreign ambassadors, he had helped to seduce Wellington from constitutional integrity, he had used every means to support the Cabinet opposition to Canning and Liverpool. Matters had come to a head at the end of 1824 when "the intemperance or miscalculation of the king" led to a premature *dénouement*.[3] Canning said that he would have resigned over South America, declared that he had been driven from office by the Holy Alliance, and allowed public opinion to run its course.[4] But the King was now undergoing a change of heart; he had decided to endure what could not be cured. On 27 April he sent Sir William Knighton on a courtesy

1 Stapleton, *Life and Times*, p. 418.
2 *George IV*, No. 1139.
3 Canning to Granville (E. J. Stapleton, I, 256). He may mean the controversy with Wellington. 4 *Ibid.*

visit to Canning who was ill; Knighton intimated that the King had changed his views, and had become reconciled to Canning. Before the end of the year Canning was freely and intimately enjoying the confidence of the King. At the same time the King was drawing closer to Liverpool in their common resistance to the Catholic claims. It is to those claims, and to their effect upon the course of Government, that it is now necessary to turn.

As England rejoiced in a new-found prosperity, as Canning wrote the name of England large upon the Liberal map, there remained the grim spectre of Ireland to haunt the minds of English statesmen. English rule was the rule of a Protestant minority, and the High Tories saw clearly something from which "liberals" always turned their faces, that, without the exclusion of Catholics from the Government, it could no longer be English. If the Irish masses—whom Pitt had indiscreetly enfranchised—returned the men of their choice, Westminster would be overrun with Irish demagogues, Dublin Castle would fall to the Catholics, and the separation of the two countries must finally ensue. This idea was the basis of Liverpool's resistance to Catholic Emancipation; it was not always possible to state the naked alternatives, and it was necessary to clothe them in the time-worn arguments of dual allegiance and the Pope's political power; but in insisting that the Irish question was not religious, that it was political and social, Liverpool had the root of the matter. The weakness of the Protestant argument lay in the necessity for suppressing social and religious tendencies in order to assert a political fact, the English hegemony. Liverpool was not an intolerant man, and his attitude to the Catholics is shown clearly by his support, in 1824, of two bills, one to enfranchise English Roman Catholics, the other to allow Roman Catholics to act as magistrates.[1] Concessions might be made to the Catholics in England, where they formed an upper class minority with little political influence; they must be resisted in Ireland, where the Catholics formed a popular majority with potential political power.

Since the House of Lords had thrown out Plunket's Relief Bill in 1821, much had happened to confirm the Protestants in their view. In 1823 all secret societies had been superseded by O'Connell's Catholic Association, a representative body of Irish Catholics which provided itself with funds by the "Catholic Rent", a subscription of one penny a month from all members. O'Connell succeeded in uniting all Irish Catholics, priests and laity, in the demand for unconditional Emancipation. Catholic Emancipation, from being the favourite project of liberal-minded Englishmen, became the popular demand of nationalist Ireland.

Friends of Ireland had hoped for happier days when Talbot, a narrow-minded High Tory, had been succeeded by Wellesley, and when Plunket went to Ireland as Attorney-General. But, in spite of Wellesley's continued optimism, matters went from bad to worse; it was necessary to apply the Insurrection Act to check the Catholic Association; bottles were thrown at the Lord Lieutenant in Dublin Theatre; Plunket failed in his prosecution of O'Connell,

---

[1] In spite of Liverpool's support the bills were lost. Part of the second allowed the Duke of Norfolk to exercise his hereditary function of Earl Marshal, but even this was refused.

and only succeeded in embroiling himself with the Orange Association. These events embittered feelings on the Catholic Question: the "Protestants" cried all the louder for resistance, the "Catholics" pointed with ever-insistent logic to the need for concession.

On 19 November 1824 the King dropped a bombshell. "The king is apprehensive that a notion is gone abroad that the king himself is not unfavourable to the Catholic claims. It is high time for the king to protect himself against such an impression, and he has no hesitation in declaring that if the present proceedings continue, he will no longer consent to Catholic Emancipation being left as an open question in his Cabinet. This indulgence was originally granted on the ground of political expediency, but that expediency dissolves when threatened rebellion calls upon the king for that which the king never will grant."[1] This letter was sent to Peel, to be shown to Wellington and Eldon. Wellington first thought that it should be kept secret—"it would really create an alarm which it is not intended to create, and can do no good"—but upon consideration he thought it should be shown to Liverpool. "When it is shown to him it becomes of no importance; as long as it is concealed from him it is of importance, and the concealment gives an air of intrigue." Liverpool saw the King and heard from him "nothing which gave the slightest uneasiness or cause for complaint".[2] Nevertheless the incident was disturbing, for the man behind the King's protest was the Duke of York, the heir to the throne and the centre of the extreme High Tory group; it seemed that pressure might soon be exerted

1 Parker, I, 349.   2 Ibid. p. 351.

to drive the "Catholics" out of the Government. Fortunately the last people who desired this were the High Tories in the Cabinet; they knew that, so long as Liverpool was Prime Minister and the question was "open", Catholic Emancipation might not pass.

Something had, however, to be done with the Catholic Question; the King had threatened to break the Government if something were not done, and Wellington had written: "If we cannot get rid of the Catholic Association, we must look to Civil War in Ireland."[1] At the beginning of the session of 1825 a bill against all Associations—preserving a show of impartiality by banning the Orange Association as well—was introduced and supported by the "Catholic" ministers. Liverpool's speech is remarkable for its extreme forbearance: "I believe there are many innocent, many well-disposed members of that Association. I believe that the great majority of the Association do not see the dangers which they are bringing on their country. But my objection to the Association is, that no such body can exist in any nation, or under any state of things, without the production of the greatest evils. I impute no special blame to it, as distinguished from similar bodies. I well know what any men so associated could do and say; of how much intemperance they must necessarily be guilty, of what endless evils their combination must be productive. ...If the Catholics of Ireland are to be permitted to associate, who would say that the Protestants also would not unite? It is the natural course of things; combination necessarily leads to counter combination. Nor, however

1 Parker, I, 348.

superior in number the Catholics in Ireland may be, are the Protestants so contemptible in point of numbers, wealth, intelligence and character, as not to constitute a formidable party; and under such circumstances, how is justice to be administered in Ireland? What must be the result of permitting the existence of rival societies, each supported by the whole strength of one religious party, and of necessity full of animosity against every other? Nothing less... than an aggravation of all the evils from which Ireland has suffered; nothing less than to give additional strength and vehemence to all those feelings, by which dissension will be fomented and religious animosities increased."[1]

All the difficulties of the Government now gathered around the Emancipation Bill introduced by Sir Francis Burdett. It passed through all stages in the House of Commons by the end of April, and awaited its fate in the Lords. Much would turn upon the line taken by the Prime Minister; should he accept the verdict of the Commons, Emancipation would not be delayed, and rumours had been industriously circulated of his "supposed conversion to popery". A denial of these rumours was inserted in the *Courier*,[2] but some still thought the language of the denial not very emphatic.

At this stage Peel intimated to Liverpool that, having been beaten in the House of Commons, he could not remain in office. Liverpool replied that if Peel resigned, he too must resign; he would resign in any case if Emancipation passed the Lords, and how could he fill Peel's office when he did not expect to remain many weeks in office

1 Yonge, III, 321-5.   2 An unusual course of action.

himself? The simplest solution would be for Peel and himself, the two Protestant ministers, to retire and leave the rest to settle the Catholic Question. The High Tories were in great alarm, and they urgently pressed Liverpool and Peel to reconsider. Liverpool showed himself full of scruples: "How could I carry on the Government with dignity or credit without some *organ* of my own sentiments, and of the Protestant feeling in the House of Commons?" he asked Bathurst, who took an unusually forward part in this matter. "You would not wish me, I am sure, to close a long political life with disgrace. This must inevitably be the case if I appear now to be clinging to office when my opinions have been overruled in the House of Commons and when I cannot expect to be able to defend the Protestant cause much longer in the House of Lords."[1] Bathurst replied by speaking of the reliance which the Church placed upon him, and concluded: "It is your duty to cling to office, when by so doing you cling to your principles and your friends."[2] And when it seemed that entreaty to Liverpool failed, Bathurst and Wellington turned to Peel; "I will not call to your recollection to what a personally painful struggle you are exposing the king, by making a change of councils necessary, nor what may be felt by the University, who placed their confidence in you at so early a period of your political life. But is it fair to the public, who are doing you at this moment justice for the firmness of temper with which you have singly as a minister in the House of Commons maintained your opinions?...I am aware of the popularity which is apt to follow any display

1 Bathurst, p. 580.　　　　2 *Ibid.* p. 585.

of indifference to office; but you will find that public men, who have by their resignations exposed the country to great trouble and sudden convulsions, are not easily forgiven."[1] In response to these arguments Peel ultimately and reluctantly withdrew his resignation, but meanwhile the existence of the Government had been saved in the House of Lords.

When, on 17 May, the peers met to debate the Catholic Bill, those in the confidence of ministers knew that more was at stake than the acceptance or rejection of the measure. If it passed Liverpool would resign, for he had written to Wellington: "The more I reflect upon the question, the more impossible it appears to me that I should be a party to the *new system*, much less the instrument of carrying it into effect."[2] If Liverpool went, the Government could not continue. The Whigs were nearer than they knew to the brink of office on 17 May.

Feelings ran high. On 25 April the country had been startled by an unexpected and unprecedented event. The Duke of York, presenting a petition against Emancipation from the Canons of Windsor, reminded the House of his father's resistance to the Catholic claims, and hinted that he might soon be in his father's place, when he said that he would continue that resistance "to the latest moment of my life, whatever may be my situation in life. So Help me God!" Encouraged by this royal example, and little deterred by Whig complaints of unconstitutional interference,

1 Parker, I, 374–5.
2 Wellington, II, 435. Canning does not seem to have been aware of this consequence, at least he gave no hint of such knowledge. Liverpool studiously refrained from making his resolution public for that would have prejudiced the question unfairly.

Protestant fervour manifested itself in every part of the country. Copies of the Duke's speech emblazoned in gold were popular purchases, and the old cry of "No Popery" was heard once more in the streets. The 17th of May was such a night as is rarely seen in the House of Lords. The debate had already gone on for several hours when the Prime Minister rose to speak; Lord Colchester, the Speaker Abbot of Protestant glory, had moved the postponement of the bill for six months; the Church, personified by the Bishops of Llandaff and Chester, had supported him; Lord Anglesey, a former friend of the Catholics, had said: "Every concession that has been made to them had been followed by increased restlessness and sedition; their conduct and the language which they have adopted are such as to show that emancipation alone would not satisfy them, and that they would be content with nothing but Catholic ascendancy." The opinion of the House seemed slightly against the measure, but its fate, if not immediately at least in the near future, depended upon the tone of Liverpool's speech. His speech was an uncompromising rejection of the Catholic claims, phrased in language far more vehement than he had ever before used. "My peculiar objection to the Roman Catholic religion is that it penetrates into every domestic scene, and inculcates a system of tyranny never known elsewhere.... I say that, if this measure should pass, the Protestant succession would not be worth a farthing.... The House ought not to deceive the people. They ought at once to declare that, if the bill were to pass, Great Britain would no longer be a Protestant State. The evil I apprehend from the passing of such a bill will not be immediate, but it will be inevitable, and it will come upon the country in a manner little expected.... Can the House...not see that a great and powerful engine is at work to effect the object of re-establishing the Catholic religion throughout these kingdoms? And if once established, shall we not revert to a state of ignorance, with all its barbarous and direful consequences? For the last hundred and thirty years the country had enjoyed a state of religious peace, a blessing which has arisen from the wisdom of our laws. Those laws granted toleration to all religious creeds, at the same time that they maintained a just, reasonable and a moderate superiority in favour of the established Church. Your lordships are now called upon to put Protestants and Roman Catholics upon the same footing; and if you consent to do this, certain I am that the consequence will be religious dissension not religious peace."[1] The result of the debate was a magnificent majority of forty-eight for Protestantism.

"God be thanked", wrote the King to Liverpool. "I congratulate you most sincerely on your successful efforts of last night."[2] "Nobody", said Canning, "expected other than a defeat; but the vehemence of L's speech was an astounding disappointment."[3] It may now be asked what were Liverpool's real sentiments upon the Catholic question; not as a matter of principle, for he had shown himself opposed beyond all hope of compromise, but as a matter of political expediency. The surprising answer is that he was convinced it must pass, was prepared to facilitate its passing,

1 Yonge, III, 331 ff. 2 Wellington, II, 451.
3 E. J. Stapleton, I, 270.

and in particular to recommend Canning to the King as his successor; to Bathurst he wrote: "The *crisis* cannot be averted many months. I should be forced out, if not by any direct act of my colleagues, by the circumstances of the Government. Whenever the *crisis does come*, the *Protestants* must go to the wall."[1] He proposed to go while he could go honourably, and to the consternation of the Duke suggested Canning as his successor. Canning seems also to have contemplated resignation. Five days after the Lords' debate, Liverpool wrote to Bathurst: "I cannot, however, agree with you that it would be right for me to let Canning resign, if the majority of the Cabinet should still be for keeping the question in *abeyance*, and then give up the Government as incapable of forming one on the exclusive protestant principle. It appears to me to be my duty to inform the king of the actual state of his Government and let him know that the formation of a Government upon the principle of resisting the Catholic claims is *absolutely impracticable*, whereas the formation of a Government upon the opposite principle, even from amongst his present servants with some few additions, is within his power."[2] Peel's withdrawal of his resignation, the genuine alarm of his colleagues, and the prospect of the King's obstruction to any "Catholic" ministry, induced Liverpool to give up this resolution. He would stay in office, but he would do nothing further to postpone the ultimate and inevitable concession of the Catholic claims.

This resolution was put to the test immediately. The Parliament had been elected in 1820, it had still a year of

1 Bathurst, p. 580.   2 *Ibid.* p. 583.

statutory life, but it was without precedent to allow a
Parliament its full statutory life. The Protestant enthusiasm
aroused by the Duke of York's speech was still running
high, and, as Canning wrote to Granville, "a dissolution at
present would give us a 'No Popery' Parliament, and array
England against Ireland".[1] For precisely this reason Wellington urged a dissolution. "It is impossible", he wrote to
Liverpool, "that, constituted as the government is, you
should dissolve Parliament upon the declared principle of
an appeal to the people upon the Roman Catholic question
...but I should contend that, viewing the question as you
and Peel do, as one of principle, and seeing the difficulties
and dangers from which by tranquillity and good management alone we recently extricated ourselves, it is a point of
duty to decide upon the period of the dissolution in reference only to the effect which that decision might produce
eventually upon the Roman Catholic Question in the House
of Commons."[2] Liverpool deferred the decision until September, and in the middle of that month a minor Cabinet
battle took place. Canning wrote very fairly to Liverpool:
"As to the general reasons for or against [dissolution],
supposing the Catholic question out of the way, I think
there can be no doubt but that those for it greatly pre-
dominate";[3] but, whether avowedly so or not, dissolution
would appear as an appeal upon the Catholic Question.
Liverpool inclined to a dissolution now, but both he and
Canning were prepared to admit the arguments of the
other. On 12 September Canning, who had been making

1 E. J. Stapleton, I, 272.
2 Wellington, II, 463–4.   3 E. J. Stapleton, I, 289.

a tour of the country houses, was more definite; the friends whom he had seen and his correspondents were as one in urging "that there is a fury upon the Catholic question, ready to break forth, the instant that the now expected dissolution takes place".[1] Liverpool's own solution, which was the one finally adopted, was ingenious: "If we can *all* agree to keep the Catholic and the Corn question in abeyance during the next session, I am very indifferent as to immediate dissolution."[2] The Government and the House of Lords were saved from the inconvenience of another pro-Catholic vote in the Commons; and Canning loyally supported Liverpool by sending a circular letter impressing upon Catholic sympathisers the inexpediency of raising the question in the last session of an expiring Parliament.

Yet the doubts and dissensions of the ministers were not at rest, and a symptom of this is the number of small but irritating problems which began to gather around the harassed Prime Minister. An unfortunate division of opinion arose over the election to a vacancy in the representative peerage of Ireland. Clanricarde, Canning's son-in-law, put himself forward, and was opposed by the Orange Lord Farnham; at home Canning urged the claims of Clanricarde, Peel took up the battle for Lord Farnham.

1 E. J. Stapleton, I, 293.
2 Wellington, II, 499; Add. MSS. 40305, f. 86, Liverpool to Peel: If the Government supporters of Catholic · Emancipation were "prepared to discourage its being brought on, and if brought on, to move a previous question or adjournment upon it...I have no desire to press the dissolution during the present autumn. I say *press the dissolution*, because I think the reasons for and against it are nearly balanced."

Liverpool had to reconcile the two and point objections to both candidates. Clanricarde had involved himself in the sedition of the Catholic Association by paying the Catholic Rent; Liverpool would overlook this youthful folly but thought his candidature would raise more problems than it would solve. Against Farnham there was a more serious objection, for he was cited as a stock example of the brutal Irish landlord; to support this there was a disgraceful incident in which, while sitting on the magistrates' bench, he had flogged a boy in person. "Indeed", Liverpool told Peel, "I do not know how I could consistently with the Principles on which I have invariably acted, press Lord Farnham upon the Lord Lieutenant."[1] The King too had his candidate in Lord Glengall, but Liverpool did not think that he would insist.[2] The Earl of Westmeath proposed himself and began to canvass. Liverpool put forward the Earl of Mount Cashell as the most unexceptionable candidate, but no sooner had he received Government support than he expressed himself violently in public against the Catholics. "Is there no other eligible person", asked Canning, "who at least has not shown himself to be such a goose? And such a violent goose too?"[3] Westmeath offered to retire and place the votes he had gained at Mount Cashell's disposal if the Government would support him in a future election; this Liverpool refused, for such a promise would tempt every Irish peer to make a similar bargain. Finally, in spite of letters written by Liverpool to promi-

1 Add. MSS. 38300, f. 194.
2 Add. MSS. 38300, f. 195: "His Majesty does not care about Lord Glengall, he was persuaded by others."
3 E. J. Stapleton, II, 300.

nent Irish peers, Protestant fury won the day for the odious
Lord Farnham.

The dissolution of Parliament brought forward another
host of problems. Wellington advised Liverpool to keep
Government influence in his own hands, "and not to allow
yourself to attend to the recommendation of anybody for a
seat in Parliament whom you should not have a hope that
he would oppose further concessions".[1] But Liverpool remained scrupulously fair; ten seats were placed at his disposal, and "Catholics" and "Protestants" were given five
each.[2] Throughout the country the division of the Tory
party was reflected upon the hustings. Canning's friend
Gladstone opposed the Beresfords at Berwick; Palmerston
with the help of Whig votes just defeated the Protestant
Goulbourn at Cambridge University; and Wellington became furiously angry when he heard reports, probably inaccurate, of free trade promises made by Huskisson at
Liverpool. To Peel's disgust Liverpool refused Government aid to Holme Sumner in Surrey, and the seat was lost
to Liverpool's Whiggish friend Pallmer. Elsewhere "No
Popery" defeated well-established Whigs; Lord John
Russell lost Huntingdonshire, Lord Howick lost Northum-
berland, Brougham failed to steal a Lowther seat in Westmorland, Taunton and Chippenham both went to High
Tories. The Tories gained in all forty-two seats in England,
Scotland and Wales, mostly won by Protestants; the Whigs
gained only twenty-three. In Ireland, however, the Whigs
gained twelve, and the Tories eight. The Government came

1 Wellington, III, 314.
2 Wellesley, II, 160.

back with an increased majority, but the division between High and Liberal Tory, between Protestant and Catholic, was more marked than it had ever been before. The position of a Prime Minister who was both Liberal and Protestant was becoming increasingly difficult; the great Tory peers were "out of sorts with the Government",[1] and the new Parliament was faced with the dangerous topic of Corn and the inevitable Catholic question.

This unpleasing prospect was not relieved by any cessation of personal quarrels. The dissolution had occasioned a fresh batch of peers; the King agreed to Liverpool's list with more cordiality than he had ever shown on such questions, but the High Tories saw in it the dread hand of Canning. "Everybody", wrote Greville, "cries out against Charles Ellis's peerage; he has no property, and is of no family and his son is already a peer....Clanricarde, too, being made a Marquis and an English peer is thought an indirect exertion of Canning's influence."[2] The Duke of Devonshire was given a Garter, in spite of a protest by Wellington.[3] Canning's friend Morley insisted that he had a claim to the Post Office, vacant by Lord Chichester's death; Wellington demanded a bishopric for his brother Gerald. Morley was least able and most disliked of Canning's friends, and Liverpool told Canning that Morley would be a most unpopular and unsuitable appointment. Morley was prepared to treat for a peerage, but Liverpool

1 Wellington's phrase: Add. MSS. 38302, f. 117.
2 Greville, 1, 160–1. Ellis was an old friend of Canning, and Liverpool's nephew; his son was Lord Howard de Walden.
3 Add. MSS. 38302, f. 117.

saw danger ahead: "Our last batch of peers", he told Canning, "is so unpopular that I am not prepared to add to the number." A solution might be to put Robinson in the Lords, Palmerston in his place, and make Morley Secretary at War; but this would be "considered at this time as an admission of Robinson's failure". He concluded that "bad as the appointment will be, and nothing can be worse in itself, I think the *single evil* less than creating new ones"; he would propose Morley to the King, but "if His Majesty objects, I do not feel called upon to press it. I am no Whig, and though I have proved that I am prepared to *press* a point when I am convinced I am clearly right, I cannot press a point upon my Sovereign when I know that I am *wrong*."[1] Apparently the King did object, for Lord Frederick Montagu was appointed Postmaster-General.

The question of Wellington's brother was peculiarly unfortunate, for, though in most ways unexceptionable, Gerald Wellesley was separated from his wife. He did not institute divorce proceedings, so the assumption was that his wife could recriminate. Lord Wellesley first advanced his brother's claims, then appeared to recognise Liverpool's objections, but wrote to Wellington urging him to press their brother's case with all the means in his power. An extremely bitter correspondence ensued between Wellington and Liverpool. Liverpool was much hurt by Wellington's accusations: he could not accuse himself of having overlooked Wellington's fair pretensions, and for his family "I have done much more...than I have for my

[1] Add. MSS. 38301, fs. 262 ff.

own".[1] Liverpool carried his point, but the incident did not improve his relationship with Wellington.

Hints had been given in 1825, and perhaps Wellington suspected Liverpool's real intentions. Those intentions he confided to Canning during 1825, and to Arbuthnot at the beginning of 1827. Canning said later that Liverpool was anxious "to have the trial of strength on the Catholic question as early as possible in the new Parliament. If the issue should be in favour of the Catholics and he fully expected it to be so—he would (in my conscience I believe) have retired, recommending to the king to form a Government fit to manage the final adjustment of the question, and to the House of Lords to acquiesce in that adjustment."[2] To Arbuthnot he said that he was determined to retire at the end of the session in 1827; he said that "not only quiet and retirement were requisite for his much shattered health, but that the time had arrived when he felt it necessary to take into consideration the Catholic claims"; he himself had taken too prominent a part against the Catholics, and he could neither desert Peel nor carry Emancipation without him.[3] Liverpool anticipated the inevitable concession; he could not take an active part in granting it, but it would be facilitated by the passive act of resignation.

With this in his mind, the action taken by the Duke of York in November 1826 was peculiarly embarrassing. In the last few years York, as the heir to a sovereign who

---

1 Yonge, III, 383–96, for the whole correspondence.
2 Wellesley, II, 160. He was slightly more definite, but still reserved as to details in January 1827 (Temperley, *E.H.R.* 1930, quoting letters of Joan Canning). See Appendix B: "Canning's Supposed Negotiations with the Whigs."   3 Parker, III, 353.

was almost a chronic invalid, had gradually come to play a more prominent part in politics. He had viewed with increasing mistrust the trend of affairs, and his good humour had not been restored by Liverpool's refusal to engage the Government to pay his debts.[1] Then in November he realised that he would never be King, that his limbs were swollen with incurable dropsy, and that his splendid constitution had given out before his brother's rotten physique and astonishing vitality. It was with the awful solemnity of one who knows his days are short that he sought an interview with Liverpool to make a protest against the whole course of government—half-measures were leading to disaster, a firm stand must be taken, an exclusively Protestant ministry must be formed—and he spoke the general alarm of Churchmen and Tory squires. Fortunately all other High Tories and the King had abandoned the idea of an exclusive Protestant ministry as an ideal not to be found in an imperfect world. Tactfully ignored by the High Tory ministers, snubbed by the King, the Duke went back to die with the pathetic knowledge of having led a forlorn hope.

One other embarrassment was to come from the royal family. When the Duke of York died, the Commandership-in-Chief became vacant. There was only one possible choice for his successor, but for some reason the King hesitated.

[1] Liverpool to Sir Herbert Taylor, the Duke's Secretary: " I am willing to deal liberally with respect to the house. It is an intelligible and a limited object. But with respect to the debts, not even the Duke himself knows what they are. I am satisfied that the Government by implicating themselves in them, might occasion a Revolution in the country ": Add. MSS. 38302, f. 21.

Wellington was prepared to see the hand of Canning even in this, but Peel assured him that the extraordinary reason was an idea of the King that he himself might become Commander-in-Chief. Liverpool called the idea "preposterous", and Wellington was appointed. The result was more satisfactory than might have been expected, for it came near to effecting a reconciliation between Wellington and Liverpool.

But before this the Cabinet quarrel had returned to the familiar theme of foreign policy, and Liverpool was able to perform one last service for Canning by aiding him to his greatest triumph. On 10 March 1826 died John VI of Portugal. His heir was Dom Pedro, the Emperor of Brazil, but the security of the kingdom was threatened by the exiled younger son, Dom Miguel, and his mother the Queen. Before his death John had appointed a Council of Regency from which both were excluded. On 22 June came news from Brazil: Dom Pedro resigned the crown of Portugal to his eight-year-old daughter and appointed his sister, Infanta Isabel, as Regent; before abdicating he had performed one act of sovereignty, he had given Portugal a constitution. This was to unite the throne with the Portuguese liberals, but there was also a strong absolutist party which looked to Dom Miguel, to the Queen-Mother Carlotta, and to her brother, Ferdinand of Spain. Canning was "*little* pleased" to hear of the constitution—which was certainly a very bad one—but his sense of humour was delighted by the spectacle of Metternich trying to prove that even a king could not introduce fundamental change. On 11 July he sent a circular to Paris, Berlin and Vienna, which denied any English complicity in Dom Pedro's action, but warned the powers against interference in Portugal. On 24 July the Ambassadors' Conference at Paris took the hint and advised Spain not to interfere. But a new situation arose when Portuguese troops attached to Miguel deserted and crossed into Spain, and Spain lent countenance and succour to these deserters who began to muster for an invasion of Portugal.

On 19 September Canning arrived in Paris on that long-promised visit to Granville. In secret meetings he brought the French and the Russians round to his side, and, when news arrived of military preparations among the Portuguese deserters, he ordered Lamb, the ambassador at Madrid, to withdraw unless they were dispersed. On the 7th he cancelled this instruction as the Spanish seemed to be complying, but England had threatened once and the threat would be carried out if the same provocation arose.

On 10 October Liverpool wrote a long and particularly interesting letter to Canning. There are those who have believed that Liverpool was simply a puppet in Canning's hands, but this letter, written during Canning's absence, showed him to be more Canningite than Canning himself. He began by expressing the hope that joint Anglo-French action might bring Spain to reason, but "Suppose, however, Spain to become the *aggressor*, and Portugal *to call upon us* as her ally?" He would first issue an order "for seizing and detaining all ships under the Spanish flag in every part of the world", declaring that they would be restored "in case just satisfaction was given within a reasonable time". He would call upon the allied powers to use their influence with Spain, "upon the principle that as both Spain and Portugal were independent kingdoms, neither had a right to interfere in the internal concerns of the other". And "I would announce to the Allies that if they declined the proposed intervention, *or* if they should fail in compelling Spain to retrace her steps, we should be forced to play the whole game of liberal institutions in Spain as well as in Portugal; that we should send the Spanish patriots now in England or on the Continent to Gibraltar, and should spare no exertion to raise the Standard of the Constitution again in Spain".[1]

Canning returned home on·25 October and found a violent opposition in the Cabinet; Wellington complained that Canning, on his sole authority, had run the risk of war by recalling Lamb, and there was the accumulated bitterness of four years in his letter to Bathurst: "Canning certainly is the most extraordinary man. Either his mind does not seize a case accurately, or he forgets the impressions which ought to be received from what he reads, or is stated to him; or knowing or remembering the accurate state of the case, he distorts and misrepresents facts in his instructions to his ministers with a view to entrap the consent of the Cabinet to some principle on which he would found a new-fangled system."[2] Liverpool supported Canning; once more the opposite parties in the Cabinet were arrayed in the familiar way; once more the Ultras had to yield.

But Spain was not to be warned; her hostility towards

1 Yonge, III, 406–7.
2 Bathurst, p. 615. Omitted without indication from Wellington, III, 403.

Portugal became more open, the raids of the Spanish armed deserters became more daring. The Portuguese Government appealed to England, and on 8 December a despatch from Sir William A'Court convinced Canning of the urgency of the matter. On the following day the Cabinet decision was taken. Three days later troops were embarking for Portugal. The gesture was rewarded with complete success; by the end of the year Portugal was peaceful within, and those who had threatened her frontiers were disarmed and dispersed by the Government which had fostered their attempt. It was Canning's greatest diplomatic triumph, it was also the occasion of his greatest parliamentary triumph. "We go to Portugal, not to rule, not to dictate, not to prescribe constitutions—but to defend and preserve the independence of an ally. We go to plant the Standard of England on the well-known heights of Lisbon. Where that Standard is planted, foreign dominion shall not come!" And later, in his reply, he placed his whole foreign policy under review and closed with that most famous declaration: "Contemplating Spain, such as her ancestors had known her, I resolved that if France had Spain, it should not be Spain 'with the Indies'. I called the New World into existence to redress the balance of the Old."

Canning and the Government had never stood higher in public estimation, yet the difficulties of that Government were no less. Liverpool knew that his time was short, perhaps in this life, certainly as head of the ministry. On 16 December he wrote to Robinson, who had found in his wife's continual ill-health an honourable excuse to absent himself from the labours of Westminster and to ask for removal to an easier office and the House of Lords:[1] "I must begin by telling you that I have been *very ill*. I am recovering, but this last illness I cannot but consider as a hint that I am better fitted now for repose than for the labours, and still more for the anxieties of the situation which I have held for so many years.... I cannot in a letter enter into all the particulars, but be assured the Government hangs by a thread. The Catholic question in its present state, combined with other circumstances, will, I have little doubt, lead to its dissolution in the course of this session; and any attempt to make a *move* now, in the more efficient offices, would infallibly hasten the crisis."[2] He had set himself two tasks—to carry the new Corn Law, and to facilitate the accession of Canning—neither was he destined to accomplish.

Upon the Corn Law "he was resolved to stake (more perhaps than any minister...has ever done upon any measure of such a nature), that eminent reputation, which was naturally most dear, as well as most honourable to an individual in his exalted station, and if necessary, that station itself".[3] After that he would recommend Canning as his successor, and he would perhaps use what remained of his authority in persuading others to accept Canning. These were anxieties enough for a man who already felt himself exhausted in body and mind.

On 16 February Joseph Planta had never seen Liverpool

1 Add. MSS. 38302, f. 113.   2 Yonge, III, 438–9.
3 Canning in the House of Commons, 1 March 1827; Hansard, XVI, 759.

"in higher force—or in more comfortable state", but that night the speaker who was never at a loss for a word, seemed to stumble and referred to the Duchess of Clarence as a "worthy and deserving object". At ten o'clock on the following morning he was found lying paralysed on the floor of his breakfast room. It was as though a pillar of the Constitution had fallen; everyone felt a loss, few a personal loss. Greville remarked how little anybody seemed to care about the man, Croker found "no grief, or even a decent pensiveness".[1] During a month of intense political speculation Liverpool lay unconscious. On 25 March he rallied sufficiently to answer a question; when Lady Liverpool hoped that he would soon be well enough to resume business, he murmured, "No, no, not I—too weak, too weak". It was his last appearance on the political stage, for his utterance "relieved the Ministers from the silence which delicacy had imposed upon them".[2] The ministry of Lord Liverpool was at an end.

Liverpool lingered for nearly two years in a semi-conscious condition before he died on 4 December 1828. On the 8th his body was taken to the family vault at Hawkesbury in Gloucestershire. His funeral was as un-ostentatious as his life, but "the absence of public splendour was amply supplied by the strongest exhibition of public feeling".[3] Of public men only his brother-in-law, the Marquis of Bristol, his Kingston friend Pallmer, Lord Sidmouth, and the Duke of Clarence followed the hearse; but the inhabitants of Kingston lined the road to pay a last

1 Greville, I, 168; Croker, I, 362.   2 Croker, I, 366.
3 This account is taken from the *Gentleman's Magazine* of 1828.

tribute. So "amid his good works and his charities and attended by the tears of the multitude, his lordship received the parting blessing of a community, to which for more than twenty-six years he had been an unceasing benefactor".

With Liverpool's funeral cortège went also the dead body of the old Tory party—the party of George III and of Mr Pitt, the party which inherited the flamboyant creed of "Church and King", the party whose honest unthinking supporters had stood behind two generations of able administrators. Canning was already dead and his followers were estranged from the party; Wellington and Peel were thinking of a strategic retreat upon the Catholic Question; Whigs had presumed to enter the Council Chamber and were hopefully awaiting the day when they might take full possession. The Tory Government had been identified with Liverpool, it was amply proved that no one could take his place.

The English party system in the 1820's did not represent a sociological division. The clash of opinions within the Cabinet did represent a clash of interest in the country at large, but it was of great value to England to have at the head of affairs a man who was an administrator rather than a partisan. Thereby England learnt a small part of the hardest political lesson, the separation of personal interests and political judgment. A bold man might have done more, he might have done much less. Nor, with all his caution, did Liverpool lack courage, and he was able, often against great difficulties, to give England the Government and the policy which he desired. Above all his great honesty made a deep impression in the country; it, as much as any other thing, helps to bar off the politics of the nineteenth century from those of the eighteenth. It was this integrity of character, combined with real but not striking abilities, which secured him at the head of the Government, and it was this, as much as the brilliance of Canning, which earned for the Government the respect of the middle classes. The greatest merit of the Government lies in the fact that it represented more than a single class, and more than a single interest; for this phenomenon Liverpool can claim as much credit as any man. If the historian feels, at times, tempted to sneer at his lack of brilliance, if his career seems pedestrian and uninspired, then the historian may call to mind Liverpool's own motto, "Palma non sine pulvere".

APPENDIX A

THE MERCANTILE INTEREST

This list includes all those who can be shown to have had immediate mercantile connections. Some, in spite of their connection, would undoubtedly have preferred to think of themselves as country gentlemen.[1] The most probable omission is of a number of West India proprietors.[2]

Alexander, J. Alexander, J. D.	Old Sarum	Connected with the E. India trade.
Astell, W.	Bridgwater	Director, E. India Co.
Attwood, M.	Callington	Banker and London merchant.
Baillie, J.	Heydon	A "nabob".
Baring, Sir T. Baring, Alexander Baring, Henry	Wycombe Taunton Colchester	Sons of Sir Francis Baring, the financier.
Beecher, W. W.	Mallow	
Bent, J.	Totnes	W. India planter.
Benyon, Ben	Stafford	
Bernal, R.	Rochester	Barrister, father a W. India planter.
Birch, J.	Nottingham	Liverpool merchant.
Blake, Sir F.	Berwick	Banker of Newcastle.
Bridges, Sir G.	London	A former Lord Mayor.
Bright, H.	Bristol	W. India merchant.
Brogden, J.	Launceston	Russia merchant. Chairman of the Committee of the House.
Butterworth, J.	Dover	A "Saint", a methodist, and a bookseller.
Buxton, T. F.	Weymouth	Brewer, philanthropist, and dissenter.
Calvert, N.	Hertford	Brewer.

1 Thus in 1826 W. W. Whitmore, a director of the East India Company, referred to himself as a member of the landed interest (Letter to the Electors of Bridgnorth). The Whitmores had been established in Shropshire for over two hundred years, so there was justice in his claim; the landed property of others was not more than a generation old.

2 Hansard, 22 May 1823. Mr Forbes "saw more clearly than ever that the West India interest in the House was paramount to every other".

Calvert, C.	Southwark	Brother to above.
Calvert, J.	Huntingdon	Cousin to above.
Carter, J.	Portsmouth	Brewer.
Chaloner, R.	York	York banker, brother-in-law to Lord Dundas.
Cherry, G. H.	Dunwich	A "nabob".
Cockerell, Sir C.	Evesham	Banker, E. India merchant.
Collett, E. J.	Cashell	Hop merchant of Southwark.
Cripps, J.	Cirencester	Banker of Cirencester.
Crompton, S.	Retford	Derby banker.
Curtis, Sir W.	London	Merchant (biscuits, fisheries, brewing).
Dent, J.	Poole	London banker.
Divett, T.	Gatton	
Ellison, C.	Newcastle	Banker of Newcastle.
Gaskell, B.	Maldon	Manufacturer.
Gordon, R.	Cricklade	London merchant.
Grossett, J. R.	Chippenham	
Gurney, Hudson	Newtown (I. of W.)	Bankers of Norwich.
Gurney, R. H.	Norwich	
Haldimand, W.	Ipswich	Bank director.
Heygate, W.	Sudbury	Alderman and banker of London.
Hodson, J.	Wigan	
Horrocks, S.	Preston	Manufacturer.
Houldsworth, T.	Pontefract	Manchester manufacturer.
Hume, J.	Aberdeen	
Huskisson, W.	Chichester	
Innis, J.	Grampound	London merchant.
Irving, J.	Bramber	London merchant.
Maberley, J.	Abingdon	Army contractor.
Maberley, W. L.	Northampton	Son of above.
Madocks, W. A.	Chippenham	
Manning, W.	Lymington	W. India merchant, Bank director.
Marryat, J.	Sandwich	London merchant.
Martin, J.	Tewkesbury	London banker.
Miles, P. J.	Westbury	W. India merchant, banker at Bristol.
Mitchell, J.	Hull	W. India planter.
Money, W. T.	St Michael's	E. India director.
Moore, P.	Coventry	A "nabob".
Morland, Sir S. B.	St Mawes	London banker.
Ommaney, Sir F.	Barnstaple	Navy agent.
Pares, T.	Leicester	Barrister, son of a Leicester banker.
Pease, J.	Devizes	Bank director.
Phillips, G. R.	Wootton Bassett	Lancashire manufacturer.
Phillips, G. R.	Steyning	Son of above.

Plumer, J.	Hindon	W. India merchant.
Pole, Sir P.	Yarmouth	London banker.
Ramsbottom, J.	Windsor	London banker.
Ricardo, D.	Portarlington	Financier.
Rickford, W.	Aylesbury	Banker of Aylesbury.
Ridley, Sir M. W.	Newcastle-on-Tyne	Banker of Newcastle.
Robarts, A. W.	Maidstone	London banker.
Robarts, G. R.	Wallingford	London banker.
Robertson, A.	Grampound	London merchant.
Rumbold, C.	Yarmouth	A "nabob".
Scott, S.	Whitchurch	Corn dealer.
Shaw, Sir R.	Dublin	Alderman of Dublin.
Smith, G.	Wendover	
Smith, S.	Wendover	Relatives of Lord Carrington, and
Smith, J.	Midhurst	members of the banking firm of
Smith, A.	Midhurst	Smith, Payne, and Smith.
Smith, Hon. R.	Berkshire	
Smith, C.	St Albans	Liquor merchant, London alderman.
Smith, W.	Norwich	London banker, a leading Methodist.
Taylor, C. W.	E. Looe	West India planter.
Thompson, W.	Callington	London alderman.
Tulk, C. A.	Sudbury	London merchant.
Walker, J.	Aldborough	Iron master of Rotherham.
Wall, C. Baring	Guildford	Related to the Barings.
Wells, J.	Maidstone	Shipbuilder.
Whitmore, T.	Bridgnorth	Bank director.
Whitmore, W. W.	Bridgnorth	Director, E. India Company.
Widman, J. B.	Colchester	W. India merchant.
Wigram, W.	Wexford	Banker.
Williams, R.	Dorchester	London banker.
Williams, W.	Weymouth	London banker.
Wilson, T.	London	Merchant.
Wood, M.	London	Alderman.

CANNING'S SUPPOSED NEGOTIATIONS
WITH THE WHIGS

In 1831 Arbuthnot told Greville (*Diary*, II, 172) that Canning had negotiated with the Whigs before Liverpool's seizure, that Brougham took the initiative from the Whig side, and that Sir Robert Wilson acted as an intermediary between Brougham and Canning. The source of Arbuthnot's story has never been discovered. On 10 March 1827 he wrote to Peel that the Duke "cannot bring himself to put trust in Canning. He thinks that in his own department there is much trickery; he sees that the sons and relations of our most vehement opponents are taken into employ; and he cannot divest himself of the idea that, directly or indirectly, there has been an understanding with some of the leaders of the Opposition" (Parker, I, 452). So in March 1827 there was only a suspicion, and in the ensuing four years Arbuthnot acquired the circumstantial evidence. Among none of the papers of the period is there a shred of evidence in support of the story, and it can only be assumed that Arbuthnot put his knowledge of the negotiations after March 1827 and his suspicion of negotiations before February 1827 together and produced the story which he told to Greville. The question has been discussed by Professor Temperley (*Foreign Policy, etc.*, pp. 521–30) and Dr Aspinall (*The Formation of Canning's Ministry*, pp. xxix–xxxi) and both have come to this conclusion. The private letters of Princess Lieven to Metternich were not, however, available to Professor Temperley, and Dr Aspinall has made inadequate use of them. The Lieven letters have to be used carefully as she was liable to repeat gossip as substantiated fact. Her story of a meeting between Canning and Lansdowne at an Inn near Marlborough may be so dismissed. But on 2 May she used a conversation with Canning as proof of the rumours she had reported. Now a report of a conversation is a different matter to a rumour, and it may be assumed that Canning did use the words, or at least the sense, which she attributed to him. Canning said: "Sooner or later, we must join with Lord Lansdowne. He is a moderate man. Lord Grey is the difficulty; with him it will never be possible to come to an agreement." Having heard previous rumours of negotiations with the Whigs Princess Lieven assumed that this proved them. Actually it does nothing of the sort, but it does throw a valuable light upon the trend of Canning's ideas at this time. He believed that the Tory party had done its great work (cf. his letter to the King, p. 245), and in 1824 he had written to Liverpool, "I think our business is to admit the extinction of party feeling rather than to show a determination to keep it alive". The great obstacle to a fusion of parties was the Catholic question, that would inevitably separate those with whom the Whigs could unite from those with whom they could not. Loyalty to Liverpool prevented Canning from precipitating the question, but Liverpool's health was so bad that there was little prospect of his staying in office for more than a year, and Canning knew that he would retire if the new Parliament passed a measure of Catholic relief. It was then but natural that Canning's thoughts should anticipate the future and that he should look forward to a Catholic coalition when Liverpool retired. But there is no evidence to show that he took any steps towards facilitating that coalition, and when Liverpool did retire he tried honestly and sincerely to form a Tory Government. It seems that not only is Canning cleared, but that he must also be credited with a loyalty to his colleagues which bade him hold his hand, even when he realised that he would probably have to seek Whig aid after Liverpool's retirement.

BIBLIOGRAPHY

This list of books used is not exhaustive and some works to which single references have been made are not noted here. The word in italics is the short reference used in the footnotes.

I. MANUSCRIPT SOURCES

Add. MSS. Additional Manuscripts in the British Museum.

The Papers of Liverpool, Huskisson, Vansittart, Peel, Ripon (Robinson), Wellesley, Aukland, and Sir Robert Wilson.

II. PRINTED SOURCES

Ashburton, Lord. "The Financial and Commercial Crisis Considered."
Aspinall. "Lord Brougham and the Whig Party."
—— "The Formation of Canning's Ministry."
—— (editor). "The Letters of *George IV*."
Bagot. "George Canning and his friends."
Bathurst MSS. Historical MSS. Commission.
"Black Book of 1820."
Buckingham. "Memoirs of the Regency."
—— "Memoirs of the Court of *George IV*."
Bulwer. "Life of Palmerston."
Buxton. "Finance and Politics."
Clapham. "Economic History of Great Britain."
Colchester. "Diaries."
Creevey. "Diary."
Croker. "Correspondence and Diaries."
Davis, H. W. C. "The Age of Grey and Peel."
—— Articles in the "English Historical Review".
Dowell. "History of Taxation."
Dropmore. Historical MSS. Commission. "MSS. of J. B. Fortescue," vol. x.
Feiling. "The Second Tory Party."
Feveryear. "The Pound Sterling."
Greville. "Journal" (ed. Strachey and Fulford).

Halévy. "History of the English People." (English trans.)
Hammond. "Village Labour."
—— "Town Labourer."
—— "Skilled Labourer." Hastings. Historical MSS. Commission.
Hansard. Old Series to 1820; New Series after 1820. Where there may be doubt a date is also given in the reference.
Heron, Sir R. "Notes."
Herries, J. C. "Memoir."
Huskisson. "Papers" (ed. Melville).
—— "Speeches."
Lieven. "Private Letters to Metternich" (ed. Quennell).
—— "Life", by H. Montgomery Hyde.
Liverpool. "Memoir" (1827).
Maclaren. "Sketch of the History of the Currency."
Marshall, Dorothy. "The Rise of George Canning."
McCleod. "Theory and Practice of Central Banking."
Newton. "Early Days of the Right Hon. George Canning."
"The Pamphleteer."
Parker. "Sir Robert Peel."
Parliamentary Reports. "On Bullion" (1810).
—— "On Cash Resumption" (1819).
—— "On Banks of Issue" (1841).
—— "On the reorganisation of the Civil Service" (1854–5).
Pellew. "Life of Sidmouth."
Phipps. "Memoirs of R. P. Ward."
Ricardo. "Political Works."
—— "Letters to Trower."
—— "Letters to Malthus."
—— "Letters to McCulloch."
Shelley, Lady. "Diary."
Smart. "Economic Annals."
Stapleton. "Political Life of Canning."
—— "Life and Times of Canning."
E. J. Stapleton. "Some Official Correspondence of George Canning."
Tayler. "History of Taxation "
Temperley. "Foreign Policy of Canning."
—— "Life of Canning."
—— Articles in "English Historical Review", 1923 and 1930.

Temperley (with L. Penson). "The Foundations of English Foreign Policy."
—— —— "A Century of Diplomatic Blue Books."
Tooke. "History of Prices."
Trevelyan. "Lord Grey of the Reform Bill."
Twiss. "Life of Eldon."
Walpole, Spencer. "History of England."
Watson, Seton. "Britain in Europe."
Webster. "Foreign Policy of Castlereagh."
—— "British Diplomacy."
—— "The Congress of Vienna."
Wellesley. "Papers" (ed. Melville).
Wellington. "Supplementary Despatches (to end of 1820)."
—— "New Series (1821 and onwards)."
Wilberforce. "Life."
—— "Correspondence."
Yonge. "Life of Lord Liverpool."

For the works used in estimating the composition of the House of Commons see p. 80.

INDEX

A'Court, Sir W., 281
Addington, *see* Sidmouth, Earl of
Angerstein, J. J., pictures purchased for National Gallery, 200
Arbuthnot, C., 28, 29, 33, 136, 144, 161, 167; letters on Wellington in the Cabinet, 68, 241, 254

Bank of England, 175, 176, 186, 211; policy in 1825, 203, 206
Baring, A., 56, 188, 205
Bathurst, C. Bragge, 65, 66, 123, 165, 166, 167
Bathurst, Earl, 48 n. 2, 73, 265
Beaufort, Duke of, 231
Bloomfield, Sir B., 122
Bristol, Earl of, 11, 283
Brougham, H., 64, 106, 184, 208
Buckingham and Chandos, Duke of, 79, 122, 150, 157
Buckinghamshire, Earl of, 24, 128
Bullion Report of 1810, 107, 176, 177, 179

Cabinet, composition of, 78; Liverpool and, 69–75; parties in, 231–2, 252
Calvert, N., 189
Canning, George, 15, 19, 23, 24, 143, 147–9, 245, 246, 270, 279, *et passim*; and George IV, 66–7, 135, 136, 157, 161, 241, 243–4, 246, 253, 257, 260; and Liberalism, 2, 230, 245; and Liverpool, 2, 7–8, 11, 12, 13, 96–7, 124, 126, 127, 128, 130, 133, 162–3, 228, 246; and Portugal, 278–81; and Radical

Agitation, 112, 116; and South America, 242 *et seq.*, 258; and Wellington, 239–41, 247–51, 253, 280; character, 124, 229–30; opinions on, 71–2, 124, 144, 280
Caroline, Queen, 118; Canning and, 129; funeral of, 141
Castlereagh, Lord (Marquis of Londonderry), 15, 125, 143, 150, 155–6; foreign policy of, 232–3; relations with Liverpool, 51
Catholic Association, the, 261
Chester, Bishop of, 267
Christ Church, 5, 6, 7, 8
Church of England, Liverpool and, 93, 199; patronage in, 92 *et seq.*
Civil Service, reform of, 91, 92 n. 1
Clanricarde, Lord, 271–2, 274
Cobbett, W., 183, 184 n. 2, 186
Colchester, Lord, 267
Commons, House of, composition of, 80, 81; corruption in, 85, 87, 95–6; management of, 87, 88, 95, 98–9, 102, 103–4, 105
Conyngham, Lady, 141
Conyngham, Lord Francis, 245, 247, 249
Conyngham, Marquis of, 141
Corn Laws, history of, 185, 214–19, 220–1; Huskisson and, 56, 214, 218, 219, 223, 224; Liverpool and, 56, 217, 218, 220, 222–3, 224, 225, 226
"Cottage Coterie", the, 67, 241, 249
Courier, the, 110